Steamers to Stornoway

Ships and shipping services to Lewis from 1750

Colin Tucker

The Islands Book Trust

Published in 2013 by The Islands Book Trust

www.theislandsbooktrust.com

ISBN: 978-1-907443-43-5

The Islands Book Trust
Ravenspoint Centre
Kershader
South Lochs
Isle of Lewis
HS2 9QA
Tel: 01851 880737

Typeset by Erica Schwarz (www.schwarz-editorial.co.uk)
Cover design by Raspberry Creative Type
Printed and bound by Martins the Printers, Berwick upon Tweed

HIE
Innse Gall
Outer Hebrides

Contents

Introduction

One of the earliest steamship companies to serve the Western Isles described its ships and services as 'Deò-Ghrèine nan Gàidheal' ('The Gaels' Ray of Sunshine'). This reflected the significant role played by these vessels and their successors in lessening the isolation of the islands of the Outer Hebrides, including the Isle of Lewis, and in opening up commerce and trade. In the early days of powered ships, it was considered that they were fit for use only on rivers and sea coasts, with perhaps an occasional short voyage on the open sea in calm weather, but once it was realised that this was not the case, services developed linking Stornoway and the mainland. These services became an integral part of both island life and West Highland shipping, described as

> a whole system of steamers … battling the Atlantic … crossing and re-crossing, plunging into the lochs, winding along the sounds, threading their way among the islands, fine pleasure boats for the flock of summer swallows, stout trading boats summer and winter serving the whole archipelago, linking with the world the lonely bay or the outer islet, freighted out with supplies of all sorts and shapes, freighted in with wool and sheep, Highland beasts and Highland bodies: surely the liveliest service in the world! (*Memoirs and Portraits of One Hundred Glasgow Men.*)

The no-longer isolated island began to be integrated with the economy of the Lowlands, changing island life for ever. Steamships made it possible to export island produce regularly, and a wide variety of goods hitherto unavailable could now enrich the Lewis people's lives. The steamers also brought 'outside ideas' and news. They helped feed the industrial revolution in the second half of the nineteenth century, both in terms of supplying meat and fish, and also in supplementing the workforce, as islanders could now leave to seek work, either on a permanent or seasonal basis. All these aspects are illustrated in a nineteenth-century Gaelic song by Mary MacPherson of Skye ('Màiri Mhòr nan Oran'), 'Oran do *Dhail na Cluaidh*', translated into English by Donald Meek as 'Song on the *Clydesdale*':

> 'Nuair lìbhrigeadh tu a' mhin 's an tea,
> Gum faigheadh tusa càise 's ìm,
> 'S bhiodh toradh mara agus tìr'
> A' falbh air prìs don Ghalldachd.
>
> 'Gur iomadh diùlnach agus òigh
> Thug thusa leat à Tìr a' Cheò,
> A' falbh a chothachadh an lòin,
> 'S gu leòr dhiubh nach do thill ann'.
>
> 'When you would deliver meal and tea,
> You would get butter and some cheese,
> And the produce of land and sea
> Would seek a price in Lowlands.
>
> 'Many a youthful lad and lass
> You took away from the Isle of Mist,
> As they went to earn their keep,
> And many did not return there.'

Her words also show how, when famine struck the islands, including Lewis, it was the steamships which enabled news of such a disaster to reach the south, and allowed relief supplies to be brought to the island:

> 'Gur iomadh frachd thug thusa leat,
> Rinn fuasgladh oirnn an àm na h-airc'
>
> 'Many a cargo you conveyed
> Which saved us in the hour of need.'

The steamers hastened the decline of traditional island social and economic systems which had survived through Lewis's relative isolation from the rest of Scotland. In all these ways, they significantly affected the lives of the people of Lewis.

The island was also opened to visitors by the development of steamer services. Henry Bell pronounced that 'the beauty of the natural scenery on the passage is not to be equalled in Europe', and this sentiment was echoed through the years as sailings to Stornoway were advertised for tourists. Today tourism is one of the main sources of employment in Lewis and visitors arrive and leave daily by ferry.

Many of the ships which have served Stornoway and the people of Lewis, by virtue of their longevity of service, achieved iconic status, and became an almost daily part of people's lives. The same can be said of the name 'MacBrayne', for under the guise of the various companies which have used the name or been associated with it, 'MacBrayne' has maintained the shipping link between the island and the mainland for the greater part of the last two centuries.

I first became aware of Stornoway and its steamer services in the late 1950s when I came across a MacBrayne steamer timetable. Not long after, I acquired a copy of Duckworth and Langmuir's *West Highland Steamers*, followed by one of MacBrayne's red guide books dating back to the end of the nineteenth century. My first visit to Stornoway, in 1964, included a crossing on the *Loch Seaforth*. To these ingredients was added seven summers employed on that steamer and other MacBrayne ships, and since then regular crossings on the various succeeding car ferries. The seeds of the book had been sown, but it has taken half a century for germination and fruition to take place.

My research could have continued almost indefinitely, but I gave myself a deadline and held to it. Thus there may be information to which I was not party, but I believe that I have been able to piece together the development of the shipping services to Stornoway. If there are any errors or significant omissions, the fault is mine. In the text I have used the word 'the' before vessels' names. In Lewis, steamers have always been referred to in this way, as in 'it was a terrible crossing on the *Lochness*'. I am aware that a number of ships carried the same names, but I have not numbered them; reference to the context should enable the reader to know which is which.

Chapter 1

Mail Packets and Schooners

The Isle of Lewis is the largest of the Outer Hebrides, lying about 50 miles west of the Scottish mainland. It has an area of 825 square miles, is about 55 miles in length from north to south, and at its greatest breadth stretches some 28 miles. The main town of Stornoway is situated on probably the best natural harbour in the Western Isles on the east side of the island. Lewis has the greatest number of inhabitants of any of the Hebridean Islands, with a population today of about 18,000, of whom just over 8,000 live in Stornoway. In 1830 the numbers were about 14,000 and 3,000 respectively; the island reached its highest population in 1911 when the number of inhabitants was just below 29,000.

For centuries people have travelled to and from Stornoway by sea. The original settlers, Mesolithic people who reached the island about 7000 years ago, must have been capable of navigating seaworthy craft. Since then, much of the history of Lewis is bound up with arrivals, departures, and other events dictated by the surrounding waters. In the ninth century the island was invaded by the Norse people, so that today their place names sit side by side with Gaelic ones – Stornoway itself is evidently derived from *Sjornavager*, the Norse for 'steering bay'. In the fourteenth and fifteenth centuries, the Lords of the Isles used the sea as the means of communication to achieve their power and dominance. Later, the power of the Macleods of Lewis was crushed by Cromwell, as was a later insurrection by the Earl of Huntly. All these different groups came by sea, as did the Fife Adventurers and Dutch fishermen in the sixteenth century. Prince Charles Edward Stuart ('Bonnie Prince Charlie') crossed by water to and from Lewis, as he escaped after the Battle of Culloden.

As fishing and trade developed, the importance of travel by sea increased. By the eighteenth century, an extensive trade was being carried on with the Baltic, Norway, Sweden, Holland, France and the north of Ireland. Later Stornoway flourished as a port of call for vessels trading to the Baltic from Liverpool and Ireland. Trading had its dangers, however: in 1799 a Stornoway ship was captured by a French privateer almost within sight of Stornoway Harbour, while also during the eighteenth century all the shipping in Stornoway's harbour, and the town itself, were 'held up' by two 'impudent' privateers which took possession of the Minch for a whole fortnight.

In the 1790s, a total of 10,945 barrels of herring, 137 tons of cod and ling, and 393 barrels of salmon were carried on ships from Stornoway, both to other UK ports and for export, even though there was no quay, and as John Knox, a Scottish bookseller and philanthropist from London, recorded on a visit in 1786, vessels had to load and unload upon the beach or in the bay by means of small boats. This information was recorded in a report to the British Society for Extending the Fisheries and Improving the Sea-Coasts of the Kingdom. In this he also described the tribulations incurred in attempting to reach Lewis from the north end of the Isle of Skye. While there was a packet which sailed every fortnight from Dunvegan, it happened to be on the other side of the Minch.

Rather than endure a long wait, he was able to board a boat carrying limestone from Skye to Benbecula. A stiff south-west wind prevented the ship from making there, and the course was changed to Lochmaddy. Eventually, having been forced to change course again and run before the wind, they arrived at Rodel, Harris. This demonstrates how haphazard travel was across the Minch in those days, with neither passage nor destination guaranteed.

Most of the islands of the Hebrides, however, had no regular service to the mainland and ships sailed only when there was sufficient cargo to justify a voyage. Any intending traveller would have to wait until a ship was ready to depart, and then travel with only the most rudimentary of accommodation and shelter. Stornoway was more fortunate; it was one of the few places to gain the luxury of a regular service to the mainland, with scheduled sailings across the Minch to Poolewe, although during winter months there were no crossings and the island was thus completely isolated. In 1756 George Mackenzie, 'Steward and Receiver of Lewis', presented a request to the Postmasters General for a weekly packet boat from Stornoway to Poolewe, with a foot-runner from there to Inverness. Apparently this request was granted the following year, and by 1759 a sailing packet had been established with Government finance, sailing once a fortnight to the 'opposite coast', carrying 'mail, byletters and passengers, and on occasion … cattle and horses'. There is no evidence to show that these packets were better than the ships carrying cargo. These latter were sailing vessels which were broad-beamed, deep-draughted schooners with one or two masts, and between 60 and 80 feet (18m and 24m) in length. They were designed more for carrying cargo than for speed or comfort. The description by John Knox of his experience of returning across the Minch in the 1780s illustrates well the conditions which travellers would have to endure. He stated that 'a packet goes from (Stornoway) to Pool Ewe (sic) on the opposite coast every fortnight, and when Seaforth (the island's principal land-owner) is in Stornoway, once every week'. He also gave details of the vessel, which was

> small, in a very improper state for going to sea, and ought to have been broken up long since. She is engaged at certain seasons in transporting cattle from Lewis to Pool Ewe, which had rotted her timbers and bottom. She was at the same time the want of necessary tacking for a voyage of forty to fifty mile (sic), in a sea that lies open to the northern ocean. The crew consisted of the master, whose name was Macleod, three men and a boy.

James Hogg, the Ettrick Shepherd, better known as a poet than as a traveller, wrote a description well illustrating the problems and frustrations encountered as he tried to cross from Loch Broom to Stornoway. At first there was no boat, but on his third day of waiting at Dundonell, he learned that the schooner *Isabella* of Stornoway had been taking on board a load of stones on the south side of Loch Broom and was awaiting only the return of one of her crew before departing. He procured a passage, and duly boarded the vessel at 1400. Due to a contrary wind and the flow of the tide, they could not sail that night, and he disembarked to spend the night ashore. Early the following morning he was back aboard, and at 0700 the crew heaved anchor and got under way. There was a small breeze blowing straight against the vessel, and the whole day was spent without getting out of Loch Broom. At the close of the day, still in the loch, a boat was sent ashore to bring a lady, bound for Stornoway, on board. She was not ready, and the master was obliged to wait for her, as she was the mother of the ship's owner. This resulted in another night in Loch Broom, and as there was no suitable mooring, the *Isabella* had to anchor in a bay. As the sea was heavy, the vessel 'wrought incessantly during the whole night'. The next morning Hogg went ashore for breakfast, but after that progress started to be made. By noon they were out of the loch and past the Summer Isles. The captain steered the ship far north in the hope of getting

The sailing smacks *Advance* and *Jessie* were typical of the sailing vessels used to convey passengers to the mainland before the introduction of steamships. They are pictured here surrounded by the local fishing fleet in Stornoway harbour

a north-east wind, but instead the wind dropped completely and they were becalmed in the middle of the Minch with 'the vessel floating with her stern towards Stornoway'.

> At one time they were on the level of the Ness peninsula, and the next they were carried southwards and found themselves off the Shiant Isles, and to make matters worse a whale kept close to the ship, and from time to time rubbed himself violently against the sides of the vessel, which alarmed Hogg and the lady very much, though the crew did not seem to worry in the least, but said to Mr Hogg, "He be wanting you to come down and have breakfast with him." He (Hogg) says neither could get off to sleep for fear of him overturning the ship. (*Tales and Traditions of the Lews.*)

After a third night, the wind rose and the ship eventually reached Stornoway about seven in the evening. It had taken over 'sixty hours for a journey of scarcely so many miles'.

Poolewe was the preferred mainland destination for the mail packet, as a better road from Loch Ewe to the East Coast had been built for the mails by the local gentry in 1768. When the British Fisheries Society started to construct their new settlement at Ullapool in the late 1780s, they were of the opinion that they could change the route of the packet to Loch Broom. This was because it was a more direct route and it was expected that a road would also be built which would be shorter than the one to Loch Ewe. This did not happen, and even with the opening of an inn at Ullapool used by many travellers en route to Stornoway, the official packet continued to sail from Poolewe. A further attempt to change the route to Ullapool had been resisted by Seaforth, partly because the passage from Ullapool was considered to be dangerous.

The *Statistical Account* of 1791–99 refers to these mail packets, stating that, around the end of the eighteenth century, it became necessary to sail more often; so the old packet was sold and a new one purchased, which then sailed weekly. The annual cost was £130; £70 of this was met by the government, and £60 by the Earl of Seaforth, then owner of Lewis, less any revenue from passengers, which apparently was not great. In 1814 Robert Heron wrote in his Agricultural Review that 'ferryboats are too few, too uncertain and irregular'. He pleaded, 'Let packet boats … be industrially multiplied'.

A number of vessels continued to provide a service between the island and the mainland. William Daniel, in his book, *A Voyage round the Coast of Scotland and the adjacent Islands*, wrote in the 1820s that Stornoway has 'a regular packet which sails to the mainland once a week with the mail and passengers,' adding that 'it is sometimes employed, though very improperly, for the conveyance of cattle to the west coast of Ross-shire.' In 1823 Mr Stewart-Mackenzie bought the *Glenelg of Glenelg*, a sailing smack of sixty tons, to run a weekly service between Stornoway and Poolewe. Less than two years later, on a stormy morning in November 1824, she was lost with all on board, soon after leaving Poolewe. One of the three passengers on board, the Rev Mr Fraser, minister of Stornoway, had 'over-persuaded' the master to attempt the crossing. The vessel which succeeded her was far from reliable, as the following account from 1836 shows:

> The packet sails once in the week from Polewe (sic) to Stornoway. It is an ill-found vessel, its tackling ill suited to bad weather and its crew insufficient, being in summer only three; a fourth is added in winter. The cabin is such that none of the passengers would venture into it, the hold affording much more preferable accommodation. The length of the passage to Stornoway is forty-two miles. A vessel leaving Polewe early may reach the Long Island before the wind changes at noon, but our passage was prolonged to seventeen hours; we deviated from our course three points, owing to the deficiency of the compass.

Other sailing ships were the smack *North Britain*, which operated for eighteen years, while the *Lady Hood*, named after one of Lord Seaforth's daughters, was one of the last sailing ships before regular communication by steam vessels was established.

Further evidence of the unreliability of both travelling to Stornoway by sailing ship and the mail service can be seen in two letters sent from a visitor to Stornoway to his wife in Gatehouse of Fleet. In the first, dated 30 September 1827, the writer described,

> I wrote (a letter) and despatched it from Portree Thursday week. I hope it reached you in due course and wd. (would) allay all your fears for my safety. I went that night on board the *Prince of Wales* and it left early on the morning before I was out of bed, so I can give no more account of it (Portree) than of Tobermory. Sunday was a remarkably hot and calm day, we did not therefore make much progress in our voyage, about sunset we were within five or six miles of Stornoway, but as it soon turned dark, Capt. Oliver did not like to risk running into the harbour, the entrance of which is confined, he therefore stayed off and on all night, and it was (early) next day before I boarded.

He added:

> I do not know my route home; the packet sails from this every Saturday morn. (morning) for Pollewe (sic) directly opposite and comes back Sunday evening and the mail goes along Loch Maree to Dingwall, but as there is no road from the coast till near Dingwall, I should prefer getting down to Skye or Mull by some vessel going that way and get within reach of a steamboat to Glasgow

> rather than run the risk of walking 40 miles thro' bogs, but we shall see.

A postscript also stressed the unreliability of the service:

> Monday morning. This letter will be taken down today to Lochalsh in the Sound of Skye and put into the Post Office there and will reach you before the departure of next packet from this place. I observe the packet has come in during the night but Mr Gillanders will be off in (when) the letters are delivered, so if there should be any from you I shall not be able to reply to them by this opportunity. Another fine day and as the wind is from the north east, the vessel will run down to Lochalsh in 8 or 9 hours.

The second letter, dated 7 October 1827, continued the same sentiment:

> The great drawback to this place seems the difficulty of communication with the Mainland. The Mail shd. in due course leave Stornaway (sic) every Saturday morning early & return on Sunday, but the Packet & the Mail are still snug in the harbour & as it is a dead calm today, the Packet may not be able to effect a passage across the Minch until tomorrow & it is likely it may be Wednesday before the Mail arrives here, or three days behind its time.

To further emphasise the problems, on the flap of the envelope of this letter was written 'Monday, I send this by Capt. Oliver's Cutter & who will put it into the first Post Office he passes by on his way to the Southward.' The letter, in fact, was postmarked 'Oban', and dated 19 October, almost two weeks after the letter was written. The introduction of steamships would remove these uncertainties.

Chapter 2

The First Steamships

The coming of steamships to Stornoway occurred in the 1820s, although it was several years after that before any regular service commenced. While the first regular steamship service had started on the Clyde in 1812, when Henry Bell's *Comet* had pioneered a service from Glasgow to Greenock, it was a number of years before a steamship ventured as far north as Stornoway. Steamers, pioneered by men such as Henry Bell, Robert Napier, James Thomson and Archibald McConnell, gradually expanded their services, creating a network of routes which spread up the sea-lochs of the Clyde estuary and then through the Crinan Canal, opened in 1817, or round the Mull of Kintyre, to the West Highlands. It was said that, with the combination of steam and the Crinan Canal, the journey from the West Highlands to Glasgow was reduced from three weeks to one. By 1819 a service had been started from Glasgow to Oban using the Crinan Canal, and soon afterwards steamers were reaching as far as Tobermory, Staffa and Iona, Isle Oronsay in Skye, and, via the Caledonian Canal, Inverness.

In 1819 Henry Bell entered into discussions and correspondence with a number of prominent Highland landowners, including J A Stewart-Mackenzie of Seaforth, one of the principal land proprietors of Lewis, and Sir Hugh Innes of Lochalsh. He proposed introducing a steamer to serve Skye and Lewis to commence in April 1820. His ship would be able to carry between eighty and ninety passengers below decks, with main and steerage cabins, two dining cabins, a steward's room and good water closets. The steamer would have two new copper boilers and a new engine. It is not known what vessel Bell envisaged for this purpose, other than that it would not have been the *Comet*. He pointed out that the steamship would provide the quickest way to transport mails, and that a steamship would benefit merchants, fishermen and the whole island community. He further suggested that the traffic would soon require a second vessel, built to carry thirty or forty tons of cargo as well as passengers. There appears, however, to have been a lack of agreement about a number of details. Whereas Bell favoured a through service from Glasgow, Mackenzie preferred a service from Crinan to Stornoway, trans-shipping both passengers and goods at the former point. This may have ensued from information he received from William Thomson of Crinan. He advised Mackenzie on the size of ship which could pass through the Crinan Canal, and also informed him that, if a ship was large enough to sail the Minch safely, she would be of too great a draught to sail up the Clyde to Glasgow, and that Greenock would be his recommendation for the Clyde terminus. The result may have been that the three went their separate ways. The *Glasgow Chronicle* announced in 1820 that Sir Hugh Innes had 'made arrangements for plying a large steam boat … between Kyleakin … and Glasgow … and that it is in contemplation to join another boat, which will ply between Kyle and Lewis'. Some subscriptions were made to the purchase of a new ship organised by Mackenzie, but this did not come to fruition. In 1820 it was reported in the *Greenock Advertiser* that:

> it is now intended that a steam-boat shall begin to ply from the Clyde to the Lewes (sic), through the Crinan Canal and the Sound of Mull … to call at Tobermory, … Isle Ornsay, Lochalsh, Castlemoil, Portree and afterward go to Stornoway'.

This may well have been the plan for the paddle steamer *Highland Chieftain* which was already sailing as far as Skye, but she was needed to replace the original *Comet* on the Fort William service when the latter was wrecked near Crinan and accordingly this did not happen. That same year a Greenock company wrote to Seaforth to consider the possibility of establishing a steamer service to Lewis. It is interesting that even at this early date the value of tourists in making the service viable was being considered, the letter pointing out that:

> there exists here and (in) Glasgow … a fanaticism for steam boat excursions in summer which we have no doubt would make the present plan pay remarkably well. The novelty of seeing the Hebrides … would attract multitudes to all parts of the North of Scotland.

Once more it seems that the scheme failed to materialise.

There are a number of claims for the first steamship to reach Stornoway. The earliest is thought to be the *Argyll*, which had been serving Inveraray from Glasgow, but on 7 February 1822 she sailed round the Mull of Kintyre to Stornoway. Three years later, on 11 March 1825, a meeting was held in the Waterloo Hotel in Edinburgh, for the purpose of 'establishing a Steam Conveyance between Greenock and Stornoway'. The vessel would not exceed 200 tons, would have two engines of forty horse-power each and copper boilers. The plan was for a weekly service during the season, the route going 'round the Mull of Cantyre (sic) during such months of the year as may be found safe and advisable'. The ship was to 'touch at every point of the voyage that is likely to encourage intercourse'. These places were to be Bute, Campbeltown, Sound of Islay, Oban, Mull, Tobermory, Arisaig, Isle Ornsay, Glenelg, Kyleakin and Portree on the outward journey, while on the return southwards, calls would be made on the coast of Harris, at Lochmaddy, Dunvegan, and Peterport (on Benbecula) before rejoining the northward route. There is no mention of what vessel might have operated this service, or whether the scheme actually materialised.

Later in the same year, 1825, on 30 July the *Inverness Journal* reported the first appearance of the '*Maid of Isla* Steam Yacht'. On board were the Seaforth family. Spectacular celebrations greeted their arrival in Stornoway Harbour:

> On passing the extremity of the rocky barrier which protects the harbour of Stornaway (sic) the approach of the *Maid of Isla* was announced by a signal gun placed on an opposite eminence; and the merchant vessels at anchor in the harbour, in all their gaudy decorations, commenced on this a *feu de joie* from their swivels and carronades.

On a newly fitted-out brig, about a hundred seamen and schoolboys perched on her rigging and spars gave three hearty cheers as the steamer passed, and a salute of twenty-one guns was fired as the party disembarked.

Another claimant to be the first steamer, in 1826, was the paddle steamer *United Kingdom* which had been built in Greenock by Robert Steele. She was the largest steamer then built with two 100 horse power engines. Carrying about 120 passengers, her maiden voyage took her from Greenock via the Mull of Kintyre to Stornoway. Here she attracted great attention, crowds of people going out in 'every boat that could float' to view her, 'to behold what had never been seen before, namely a steam vessel'. This was quite unlike the response on some other islands, where the arrival of a steamship with belching black smoke from her funnel caused panic-stricken locals to run away in terror. From Stornoway she continued round the north of Scotland to Orkney before finishing up at Newhaven, on the Firth of Forth. It is also claimed that the

Aimwell left Greenock to become the first vessel to steam into the harbour at Stornoway in 1828. She was a paddle steamer originally built on the River Thames and later serving across the Irish Sea. Other early steamers to reach Stornoway were the *Glasgow* and the *Commodore*, the latter gaining the dubious distinction of becoming the first, but by no means the last, Stornoway steamer to be wrecked on the rocky shores of the west coast when she ran aground off Campbeltown in 1831.

In June 1828 the following advertisement appeared in the *Glasgow Herald*:

> *BEN NEVIS* is appointed to sail ... betwixt Glasgow and Stornoway. The *Ben Nevis* will therefore leave the Broomielaw every alternate Tuesday and Stornoway every intervening Tuesday.

This would suggest that the *Ben Nevis* was to operate a regular service, but it is doubtful if this was in fact the case as, her sailings to Lewis appear to have been an extension of her regular route from Glasgow to Portree and this extension north to Stornoway most likely occurred only intermittently. In spite of that, the steamer, built in 1824 and owned by Jas. Lang, but operating for the Ben Nevis Steamboat Company, was, in fact, registered in Stornoway from October 1829. Several sailings must have taken place, however, for it was on one of these, returning to Glasgow from Stornoway, that she was wrecked at Carskey, twelve

The paddle steamer *Duntroon Castle*, which sailed to Stornoway during the 1850s, is a good example of the early steamers which sailed to the Hebrides. This painting, which must be one of the earliest of a West Coast steamship, appropriately depicts her passing Duntrune Castle, in Argyllshire. (PS *Duntroon Castle*, unknown artist, Glasgow Museums T.1940.48 (Digitally enhanced detail, reproduced by kind permission of Glasgow Museums))

miles south of Campbeltown on 18 August 1831. *The Scottish Tourist's Steam Boat Pocket Guide*, published by McPhun in 1835, mentions that 'steam-boats sail pretty frequently during the summer from Glasgow to Tobermory … touching at Oban on the way', and that 'the *Glen Albyn*, *Foyle* and *St Columb*, during the summer months make some delightful pleasure excursions round all the West Coast, stopping a few hours for the accommodation of tourists at each place'. While St Kilda, the Caulin (sic) Hills and the Spar Cave on Skye are included, there is no mention of any sailings to Stornoway. In the Guide's list of 'Steam-vessels in the Trade of Clyde', none are shown trading to Lewis, and only one, the *Maid of Islay No 2*, sailing to Skye, from West Loch Tarbert. A year earlier Anderson's *Guide to the Highlands and Islands of Scotland* recorded that 'a steam boat, in the summer season, makes occasional trips from Glasgow to Stornoway.' Thus, while the west coast mainland and the islands as far north as Skye were receiving regular steamship services from Glasgow, it would not be for another 15 years that this was provided for the people of Stornoway and Lewis. Meantime they had to trust to the sailing packet carrying mails to Poolewe or an irregular visit by a steamer from Glasgow. This situation is aptly described in an extract from an article in the *North British Daily Mail* which paints an interesting picture of Stornoway in the 1840s, when the harbour would be home to both sail and steam vessels:

> Sometimes the postal bags would be windbound with the old packet for a fortnight or more. Once a week a steamer from Glasgow crept into the harbour, and caused commotion, and then the people, young and old, would crowd the little quay like bees … about to swarm. The event caused a ripple in the smooth surface of Stornoway life, but when the steamer left there was the old calm.

The article then goes on to show how the service to the mainland was at the mercy of the mail boat's master:

> Postal communication was by packet to and from Poolewe twice a week. Old Captain Leslie was commander. Cautious old salt was he! He never risked his frail barque in a gale if he could help it. If there were two mare's tails in the sky boding wind, or a puff or two from the wrong direction, then he was off into shelter until there was a reliable breeze. And when the good folks, with a little irritation, would say, 'What was keeping you?' he would reply, 'My anchors, of course.' The consequence was that sometimes there was no post for a fortnight.

That Captain Leslie was a 'character' is further illustrated by comments made in the same publication in January 1910, when he was described as a 'trig little Englishman'. On one occasion on his arrival in port he was asked, 'What news, Captain?' to which he replied, 'Oh! It's all under me oxter.' The mail bag in those days was no larger than a schoolboy's satchel.

The same captain was involved in an unusual occurrence while he was on passage between the mainland and Lewis. This was described in the book *Gairloch in North-West Ross-Shire* under the heading 'The Stornoway Packet and the Whale.' It relates that:

> the smack *North Britain*, Captain Leslie (in command), was carrying the mails between Poolewe and Stornoway for eighteen years. Leslie had four of a crew besides himself. Murdo Macdonald was at the helm when the smack struck a whale. She was running with a two-reefed mainsail and slack sheet. She ran on the back of the whale and cut it through to the backbone; seven feet was put out of the cutwater of the packet; it was a severe stroke! When the smack ran up on to the back of the whale her stern went under to the companion. The whale sank down, and so the smack went over her, but made so much water in the hold that they were obliged to run her ashore. They got her to Bayhead, inside the pier at Stornoway. The whale went ashore in Assynt, and they found the cut on her.

Steamship sailings would be advertised in the local newspapers, such as the *Inverness Journal*, which in March 1836 announced that the steam packet *Inverness*, with Captain MacNeill in command, would sail on 21 March at noon for Oban, Tobermory, Portree and Stornoway, returning on the twenty-fifth for Glasgow. It was also mentioned that the vessel was provided with comfortable sleeping berths, and that 'goods for shipment must be along-side half an hour before the Advertised time of sailing, otherwise they cannot be taken'. This was unusual, as most of the steamships carried passengers only, leaving carriage of goods to the established sailing vessels. There was indeed a not inconsiderable amount of goods being traded to Stornoway by sailing ships; in 1834 sixty-seven vessels, including one foreign ship, imported cargo to the island. Amongst this was grain for the distillery which was unloaded at the door directly from the ships.

Chapter 3

Conditions for the Early Traveller

A traveller on one of the early steamships would have experienced a journey which would have lasted the best part of a week, or even longer:

> In the olden days it sometimes took a couple of weeks to sail to Lewis from Glasgow; and within living memory the outward journey frequently occupied five or six days, because the steamer called with the odd passenger and sundry cargoes at innumerable little ports on the way, and often steered as far north as Aultbea and Lochinver before crossing the Minch. It must be remembered, too, that there were no sailings on Sundays; and this sometimes added an extra day to what was already a tedious voyage. This day was spent at the last port at which the steamer called on the Saturday afternoon.

Conditions on board were also far from sophisticated, as the following description shows:

> First-class passengers had a small saloon under the deck house, affording good views of the now renowned romantic Highland landscape, (but) the second-class passengers had to make do with the cramped benches in the tiny forward cabin. Here the headroom was so low that, even when sitting, the taller passengers had to stoop. … There was a captain and a crew of seven, one of whom was a salaried piper. Passengers often enjoyed dancing on the deck – it was one way of keeping warm. Gentleman would, naturally, be accompanied by a personal servant, who would serve a picnic meal in the saloon. At night the … (vessel) moored. Gentlemen would perhaps avail themselves of an introduction to one of the noblemen whose landed properties lined the route (Lumsden's *Steam Boat Companion* thoughtfully provides the owners' names, so that the well-connected could make contact). Those of more modest means would have to put up with the doubtful comforts of a local hostelry, while the poor, including the evicted clansmen driven from their glens to seek work in Glasgow, would wrap themselves in their plaids and sleep in the stuffy cabin or in the heather. (*The Discovery of the Hebrides*)

Schedules might not be followed, and the journey could have been far from safe as J E Bowman describes in his *Highlands and Islands – a Nineteenth-Century Tour*:

> The *Ben Nevis* steamer appeared within the Sound of Kerrera, and when she stood under the pier at Oban, her deck presented such a scene of tumult and disorder that we were at a loss to assign the cause. She was altogether so unsteady, that her wheels were lifted alternately out of the water. We, however, got on board, and with some difficulty made our way to the stern; where we learnt that she had a double complement of passengers (280 were on board) in consequence of the *Comet* being under repair in Glasgow. The captain also was extremely drunk.

Weather conditions could also make for an unpleasant journey. A graphic picture of the stormy nature of conditions which might be experienced is given in *Sketches of Highland Character*.

Conditions were sometimes harsh on early steamers rounding the Mull of Kintyre

A passenger boarding a steamer lying at Greenock, ready to start for the West Highlands, overhears the following conversation:

> "Ye'll think it's a plowy nicht?" said a hairy-faced fellow, who had a plaid rolled tight round his neck, as if he had serious thoughts of doing himself an injury.
>
> "Aye will it," answered a short squat man in moleskins, all covered over with coal dust. "Ye see the clouds, hoo they chase ane anither; that's a gran' sign o' wind. We'll hae a dance on the Moil the nicht, or I'm mista'en. There is plenty o' that afore us, or the winter is ower."
>
> "No doot o' that; but ye're accustomed to it, and 'ill no mind it."
>
> "We wadna need, Dugald, for mony's the awfu' nicht we hae o' it on the Mull of Cantyre."
>
> "It'll pe sometimes washing ower the fessel?"
>
> "Washing ower the veshel! Ay man, sometimes washing ower the funnel and near puttin' out the fire on us, and wad do sae if the smoke dinna keep it frae coming doon."

If conditions for the passengers were poor then, things were no better for the crew. A contemporary account states that:

> we can hardly expect the stoker to remain below longer than necessary, hence his tendency to shovel in a good quantity of coal at a time and then ascend to the deck for a smoke himself. In the old days it was considered the proper thing to have a long pennant of black smoke streaming from the high and narrow funnel.

George Clayton Atkinson made two expeditions to the Hebrides in the 1830s, providing details of both places and conditions of the time. The second of these journeys took place in 1833 and as part of his expedition to the Feroe (sic), Westman Islands and Iceland, he voyaged from Glasgow to Stornoway on the steamer *Highland Chieftain*. This ship had been built in 1817 as the *Duke of Wellington* and was enlarged and renamed in 1820. She replaced the *Comet* sailing to Fort William, and then passed through various owners and sailed to a number of destinations including a weekly sailing from the Clyde to Inverness via the Caledonian Canal. It is not clear whether she sailed on only one occasion to Lewis or provided a regular service. If it was the latter, then it would not have been for long, for in 1834 her engines were removed, and she became a sailing schooner until broken up in 1838.

Atkinson described how his party 'went down to the Broomie Law (sic) … to inspect the *Highland Chieftain* which is destined to convey us to Stornoway'. He considered her 'an old friend as (he) had partaken of its accommodation and dis-accommodation in visiting some of the Hebrides two years since'. He did not consider the steamer to be an imposing one, hinting to a member of the party 'that his eye seemed engaged in looking for it among the vessels of too magnificent an aspect – (he) was scanning the second or third rates'. He went on to explain:

> that as she takes the short cut to the islands through the Crinan Canal, instead of round the Mull of Kintyre, she must of necessity be so small as to pass the locks of the canal … One consequence of her smallness is that she has no sleeping room, but lands her passengers each night at different stations for that purpose – a misery or not according to taste.

The *Highland Chieftain* left Glasgow at twelve o'clock with not many on board. 'There seemed to be very few cabin passengers; only one, a stout gentleman of the name of MacIver went further than Greenock'. He turned out to be 'a confirmed bore of the old school … much given in confidentialities with the people on board, and to drink whisky when *we* paid for it'. They reached Crinan just after midnight and 'with some difficulty got ashore, and the people at a house there (were) round(ed) up', allowing them to have a bed for the night. The next day Atkinson described how, 'as our stout friend, Mr MacIver, had slept in the cabin, as well as the captain and mate, it was (on entering it this morning at 7) … very frousty (sic), and we gladly preferred walking along the banks of the canal as the steamboat worked slowly through'. He had little complimentary to say about the ship or the rest of the second day's journey. 'Our vile, small, undignified steamer stopped at Oban to renew its stock of coals, and we … rambled on shore … till recalled to the boat by the most indefatigable ringing of a badly toned bell, and a long column of insurgent steam'. The second night was spent at Tobermory where, 'after hunting about we at length established ourselves in Mrs Cuthbertson's lodgings, had a glorious tea, and went to bed'.

The next day's voyage from Tobermory to Portree was described as generally tedious, due to 'the number of intervening places at which it is necessary to call for the delivery of packages and people'. On the final leg of the voyage, the steamer left Portree at five in the morning and Atkinson described how the tedium of the crossing was broken, when

> from Hunish we dashed on into the Minch … and in a couple of hours came to the Shiant Islands. Our worthy captain, as the weather was nothing particular, steered the steamer through the channel which divides them, and lowering his boat, landed us for an hour upon the northern of them.

Stornoway was finally reached at three o'clock, after a crossing of ten hours.

Chapter 4

Sir James Matheson and the *Mary Jane*

It seems likely that the first regular sailings were organised not from Glasgow but from Stornoway. In 1844 Sir James Matheson bought the island of Lewis and set about trying to improve conditions on the island. It was reported in the Inverness Journal that he intended to spend £40,000 to £50,000 on improvements. As well as road construction and drainage schemes he was dissatisfied with the irregular shipping services to the mainland and wished to improve matters. Perhaps the £500 he offered as an annual subsidy to operate a mail service to the mainland was too meagre for it did not attract any takers. He therefore became a part owner of the *Falcon*, a steamer which ran from Ardrossan to Stornoway in 1845, but ceased to operate in October of that year, having caught fire. This necessitated her having to be scuttled. Even in these early years the wealthy people in Stornoway had come to rely on steamers providing foodstuffs and luxury items, and it was claimed that the loss of the steamer caused Stornoway to run out of goods: there was 'not one pound of tea or sugar or tobacco or snuff in the place'.

In 1846 James Matheson then went to the Clyde shipbuilders Messrs Tod & MacGregor and had the paddle steamer *Mary Jane* built. She was named after his wife, Lady Matheson. The ship was described as a flush decked steamer with fiddle-bow and bowsprit, two masts and a single cylinder steeple type engine and was steered by a wheel at the stern. The term flush deck indicates that, like every steamer of the time, all the passenger accommodation, such as it was, was below deck. When built she was 150 feet (45m) in length, more than three times that of the original *Comet*, showing how steamships were quickly developing. She was originally built as Matheson's private yacht, but with the lack of a steamship service after the loss of the *Falcon*, she was put into service for the public good. Another theory, since discounted, claimed that she was originally built as the *Windsor Castle* for the Castle Steam Packet Co. on the Clyde.

She commenced a regular weekly service between Stornoway and Glasgow. Her first voyage finished in Stornoway on 4 June 1846 after a passage of twenty-eight hours. It is reported that a large crowd assembled on the beach to witness her arrival, only too pleased to see a steamer which would link their island regularly with Glasgow. In addition to passengers she would carry to Glasgow the produce of the island: dry salt fish, whisky, paraffin, black cattle hides, tallow, salmon whelks, lobsters and eggs. From Glasgow general goods for the island would fill her holds. Until the first quay was built at Stornoway, she would berth alongside an old hulk called the *Amity*, using this as a gangway to the landing stage. Today the name is remembered in the offices of the Stornoway Harbour Commission, located in Amity House on the quayside. The merchants of Stornoway appreciated the decrease in journey time to the mainland, saying it was 'such an advantage to them that they could turn over their capital three times before their bills became due, whereas formerly, when they depended on sailing vessels, their bills often became due before their goods arrived.' The *Mary Jane*'s regular Glasgow run made calls at Portree, Broadford, Kyleakin, Armadale, Tobermory and Oban. In addition she called at Lochinver on alternate Mondays. Under the headline 'More Steam to Sutherlandshire' the *John O'Groat Journal* of 3 August 1846 described an arrangement made between the Duke of Sutherland and James Matheson for the *Mary Jane* to visit Lochinver once a fortnight. It described how this would be a:

> Great boon to the tenantry on the West Coast of Sutherlandshire, and will be the means of transporting their stock and other produce to Glasgow, in about thirty hours after shipment. By this arrangement, an excellent opportunity will also be afforded to tourists, of visiting the West Coast from Skye to Lochinver.

After only a month she also started calling at Balmacara to connect with a mail coach which had commenced between there and Dingwall.

This, in fact, set the pattern of services to Stornoway which was to last for more than the next hundred years, consisting of a combination of 'all-the-way' sailings from Glasgow and the short crossings to ports such as Poolewe, Ullapool and Kyle of Lochalsh. This made sense; in the early days, transport by land was slow and uncomfortable, and it was easier to reach Glasgow by sea than by a combination of water and land, but there was also a need to have contact with places such as Dingwall, county town of Ross and Cromarty, of which Lewis was a part, and Inverness, the main centre of the Highlands.

On one voyage in December 1847, the *Mary Jane* had the misfortune to run down the steamer *Lochfine*, which was on her maiden voyage. It was thought there was little damage to either vessel, but the *Lochfine* evidently started leaking on her return voyage from Oban back to Glasgow, and had to be taken in tow by a tug-boat off the Cumbraes before finally sinking in

The *Mary Jane* was built for Sir James Matheson in 1846 and sailed between Glasgow and Stornoway before being sold for service on the Clyde (drawing by the author)

Cartsdyke Bay. On another occasion in the same year, Matheson used his ship to provide free transport to Broomielaw for 200–300 seasonal migrants from Lewis, Harris and Skye, and by the end of that year she had carried to Clyde ports no fewer than 2,256 people from the Hebrides looking for work.

The *Mary Jane* herself had an extremely long life for a ship. After only five years she was bought by the Glasgow and Lochfyne Steam Packet Company which operated her on the Clyde between Glasgow and Inveraray. She then passed into the Hutcheson fleet in 1857 and in 1875 she was considerably altered. She was lengthened by fifteen feet (5m), given a new slanting bow without the bowsprit and an aft deck-saloon. In this guise, and with the new name *Glencoe*, she became well known on the West Coast serving such places as Oban, Tobermory, and Loch Scavaig before sailing for many years as the Portree mail steamer. The changes to both her appearance and service were described by Andrew McQueen in his book *Echoes of Old Clyde Paddle-Wheels*. On board a steamer, the writer fell into conversation with a fellow traveller who informed him that,

> the *Glencoe*, the auld *Mary Jane* … used to be on the Inveraray rin … her an' the *Inveraray Castle*; they ran day aboot … (She) had fiddle-bows an'twa masts, but by an' by they ta'en the *Mary Jane* aff the rin, an' pit a saloon in her, tae mak' a tourist steamer o' her. They ta'en oot yin o' the masts, an' ta'en the bowsprit an' heidboards aff her, an' ca'ed her the *Glencoe*.

Under both the names *Mary Jane* and *Glencoe* the ship did return to Stornoway on a number of occasions. It is recorded that she called there from Glasgow, under her original name, in 1869, 1871 and 1874. In the summer of 1877 she ran a scheduled service from Gairloch to Stornoway every Thursday, arriving about 2200 and leaving on the return at 0600 the following morning; this was described in the press as Messrs Hutcheson including Stornoway 'in their circle of operations, thus receiving *Ultima Thule* into the category of islands placed within easy reach by their fleet of steamers.' The article did stress, however, that it was not the best sightseeing trip, as the tourist 'sees little to interest … having only time to run to and from his hotel,' and further discouraging the visitor by adding, 'he has, besides, to encounter the unpleasant situation which the odour of the briny Minch produces, and which often lays low the heads of folks with feeble stomachs.' Later in the year, on 4 October, the *Glencoe* arrived at Stornoway from Oban, carrying 'passengers only'. Between 1880 and 1882 she made nine passages from Strome Ferry. In 1909 she took the place of the broken down *Gael*, which was in turn relieving the *Sheila*.

In 1931 the *Glencoe* was still able enough to rescue the *Lochmor* and the *Lochearn*, then brand new motorships, which had somehow both contrived to go aground at Kyleakin (one unsuccessfully attempting to pull off the other). Later during the same year she was brought to the Broomielaw in Glasgow to lie alongside the newly-built *Lochfyne*, contrasting the old with the new. The ship was then laid up in Bowling Harbour, on the Clyde. The rather sad sight of her lying there was described by Andrew McQueen:

> Towards the western end of the bay … one may … see an old stager from the outer waters of the Western Highlands, with engine of the long-discarded steeple type and funnel perched well aft in the fashion that prevailed when the nineteenth century was still youthful. Her dreams (doubtless in Gaelic, for long service in the North must have made her familiar with the language as she is with every sound and headland between the Mull of Kintyre and far-off Stornoway) will surely conjure up scenes of lofty mountains, with little thatch-roofed hamlets at their

> base, and broad-beamed ferry-boats rowed by brawny Highlandmen, as shaggy as the long-horned cattle on the shore, bringing alongside incredible loads of sheep, with, now and then, an odd passenger or two.

She was finally broken up in the same year at Ardrossan, after a service of eighty-five years, much to the regret of many Highlanders who had sentimental (and for some probably less kindly) feelings for her.

Throughout her long career she was powered by a steeple engine (so called because of its resemblance to a steeple, as the cylinder was placed vertically and drove a crosshead which travelled up and down, being visible above the engine house). There is a lovely description of this anachronistic piece of machinery, written by Malcolm Laing from South Uist, and translated by Donald Meek:

> We went below to view the wonderful engine that gave the *Glencoe* her motive power. If any others of the kind were to be seen, it was surely in a museum. The engineer was standing with a crowbar in his hands like a soldier with a musket. When the telegraph rang, he thrust the point of the crowbar through a hole in the end of a stout axle and he worked it against his shoulder with all his might until the shafts of the engine began to move in conjunction with one another's notches. This caused the mill wheels on either side of the ship to chew the brine. She had to go a short distance astern (this was leaving Mallaig) before her bow would point directly at the harbour passage. When the telegraph rang again, the man with the crowbar had to aim it successfully into the hole, stop the engine, and turn the axle in the other direction to propel the ship ahead.

It was considered that the *Mary Jane* was too small for her required purposes and Sir James Matheson, together with the Duke of Sutherland, ordered a larger vessel from Messrs John Reid & Co. of Port Glasgow. She was launched on 29 September 1848 and named the *Marquis of Stafford*. She duly replaced the *Mary Jane* in March of the following year, adding Ullapool to the ports of call. This call was on a monthly basis, as reported in the *Inverness Advertiser* which announced in January 1849 that 'the *Marquis of Stafford* paid her monthly visit to Ullapool on her way from Glasgow to Stornoway, carrying goods and passengers, and picking up a considerable number of barrels of herring bound for Glasgow'. However she proved to be too large for the service and was withdrawn in 1851. She had been unsuccessfully offered for sale the previous year; a prospective buyer hoping to establish a service from Ballyshannon in Northern Ireland to Great Britain could raise only £3,000 against an asking price of £8,500 and the scheme faded out. Financially the service had not been a success. Reporting later to the Napier Commission (a public enquiry into the condition of crofters and cottars in the Highlands and Islands), William Mackay, Chamberlain on the Lewis estates, stated that the *Mary Jane* and the *Marquis of Stafford* had caused Matheson a loss of £15,000, while the loss on the contract for carrying the mail five times, rather than twice, per week was £16,800.

At the end of 1851 the *Marquis of Stafford* was involved in carrying emigrants from Lewis to Canada. Following a tour of Lewis to ascertain the number of tenants who were to be helped to emigrate, Sir James Matheson had great difficulty in finding ships to use for this purpose. He was able to use the *Marquis of Stafford* as one of six ships to carry emigrants that year. As well as obtaining the ships he also provided bread, meal, tinware and bedding, and tried to find a contact who would move the emigrants 'up country' upon their arrival in Quebec. The *Marquis of Stafford* was to carry 500 emigrants from Lewis to Troon. Many came from the Uig district in Lewis, boarding the ship in the Sound of Bernera. This must have been a slow process as passengers, including some from Tolsta Chaolais and Carloway, were still coming aboard with their luggage after two days. The mate was instructed to allow no more luggage on board as the remaining space was required for the emigrants from Ness. Sir James Matheson visited the steamer in a gale of wind and a heavy sea, to observe an allowance of biscuit equal to one pound being given to each passenger, along with tinware to each passenger who could afford it. There then followed prayers and praise by the Rev Campbell. More would-be emigrants were refused boarding to keep room for those promised a passage from Ness and Tolsta. Finally, the *Marquis of Stafford* raised anchor and sailed with 400 emigrants on board to Troon, on the first leg of their journey to the New World. She did not stop to pick up the emigrants from Ness, as those already on board feared the Ness people would bring the smallpox virus on board. The ship was then sold to Italian owners and renamed *Piemonte*. In 1860 she was acquired by Garibaldi to take part in the Spedizione dei Mille (Expedition of the Thousand). This involved a landing of a corps of volunteers to conquer Sicily as part of the unification of Italy. The steamer was captured, but later preserved at Naples, by decree of Garibaldi 'in memory of the initiative of the Italian people'. She was finally sold and broken up in 1866.

To take the place of these ships Sir James Matheson entered into an agreement with James Ramsay of Kildalton. The arrangement was that the latter's iron paddle steamer, the first *Islay*, would extend her sailings to both Skye and Lewis. She had been built in 1849, with a clipper bow, two masts and one funnel behind the paddle-boxes, and was described as 'powerful and fast-sailing'. She originally sailed between Glasgow and Islay, but in April 1851 the extension to her route was announced with the first actual sailing due to take place on 19 May of that year, and regular departures from the Broomielaw every Monday

The paddle steamer *Piemonte* was originally the *Marquis of Stafford*. She was sold in 1851 for service in Italy – a well-travelled Stornoway steamer

The *Islay* sailed to Stornoway between 1851 and 1868

after that date. However, the steamer may not have taken up the service until a later date, the *John O'Groat Journal* of 23 May 1851 stating that 'until the *Islay* is got ready, the *Duntroon Castle* is on the line 'twixt Stornoway and Glasgow'.

The *Islay*, too, was involved in carrying emigrants, picking up a sizeable number from the Ness district. This steamer did not have a trouble-free career; in 1857 she went aground at Port Ellen, and nine years later again went on rocks but on both occasions she was refloated. In 1868 she was purchased by Messrs Hutcheson, renamed *Dolphin*, and put on to a service between Glasgow and Loch Fyne before being sold again, this time to sail between Portpatrick and Donaghadee.

An insight into aspects of shipping services at Stornoway of that time, including the changeover of ownership described above, appears in a diary written in 1851 by John Munro Mackenzie. At the time he was chamberlain, or manager, for Sir James Matheson, and amongst many other jobs including fixing and collecting rents, settling disputes between tenants and administrators, and upholding the Poor Law, he was responsible for organising transport to and from the mainland through the packet boat provided by his employer.

This last-mentioned task was far from a straightforward one. At the beginning of 1851, the earnings from the *Mary Jane* hardly met the working expenses, the result of a combination of few passengers and a decrease in goods traffic. This was brought on by the 'poor state of the Highlands and partly by the effects of the opposition, the greater part of the Goods and Passengers to Oban & Mull being conveyed in Steamers passing through the Crenan (sic) Canal'. This suggests that only a small part of the revenue was derived from passengers and goods to Stornoway. In addition there were arrears of freight payments, some dating back to when the steamer commenced sailing in 1846. On a lesser scale, Mackenzie had to deal with a problem regarding missing egg boxes. In March he made an application to the Northern Lighthouse Commissioners to 'get free of light dues as the steamers carried mails'. He then had a 'discussion' with the skipper of the *Mary Jane*, Captain Hudson, who 'did not approve of calling at Eigg with mails'.

It has been suggested that it was the lack of revenue, and also the cost of repairs to his steamers, which 'continue(d) extravagant', that made Sir James Matheson enter into the agreement with the owners of the *Islay* 'for supplying the Lews with steam communication'. For this purpose Matheson and Mackenzie, accompanied by Lady Matheson, departed for Glasgow at the end of April 1851. Details of the journey give an idea of the times involved on such a voyage. They left Stornoway at 0630 on the thirtieth and had a 'pleasant passage and nothing occured (sic) in the way of business' until they reached Oban at 2130, when their Edinburgh agent and an Officer at Arms came on Board to serve a summons on Sir James. There is no mention of what this was for but it necessitated only a stop of half-an-hour, and with the weather still fine they made a steady passage to arrive at Greenock at 1130 the following morning. Plans for the change of steamer ownership must have already been initiated, for Mackenzie then ascertained that arrangements had been made for the *Duntroon Castle* to sail to Stornoway in place of the *Mary Jane* until the *Islay* was ready. The captain of the *Duntroon Castle* was duly informed as to where and when to pick up sheep on the voyage, including some from Balmacara. Ten days later the *Duntroon Castle* arrived in Stornoway from Lochinver, having experienced 'problems over the carriage of sheep'.

By 7 May the *Mary Jane* had been sold to a Mr McArthur, who went to 'value stages, planks etc on the quay, belonging to the *Mary Jane*'. He was 'entitled to all furnishings found on the *Mary Jane* as he bough(t) her as she stood with all furnishings on board'. There was, however, a delay in the change of management of the steamship services. Initially Messrs McEwan and Ramsay, owners of the *Islay*, did not sign the contracts, and Sir James Matheson then intimated that he would resume the service with the *Marquis of Stafford* if the contract was not signed. Shortly afterwards he received a letter from McEwan and Ramsay 'promising to carry out the Stornoway trade without signing a contract'. This must have been acceptable for arrangements were then made regarding sailing dates. It was also arranged to let the 'Store and Steamer Pier' in Stornoway to the new ship owners for one year at a sum of forty pounds.

In these days the arrival in Stornoway of two steamers on the same day would have been an unusual occurrence, uncommon enough for Mackenzie to have recorded this fact on 25 May. The regular steamer, by now the *Islay*, arrived at 1100, having been preceded five hours earlier by the *Glow Worm*, owned by the Ardrossan Steam Navigation Co. but chartered by a Mr William Morison to run in opposition to the *Mary Jane* and her successor. The following month this vessel was involved in a dispute regarding berthing. She had tied alongside the *Islay* and unloaded her cargo over that ship on to the quay. The quay gates were kept shut to prevent the goods being delivered further. The captain of the *Glow Worm* was then presented with two options. The first was to pay twenty shillings as quay dues for that trip and then 'not persisting' in using the wharf let to the *Islay*, in which case the cargo would be allowed to be landed. The other choice was to remove the *Glow Worm* at once. Rather than pay the fine the steamer was immediately removed to the Public Quay.

In 1868 the *National Gazetteer* stated that 'two steamers ply regularly between Stornoway and Glasgow, and there is a mail packet twice a week via Poolewe to Dingwall', indicating that, with the demise of the *Marquis of Stafford*, the short crossing had reverted back to sailing vessels carrying the mails. It would be another twenty years before a steamer service would again link Stornoway with the west coast mainland.

In January 1853 another attempt was made to instigate a steamer service between Glasgow and Stornoway. This appeared in the form of an advertisement providing details of a proposed weekly service by Messrs Orme Bros & Co., a company which much later merged with John McCallum & Co. to form McCallum, Orme & Co. Ltd, well-known for providing a service to St Kilda. The steamer was to be the *Queen*, an iron-hulled, three-masted ship with figurehead, bowsprit and square stern, a speed of twelve knots and a gross tonnage of 275 – a fairly typical steamer of the time. She was to carry cargo and twenty-three passengers. The Stornoway Harbour authorities, however, refused to provide berthing facilities because they had commitments to other companies, and the service was then amended to serve Islay, Oban, Mull and Skye, while the *Queen* was eventually sold to Australian owners.

Chapter 5

David Hutcheson Takes Control

It will already have become apparent that there was a variety of owners amongst the ships sailing to Stornoway, and, if the whole of the West Highland trade is considered, then the number becomes even greater. Gradually, however, mergers and take-overs took place and by the late 1840s most of the services were under the control of G & J Burns. In 1851 a general rearrangement of the management of West Highland services took place. Messrs Burns decided to concentrate on their more profitable Irish Sea shipping, passing control of the West Coast services to a new company, Messrs David Hutcheson & Co. The three partners of this company were David and Alexander Hutcheson, who had been Heads of Departments with G & J Burns, and David MacBrayne. The last mentioned was a nephew of the two Burns brothers and it was a condition of the sale that he be made a partner. This was the first appearance of the name which became almost synonymous with West Highland shipping, although it would not be for almost another thirty years that his name would head the company.

The Hutchesons quickly set about building new ships. The first actual Hutcheson ship to serve Stornoway was the *Chevalier*. She was launched in 25 March 1853, with a raised quarter deck, two masts and a square stern and was fitted with oscillating engines. She was described 'as sleeping 50 passengers and with decoration of a superior class'. It is likely that she called only irregularly at Stornoway as an extension of her service from Glasgow to Oban and Skye via the Mull of Kintyre, continuing an established pattern of service. This was run in conjunction with the *Islay*, which was still privately owned. The *Chevalier* did not last long, however, being wrecked in the Sound of Jura after less than two years' service.

She was replaced on the run from Glasgow to Stornoway, with calls at Oban and Skye, by the paddle steamer *Clansman*. She was built by Messrs J & G Thomson, and was the first of five ships to bear this name. This ship was unusual in having three masts and it is also recorded that she was a fast vessel for her time with an average speed of thirteen miles per hour. She provided a regular service between Glasgow and Stornoway, being advertised as 'The Splendid New Steam Ship *Clansman*,

The paddle steamer *Chevalier*, built in 1853, was the first ship built by David Hutcheson & Co. for the Glasgow to Stornoway route

Drawing by the author of the *Clansman*, the first of five ships to bear the name. She served Stornoway between 1855 and 1869

intended to leave Glasgow on 3 August 1855 for Stornoway' and that she 'will call at Tarbert in the Harris on Monday 3 September, weather and circumstances permitting'. From time to time she also extended her sailings beyond Stornoway, as was reported in the *John O'Groat Journal* of 29 August 1861, which announced that the '*Clansman* (was) to make her usual trip from Scrabster roads for Stornoway, Portree &c on Monday 9 September for the purpose of conveying back the men at the close of the fishing'. In the same year she was joined on the run by the paddle steamer *Dolphin*. This was a different steamer from the one of the same name already mentioned; she had been built in 1844, and was the first iron-hulled steamer in the Hutcheson fleet, easily recognisable by her figurehead comprising a dolphin and a mermaid. She had previously sailed on a variety of routes from Oban, including to Staffa and Iona and then only sailed to Stornoway for one year. Her successor came in 1858 in the form of the *Duke of Argyll*, whose career did not last long. Her loss was reported by the *Clansman* in January of that year on her arrival in Glasgow from Stornoway. The *Duke of Argyll* had anchored in Salen Bay, but when the wind shifted she had swung round on her anchor and struck a sunken rock. This caused her to sink shortly afterwards, although her crew and passengers managed to reach shore safely, while the *Clansman* had taken off a large part of her cargo. When the *Clansman* had left her, water was washing over the *Duke of Argyll*'s deck, and she had opened up, suggesting that recovery was doubtful.

The *Duke of Argyll*, in turn, was replaced by the *Stork;* this paddle steamer had been built in May 1851 for Messrs Burns' Irish Sea services and had been acquired six years later by Hutchesons. She was described in the *John O'Groat Journal* as a 'beautiful iron boat, swift, strong and handsomely fitted out'. She sailed between Glasgow and Stornoway until 1861 when she was sold to the Italian Government. In 1861 the *Stork* was replaced by the *Fingal*, the first screw steamer owned by Messrs Hutcheson. She was recognisable by her tall funnel which was placed quite far forward, and like most other ships of the time she was still square-rigged for sail. She was 178 feet in length, more than twice the length of the *Ben Nevis* built about forty years earlier. However, the inhabitants of Stornoway would have had little time to become familiar with her for after only four months she was sold. Before that she did make the headlines in the press when it was reported that a serious riot had occurred on board. On a voyage north she:

> received on board at Oban about two hundred fishermen belonging to Lewis, Harris and other of the Western Isles who were on their way home from the Wick herring fishing, having reached Oban via the Caledonian Canal. When the *Fingal* was about half way between Tobermory and Ardnamurchan, the fishermen, many of whom were drunk, became very riotous, and finally assaulted Captain McCallum, who was on the bridge. He put the steamer back to Tobermory, where five of the chief rioters were taken into custody, after which he resumed the passage.

Her destination on being disposed of might have been promoted as the 'South America Trade', while her purchaser could have been 'a Spanish firm' or more likely 'the Emperor of China', for David Hutcheson saw fit to sell her as a blockade runner and she became the Federal gunboat USS *Atlanta*, and these were the phrases used to cover up such deals. This was not something unusual during the American Civil War – Scottish shipowners saw the chance of selling ships for a good profit, and Americans were desperate to obtain ships. Some were even bought before they had been launched.

The rest of the *Fingal* story makes fascinating reading. She was chartered in October 1861 by a Captain Bulloch, a Southern US naval agent, with the option to buy at a moment's notice. This meant she would appear British, but be under Confederate control and could become an American ship if the situation demanded. She loaded a cargo on the Clyde of 14,000 Enfield rifles, 1 million cartridges, 3,000 sabres and other weapons, uniforms and stores, all this indicating that supplies were as important as ships to the Confederates. She then sailed to Holyhead to pick up Bulloch. However, entering that port in darkness she rammed and sank a sailing ship. In order not

The *Fingal* sailed to Stornoway for only a few months in 1861 before being sold for service in the American Civil War. She is shown here after being rebuilt in America as an 'ironclad' and renamed *Atlanta*

to be conspicuous, the British agent there was ordered to pay damages, and, while *Fingal* picked up the survivors, Bulloch quietly went aboard and the ship disappeared across the Atlantic. In thick fog she slipped through the Union blockade, and reached Savannah where she unloaded her much-needed cargo. She then loaded cotton to export to the UK, but by now the Union had the estuary blocked so *Fingal* was taken over by the Confederate navy. The vessel was then considerably altered – an armoured roof and reinforced bows converted her to an ironclad and in July 1862 she was renamed *Atlanta*. She was not a success – she was slow, slow to turn, the roof leaked and stopped air circulation below. However, several abortive attempts were made to break out, until finally in September she ran aground twice, and was captured by the Union. The Federal navy improved her, and she operated now to blockade the Confederates in the port of Richmond. At the end of the Civil War, she was decommissioned, and the last that is heard of her is sinking under tow en route to Haiti.

To take the place of *Fingal*, Messrs Hutcheson chartered the steamer *Ariel*. She had previously belonged to the Dublin & Glasgow Sailing and Steam Packet Co., but was now owned by the shipbuilders J & G Thomson. This enabled the Company to maintain the weekly two-ship service, while J & G Thomson was building a new ship for the route. This new vessel was launched in 1862, and named *Clydesdale*. She set the trend in design for the next few boats, namely having a clipper bow with a bowsprit, two tall masts and still with a sail plan. In addition she had a distinctive whaleback forecastle. She was described as 'making 'a beautiful picture entering Stornoway harbour but (was) an awkward boat to bring alongside a pier. There was no mechanical power to operate the rudder but she was manhandled by a wheel and two men to operate the rudder.' (*Tales and Traditions of the Lews*) Conditions for passengers were also now much improved, with deck houses built on the main deck, so that not all accommodation was below or near the water-line. She originally had one funnel, but after a second re-boilering in 1893, she had two funnels fitted, considerably altering her appearance.

Another of the Hutcheson fleet to call at Stornoway was the *Inverary Castle* (sic). This steamer, built in 1839, had been acquired in 1851 by Hutcheson from the Glasgow & Lochfyne Steam packet Co. She had seldom ventured further than between Glasgow and Inveraray, operating on that route for many years with the *Mary Jane*, but Stornoway Port Authority's 'Arrivals and Departures' book records her arrival from Glasgow on two occasions, in 1866 and 1873.

A description of journeys taken on the *Clydesdale* in 1872 as she sailed between Glasgow and Stornoway was written by Tina Brooke and Bell Munro in their book *A Trip to Skye*. They travelled from Mull to Skye and back, a journey which was much more straightforward then than it is today. In the nineteenth century it involved simply one sea trip, whereas today it would entail two car ferries and a winding drive of some sixty miles. Their voyage was not totally without its troubles, however, as the *Clydesdale* was about five hours late arriving at Craignure to pick them up, and then never seemed to travel at any great speed. There were numerous calls at places en route, which also added to the length of the journey. These included a call at Arisaig, described as 'one wild-looking place', where 'the steamer waited a very long time and Tina was much astonished to notice the great boxes of soap that were here landed, and more especially as there only appeared to be one human habitation within sight, and that a small inn.' From there the steamer diverted its way into Loch Nevis to land some passengers travelling to a shooting lodge. 'It was quite a little variety to watch the party going on shore which they did in little boats, rowed by some smart-looking sailors belonging to Mr Baird's fine yacht, which lay close at hand.' Although they had reserved a cabin this failed to be available and they had to resort to using the saloon where they tried to sleep amongst whisky drinking, conversations and laughter. This proved impossible, and about midnight they sat up and ordered the steward to bring them some sherry and lemonade.

On their return journey, aboard the same steamer, they were to leave from Broadford, where the sailing time was five o'clock in the morning, but the *Clydesdale* was again running late, not coming into sight round Scalpay until about two hours later. 'Then it became evident that the passengers were to row out to her, though how they were to get down into the small boat awaiting them seemed a difficult question to solve, for, the tide being low, the pier was at least six feet above the water'. Somehow they managed to get on board. There they found conditions were not ideal, and 'as there was a general air of discomfort pervading everywhere, and the decks were still in a very moist state from their recent scrubbing, Tina suggested retiring at once to the deck-cabin, which they had previously secured'. Again there were diversions, this time to Inverie on Loch Nevis to load wool, which added a further two hours to the journey. There were advantages to be gained from the ship's unhurried progress: 'just ere leaving (Inverie) the captain called out something in Gaelic to the men in one of the boats and instantly a large net was lowered and a great draught of fine fresh herrings (sic) put on board. They appeared on the table for evening tea.'

It cannot be envisaged that this would happen on today's car ferry, although it was fairly common for fresh fish to appear on the high tea menu on the *Loch Seaforth*, the cook having been given a bucket of herring or haddock by the skipper of a fishing boat tied up at Mallaig.

For the next thirteen years, the *Clydesdale* operated on the bi-weekly Glasgow run, for the first six of these in conjunction with the *Clansman*. In 1869, after fourteen years of sailing between Stornoway and Glasgow, the career of the *Clansman* came to an end when she went aground in thick fog on Sheep Island, off Sanda, on 21 July 1869. The first officer had been on watch, but, as he was concerned about navigating blind, he called Captain Sinclair to the bridge. He reduced speed to the slowest possible, but the steamer ran aground. All efforts to refloat the vessel using her engines failed, and word was sent for another steamer to come to assist. Some passengers were taken off by the *Celt*, which was sailing from Glasgow to Islay. Others remained on board awaiting the arrival of another MacBrayne ship. The *Celt* also took off the deck cargo of the *Clansman*, while the sheep on board were landed on the island of Sanda. It was initially thought that the ship would be refloated at high tide, but this failed and later the stern sank in deep water. The remaining passengers were taken off on board the *Swan*, which then returned for any cargo still on board. The *Clansman* finally broke into three pieces, and had to be declared a total loss. The *Clansman* was the last paddle steamer to sail regularly to Stornoway. In September of that year Hutchesons chartered the steamer *Snipe*, a large ship belonging to G & J Burns, to maintain the service alongside the *Clydesdale* until a permanent replacement was ready early in 1870. This new ship was the second *Clansman*, whose career will be dealt with later.

There are a number of literary references to the first *Clansman* which give an idea of what conditions were like at that time for travellers to and from Stornoway. Perhaps the best known is that by Alexander Smith in his book *A Summer in Skye* in which he describes his return journey to the Clyde, joining the steamer in Portree en route to Glasgow.

> The *Clansman* reached Portree Bay at eleven PM, and I went on board at once and went to bed. When I awoke next morning, the engines were in full action and I could hear the rush of water past my berth. When I got on deck we were steaming down the sound of Raasay … A lot of sheep were penned up near the bows, amidships were piles of wool, groups of pointers and setters were scattered about and at the breakfast table were numerous sportsmen returning to the south. … The breakfast

party, too, consisted of all orders and degrees of men. There were drovers going to, or returning from markets; merchants from Stornoway going south; a couple of Hebridean clergymen, one of whom said grace; several military men of frank and hearty bearing; an extensive brewer; three members of parliament who had entirely recovered from the fatigues of legislation; and a tall and handsome English Earl of some repute on the turf. Several ladies, too, dropped in before the meal was over. We were all hungry and fed like Homer's heroes. The commissariat on board the Highland steamers is plentiful and of quality beyond suspicion; and the conjunction of good viands and appetites whetted by the sea-breeze, results in a play of knife and fork wonderful to behold.

The long-looked-for dinner was served after we had passed Kyle-Rhea and were gliding down into Glenelg. For some little time previously, savoury steams had assailed our nostrils. We saw the stewards descending into the cabin with covered dishes and at the first sound of the bell the hurricane deck, crowded a moment before, was left entirely empty. The Captain took his seat at the head of the table with a mighty roast before him … the covers were lifted away by deft waiters and we dined that day at four as if we had not previously breakfasted at eight and lunched at one …

In autumn the voyage to the south is lengthened by stoppages and frequently the steamer has to leave her direct route and thread along inland running lochs to take wool on board … At Armadale we stayed for perhaps half an hour and then struck directly across the Sound of Sleat and sailed up the windings of Loch Nevis. When we reached the top there was an immense to-do on the beach; some three or four boats laden with wool were already pulling out towards the steamer, which immediately lay to and let off noisy steam; men were tumbling bales of wool into the empty boats that lay at the stony pier and to the pier laden carts were hurrying from the farmhouse that stood remote. The wool boats came on either side of the steamer; doors were opened in the bulwarks, to these doors steam cranes were wheeled and with many a shock of crank and rattle of loosened chain, the bales were hoisted on deck and consigned to the gloomy recesses of the hold.

As soon as a boat was emptied, a laden one pulled out to take its place; the steam cranes were kept continually jolting and rattling and in the space of a couple of hours a considerable amount of business had been done. On the present occasion the transference of wool from the boats to the hold of the steamer occupied a longer time than usual; sunset had come in crimson and died away to pale gold and rose; and still the laden boats came slowly on, still storms of Gaelic execration surged along the sides of the ship and still the steam cranes were at their noisy work. The whole affair, having by this time lost all sense of novelty, was in danger of becoming tiresome, but in the fading light the steward had lighted up the saloon into hospitable warmth and glow, and then the bell rang for tea.

The next morning the *Clansman* had left Skye and Arisaig behind.

Eig (sic) rose opposite, with its curiously-shaped scuir; Muck lay ahead. The *Clansman* soon reached the open sea and we began to feel the impulse of the Atlantic. By the time the passengers began to appear on deck the ship was lurching heavily along towards the far-stretching headland of Ardnamurchan. … Great glittering watery mounds came heaving on, to wash with unavailing foam the rocky coast; and amongst these the steamer rolled and tossed and groaned, its long dark pennon of smoke streaming with the impulse of the sea. The greater proportion of the passengers crawled amidships – beside the engines and the cook's quarters, which were redolent with the scent of herrings frying for a most unnecessary breakfast – for there the motion was at least felt … Now I beheld the steersman against the sky on the crest of an airy acclivity, now one bulwark was buried in surge, now the other and anon the sheep at the bows were brought out against a foamy cataract.

But with all this turmoil and dancing and rolling, the *Clansman* went swiftly on and in due time we were off the Ardnamurchan lighthouse. Here we rolled and tossed in an unpleasant manner – the smitten foam springing to the top of the rocks and falling back in snowy sheets – and seemed to make but little progress. Gradually, however, the lighthouse began to draw slowly behind us, slowly we rounded the rocky buttress, slowly the dark shores of Mull drew out to sea and in a quarter of an hour, with dripping decks and giddy brains, we had passed from the great bright heave and energy of the Atlantic to the quiet waters of Loch Sunart, and, sheltered by Mull, were steaming towards Tobermory … The steamer is usually detained at Tobermory for a couple of hours and during all that time there is a constant noise of lading and unlading. I became tired of the noise and tumult and experienced a sense of relief when steam was got up again and with much backing and turning and churning of dirty harbour water into questionable foam, the large vessel worked its way through the difficult channel and slid calmly down the Sound of Mull.

The longest delay during the passage is at Oban, but then we had dinner there, which helped kill the time in a pleasant way. The *Clansman* had received a quantity of cargo at Tobermory, at Loch Aline a flock of sheep were driven on board, goods were taken in plentifully at other places in the Sound at which we touched and when we received all the stuffs waiting for us at Oban, the vessel was heavily laden. The entire steerage was a bellowing and bleating mass of black cattle and sheep, each "parcel" divided from the other by temporary barriers. The space amidships was a chaos of barrels and trunks and bales of one kind or another and amongst these the steerage passengers were forced to dispose themselves. Great piles of wooden boxes containing herring were laid along the cabin deck, so that if a man were disposed to walk about it behoved him to take care of his footsteps.

Later that night the steamer made its way round the Mull of Kintyre:

The ship was labouring heavily, I heard the voices of the sailors flying in the wind, I felt the shock of solid and the swish of broken seas. In such circumstances sleep, for me at least, was impossible, so I slipped out of bed and, steadying myself for a favourable moment, made a grab at my clothes. With much difficulty I dressed, with greater difficulty I got into my boots and then I staggered on deck. Holding on by the first support, I was almost blinded by the glare of broken seas. From a high coast against which the great waves rushed came the steady glare of a lighthouse and by that token I knew we were "on" the Mull of Cantyre. The ship was fuming through a mighty battle of tides. Shadowy figures of steerage passengers were to be seen clinging here and there. One – a young woman going to Glasgow as a housemaid, as she afterwards told me – was in great distress, was under the impression that we were all going to the bottom and came to me for comfort. I quieted her as best I could and procured her a seat. Once, when the ship made a wild lurch and a cloud of spray came flying over the deck, she exclaimed to a sailor who was

> shuffling past wearing a sou'wester and canvas overalls, "O sailor, is't ever sae bad as this?"
>
> "As bad as this," said the worthy, poising himself on the unsteady deck, "as bad as this! Lord, ye sud jist a seen oor last vi'age. There was only three besides myself o' the ship's crew able to haud on by a rape." Delivering himself of this scrap of comfort, the sailor shuffled forward.
>
> Happily the turmoil was not of long duration. In an hour we had rounded the formidable Mull, had reached comparatively smooth water and, with the lights of Campbelton (sic) behind, the pallid glare of furnaces seen afar on the Ayrshire coast and the morning beginning to pencil softly the east, I went below again and slept till we reached Greenock.

A second description is found in *A Princess of Thule*, written by William Black and first published in 1873. Two different crossings of the Minch provide further evocations of a voyage in the 1860s. The first describes how

> Two young men (were) seated in the stern of the steamer *Clansman* as she ploughed her way across the blue and rushing waters of the Minch … (One) lounged about the white deck in the glare of the sunlight, steadying himself from time to time, as an unusually big wave carried the *Clansman* aloft for a second or two, and then sent her staggering and groaning into a hissing trough of foam … (He would then) start off on his unsteady journey up and down the white planks. Both men were good sailors, and they had need to be, for, although the sky above them was as blue and clear as the heart of a sapphire, and although the sunlight shone on the decks and the rigging, a strong north-easter had been blowing all the morning, and there was a considerable sea on. The far blue plain was whitened with the tumbling crests of the waves, that shone and sparkled in the sun; and ever and anon a volume of water would strike the *Clansman's* bow, rise high in the air with the shock, and fall in heavy showers over the forward decks. Sometimes, too, a wave caught her broadside, and sent a handful of spray over the two or three passengers who were safe in the stern; but the decks here remained silvery and white, for the sun and wind speedily dried up the traces of the sea-showers.
>
> "How far to Stornoway, yet?"
>
> "An hour."
>
> "By Jove, what a distance! All day yesterday getting up from Oban to Skye, all last night churning our way up to Loch Gair, all to-day crossing to this outlandish island, that seems as far away as Iceland – and for what?"
>
> "But don't you remember the moonlight last night, as we sailed by the Cuchulins? And the sunrise this morning as we lay in Loch Gair? Were these not worth coming for?"
>
> The pale blue cloud that for some time had been lying faintly along the horizon now came nearer and more near, until they could pick out something like the configuration of the island, its bays, and promontories, and mountains. The day seemed to become warmer as they got out of the driving wind of the Channel, and the heavy roll of the sea had so far subsided. Through comparatively calm water the great *Clansman* drove her way, until, on getting near the land, and under the shelter of the Peninsula of Eye, the voyagers found themselves on a beautiful blue plain, with the spacious harbour of Stornoway opening out before them.
>
> The steamer was moored at last; the fishermen and loungers drew near to meet their friends who had come up from Glasgow – for there are few strangers as a rule, arriving at Stornoway to whet the curiosity of the islanders.

On that occasion, the two travellers were sailing to Stornoway to meet Sheila, the heroine of the novel, who lived on an island off the west coast of Lewis. On a second voyage, one of them, now under Sheila's spell, is hoping to meet with her and voyage together from the Clyde to Stornoway.

> Next morning he went down, long before any passenger could have thought of arriving, to the *Clansman*. He did not go near the big steamer, for he was known to the captain and the steward; but he hung about the quays, watching each person who went on board. Sheila certainly was not among the passengers by the *Clansman*.
>
> But she might have gone to Greenock, and waited for the steamer there. Accordingly … he took rail for Greenock, where he arrived sometime before the *Clansman* made her appearance. He went down to the quay. Far away beyond the pale blue mountains opposite lay the wonderful network of sea-lochs and islands through which one had to pass to get to the distant Lewis. How gladly, at this moment, would he have stepped on board the steamer, with Sheila, and put out on that gleaming plain of sea, knowing that by and by they would sail into Stornoway harbour … They would not hasten the voyage. She had never been round the Mull of Cantyre; and so he would sit by her side, and show her the wild tides meeting there, and the long jets of white foam shooting up the great wall of rocks. He would show her the pale coast of Ireland; and they would see Islay, of which she had many a ballad and story. They would go through the narrow sound that is overlooked by the gloomy mountains of Jura. They would see the distant islands where the chief of Colonsay is still mourned for on the still evenings, by the hapless mermaid who sings her wild song across the sea. They would keep wide of the dangerous currents of Corryvreckan; and by and by they would sail into the harbour of Oban.
>
> In the distance he could hear they throbbing of *Clansman*'s engines, as the big steamer came on through the white plain … The *Clansman* sailed into the quay, and there was a flinging of ropes, and general hurry and bustle, while people came crowding round the gangways, calling out to each other in every variety of dialect and accent.

Sheila was not there, but, as in all the best romantic novels, the two do get together and after many misunderstandings, trials and tribulations, they settle happily in the Western Isles. What is perhaps more interesting is that David MacBrayne later named one of his ships *Sheila*, after that very heroine, and this steamer, as will be seen, sailed for many years to Stornoway.

William Black also wrote a factual description of crossing the Minch on the *Clansman*, which appeared in *Harper's Magazine* in 1875. He describes his voyage in the romantic way in which many Victorian travellers must have viewed their venture to the Outer Hebrides.

> We are on the deck of the great steamship *Clansman*, which is plowing (sic) its way across the Minch – the rough and rushing northern sea which lies between the mainland of Scotland and the far Hebrides. It is a brilliant July day; there is a blue sky overhead; but there is also a stiff north-easterly breeze blowing, and every minute or two one of the huge green waves dashes against the *Clansman's* bows and sends a shower of salt foam over her white decks. The fierce blowing of the wind, the southward rushing of the sea-green seas, the moving of sharply defined shadows on the sunlit decks as the steamer rises on a mighty wave and then plunges forward into the trough – all this gives one a sense of hurrying motion and expectation; and still, scan the horizon as we may, there is as yet no sign of the "stormy Hebrides."

The Greater Minch is only about twice as broad as the Channel between Dover and Calais; but whoever has been to the Isle of Lewis knows that ever after it remains in his memory as a strangely remote and inaccessible place. It seems to be farther away than Gibraltar, or Newfoundland, or St Petersburg, or any spot, indeed, that is a familiar geographical expression. Doubtless this fancy arises in part from the exceeding loneliness and desolate grandeur of the scenery on the west coast of Scotland past which the Stornoway steamer churns its way during two long days and nights. There are some of us on board who have come all the way by steamer from Glasgow – round the rocky Mull of Cantyre, where five tides meet and roar; through the Sound of Islay, and under the gloomy Paps of Jura; catching a glimpse of the mystic Colonsay, where the sound of the mermaid is still heard at night mourning for the chieftain who deceived her; keeping wide of the swirling currents of Corryvreckan –

> "As you pass through Jura's Sound,
> Bend your course by Scarba's shore;
> Shun, O shun the gulf profound
> Where Corryvreckan's surges roar" –

Until at length the *Clansman* sailed into Oban Bay. There are others of us who boarded her yesterday morning, and have even now but a misty recollection of that endless series of great and lonely mountains, of desolate islands set in a restless sea, of long bays and shores where no sign of life was visible but the countless flocks of seabirds calling and screaming to each other over the breaking waves. Last night, as the sea darkened and the stars began to appear, we sailed under the coast of Skye, and the blackness of the wild Cuchullin Hills seemed to overshadow us. By-and-by, as we can remember, the moonlight rose behind the sharp and jagged peaks, only to render the awful gloom and majesty of them more impressive. This morning, too, did we not see a rosy sunrise flush the smooth waters of Loch Gair (sic) and light up the soft green hills around? It was our last look at the mainland. Now we have left calling in at these various ports, and are standing right out to the Minch, far away on the other side of which, and as yet hidden by the white heat of the sun and the white spray of the sea, lie the long, low islands that we seek.

At length a pale blue streak along the horizon becomes visible; as we draw nearer, the outline of the bay and hill grows more and more distinct; and finally, the *Clansman* getting into smoother water, we make our way into the spacious harbour.

Chapter 6

Stornoway to Ullapool in the 1870s

Sir James Matheson returned to operating steamers to Stornoway for the last time in the 1870s. In January 1869 a 'memorial was made by the inhabitants of Stornoway to the Postmaster General praying for proper postal accommodation'. Two years later the Postmaster General was reminded about this in Parliament, and it was also suggested that Lewis should receive a similar service to that being introduced to Orkney, namely a daily service in summer and thrice-weekly in winter. The response was that any extra expense incurred would result in a loss to the Post Office, while in any case there could be no comparison with Orkney as the distance to Stornoway was greater and therefore the costs would be greater. The Postmaster General concluded that he had no intention to make any change. However, after further discussion, progress was made, and a subsidy of £1,300 was offered by the Post Office to run a steamship to carry the mail.

Once again, no-one was willing to take up the offer, so Sir James took it upon himself to provide the service for ten years. To do this, he purchased the paddle steamer *Ondine* in October 1871. She had been built in London twenty-four years earlier. Like most steamers of her day she had two masts and one funnel abaft her paddle boxes. She ran between Stornoway and Ullapool, the change from Poolewe taking place because a coach service, taking five hours, now connected Ullapool with the newly opened railway at Garve. This gave an improved, yet still slow and inconvenient, through link to Dingwall and Inverness. The *Ondine* made her first recorded crossing on 20 July 1872. A daily service was provided during the summer months, while in winter it was reduced to thrice weekly. There were occasions when severe weather caused delays in the mail reaching Stornoway, caused less by the steamer being delayed than by problems on land. In December 1878, a month which incurred heavy snowfalls, the mails due in Stornoway on the fifteenth did not arrive on the *Ondine* until the evening of the eighteenth, having been brought from Garve to Ullapool on horseback. Because of the importance of carrying the mails the Stornoway Pier and Harbour Commission offered Sir James Matheson free berthing for the *Ondine*, stating what a 'great boon it has been to the community to have such a regular mail connection'. The offer was, however, declined, Matheson opting to pay the sum of £20.

In his book *Tales and Traditions of the Lews*, Donald Macdonald suggests that in addition to the *Ondine*, which he refers to as the *Undine*, two other steamers, the *Stornoway* and the *Tusker*, sailed between Stornoway and Ullapool. He describes an incident in which the latter 'had a breakdown near Arnish lighthouse and began to drift with a south-west wind towards the "Chicken Rock". The late Rev James Grenfield was aboard and mothers remarked about James, who was the best swimmer in Lewis at the time, "If James can see land I am quite sure he will make it". The *Tusker* was saved.'

Two descriptions of voyages across the Minch in the 1870s were written by J T Reid in his book *Art Rambles in the Highlands and Islands of Scotland*. He made the crossing from Gairloch, evidence that steamers were serving Stornoway from there as well as from Ullapool. His description starts as he waits for the steamer in a hotel:

> It came the midnight hour. Boots pledged his word he would watch for the steamboat, which even then was much past its advertised time – a circumstance caused by the sheep-lifting, and traffic of that kind required for the large autumn markets … At the pier I waited for the transport boats, seen in dim shadowy form coming from the steamboat that lay out in the bay, and listened to the plash of oars. They had much goods for Gairloch and not a little to take on board. Once on board I took a look below, where many men were spread as comfortably on the saloon sofas as circumstances would permit, and finding a vacant space sufficiently large to stretch my full complement of feet and inches on, I tried to fall asleep before we got into rough water; but with the first movement of the screw I was on my feet and on deck.
>
> As we receded from the mainland … mountain ranges (grew) fainter and fainter and the Isle of Lewis loomed

The *Ondine*, owned by Sir James Matheson, sailed between Stornoway and Ullapool between 1871 and 1879. This view shows her at Stornoway, along with an unidentified steamer, sailing schooners and fishing boats

> bigger and broader, till we steamed alongside of the pier and were landed "mid the curing of a fine catch of herring taken during the night".

On his return journey he travelled on board the *Ondine*, which he describes as the 'Ullapool packet'. The crossing took place near the end of October, and the steamer's early start necessitated him joining the boat while it was still dark:

> The warning bell rung on board the steamer told me their time was ahead of mine. I hastened to embark. A sailor put the knapsack in a corner of the saloon beside the luggage of the only other cabin passenger we carried. There was discontent audible among the ruling powers in regard to goods someone wanted to put on board. We had for cargo many barrels of salt from the Stornoway Salt Store, which supplies many ports on the mainland. To the advertised minute the steamer kept. For a time it was hard to reconcile the Stornoway people to this punctuality, and more than one passenger had to be taught that it is not the duty of the captain to wait for lag-behinds, by being left on the island till the next sailing. The turning of our head safely accomplished, we steamed slowly past Goat Island, seeing the gleam from the lighthouse at intervals as it shone amid the darkness. A few ships' lights were rocking about as the swell from without told on the waters of the bay; and soon we were outside, buffeting and o'ertopping the unseen waves: dark they seemed, and dark overhead was the starless sky; all we could see from the bridge was what our mast-light shone on; the brightest light fell on our own deck, and the barrels of salt firmly roped to the ship's side. Our bow ploughed into the waves, sending the white foam to the right and to the left of her onward course; the wind whistled through the rigging. With a dancing motion we bounced over the waves or charged them, and were drenched in a shower of spray after the shock. The man on the outlook being in danger, was ordered abaft. Slowly the grey light heralded the dayspring, and the waves and white crests that crown their soarings became traceable. The light increased, and a faint gleam of ruddy hue ahead streaked the horizon, and discovered to us the mainland mountains calmly slumbering in a bed of mist: gently the roseate light stole over their heads, as if unwilling to disturb the sleepers in the spellbound land. There is no steward on board, and the keen sea-air has a tendency to give one an appetite. My fellow-traveller was made aware of this before he left Lewis, and had quite an ample store and every requisite from Stornoway Castle: he got a sailor to make tea, and invited me to have a share, – an invitation I gladly accepted. As we sailed into Loch Broom, the sun shone on the numberless rocky isles and islets we passed, and we had a fine panorama of mountains inland and to the north and the south.'

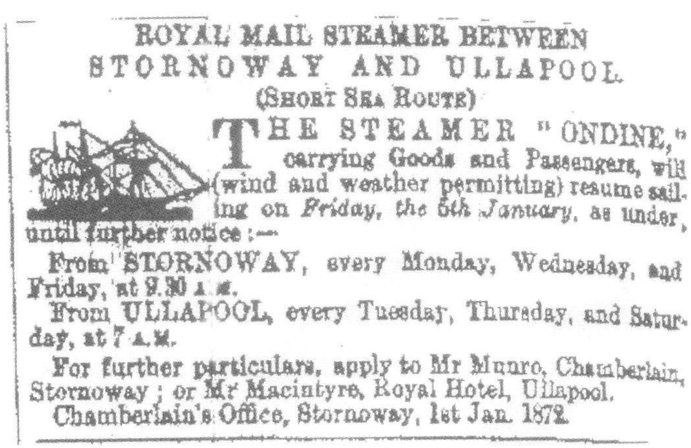
ROYAL MAIL STEAMER BETWEEN
STORNOWAY AND ULLAPOOL.
(SHORT SEA ROUTE)
THE STEAMER "ONDINE," carrying Goods and Passengers, will (wind and weather permitting) resume sailing on *Friday, the 5th January*, as under, until further notice:—
From STORNOWAY, every Monday, Wednesday, and Friday, at 9.30 A.M.
From ULLAPOOL, every Tuesday, Thursday, and Saturday, at 7 A.M.
For further particulars, apply to Mr Munro, Chamberlain, Stornoway; or Mr Macintyre, Royal Hotel, Ullapool.
Chamberlain's Office, Stornoway, 1st Jan. 1872.

An 1872 advertisement from the Inverness Courier shows details of the *Ondine's* sailings

Chapter 7

The Coming of the Railway

The inconvenience of the route travelling over the Minch and then across the mainland of Scotland to Inverness was succinctly summed up by Macleod of Dunvegan, when he stated in 1864 that there was 'very little communication betwixt west coast and the town of Inverness. The town is undoubtedly the county town, but at present, I call Glasgow my county town because I go there for everything I want by means of the steamers.'

This sentiment would have been strongly echoed by the inhabitants of Lewis, in their case Glasgow being the substitute for Ross and Cromarty's county town of Dingwall. It therefore came as no great surprise that proposals were made to construct a railway line to Kyle of Lochalsh from the east coast. An Act of Parliament was passed in 1865 to allow construction of the Dingwall and Skye Railway but financial constraints meant that the line was completed only as far as Strome Ferry on the south side of Loch Carron, about fifteen miles from the open sea. A sizeable pier was built with the railway line running on to it, and the line was opened to traffic on 19 August 1870.

The Railway Company invited Messrs Hutcheson to divert their steamers to the pier en route to Portee and Stornoway, but this was declined as the detour was too great. Hutcheson wrote to the Railway Company:

> that we could not run a steamer or steamers in connection with the trains of the Dingwall & Skye Railway without a serious loss of money and we have therefore resolved not to take it. But if there is any way whereby we can work in with the line with our present boat to our mutual advantage we shall be glad to do it.

Perhaps the fact that the passage up Loch Carron to Strome was not the easiest to navigate also influenced the decision; it became necessary for the Railway Company to provide buoys and lights to ensure safe navigation of vessels. As a result of the Hutcheson ships not extending their voyages to Strome Ferry, the Dingwall and Skye Railway Co. was obliged to purchase two steamers to operate services to Skye and Lewis. They were obtained from Messrs William Sloan & Co. of Glasgow. The *Jura* had been built in 1857 as the *Admiral Cator* for the West Hartlepool Steam Shipping Co., while the *Oscar* was seven years older. With these two ships, sailings were inaugurated from Strome Ferry to Portree and Stornoway. Portree was served daily, while the service to Lewis by the *Jura* sailed thrice weekly, on Tuesdays, Thursdays and Saturdays. The Stornoway steamer connected with the morning train which left Inverness at 0915, reaching Strome Ferry at 1315, and gave an arrival time in Stornoway of 2245.

The service was not a success. It had an inauspicious start when it was reported that on the opening day one of the captains had so much to drink during the festivities that he could not reach the bridge of his vessel. In a private letter, which wrongly named the owners of the ships, it was described how, 'MacBrayne's steamer waited for an hour to collect the captain and he certainly could not go on the bridge'. The hoped-for trade, consisting not just of passengers but also fish and livestock, did not materialise. Harbour dues at Stornoway were also a problem – the Railway Co. complained that they were charged more than other companies. The elderly steamers struggled to maintain the schedules and the service proved to be unreliable. As a result, the service to Stornoway was withdrawn in the winter of 1870, and did not re-commence the following summer. At the annual general meeting in October 1871 shareholders in the Railway Company were informed as to why sailings to Stornoway had been discontinued. The chairman reported, 'We have ceased to go to distant ports where the traffic was inadequate to meet the expenses involved in the long sailings'. He also mentioned that 'there is no doubt that we have been somewhat unfortunate with our steamers the first year and I hear it sometimes that it was a pity we did not get new steamers instead of the second hand ones we procured. But the answer to this is – we had not the capital'.

A further setback occurred when the *Oscar* ran aground on rocks near Applecross, and could no longer be used, meaning that the *Jura* had to serve Portree. She in turn was replaced by another second-hand purchase, the paddle steamer *Carham*, purchased from the North British Railway, which had operated her on the Clyde. Sailings to Lewis were not resumed. Instead, passengers wishing to travel there had to take the service to Portree and connect at that port with the *Clydesdale* or *Clansman* en route from Glasgow to Stornoway. By the end of 1873, the *Carham* was unfit for further service, requiring new boiler, funnel, safety valves and steam chest casing. It was thought wise to replace her, and by good fortune the Company was able to

The Pier at Strome Ferry. Sailings to Stornoway operated by the railway company commenced in 1870 but were withdrawn the following year before being reintroduced in 1874 using the steamer *Ferret*

purchase the *Ferret* from G & J Burns. She took up the Portree mail run in January 1874, with the new mail contract including a weekly sailing to Stornoway which commenced in May of that year and eventually included a winter sailing. The *Carham* must still have been serviceable, for she is recorded as sailing to Stornoway in 1877 and 1880, relieving the *Ferret*. The timings of the Stornoway service have been described as 'engagingly non-committal', with an 1878 timetable advertising that the steamer would 'leave Strome Ferry every Wednesday not earlier than 2.30pm, Portree about 6.30pm reaching Stornoway about 1.30am on Thursdays except the fourth Thursday in February on which date the steamer will reach Stornoway about 10.0am'. This variation was due to a once-a-month sailing to Gairloch, Aultbea and Poolewe which was incorporated into the sail to Stornoway. The Highland Railway took over the operation in 1878 but they, too, incurred losses. The steamer accounts registered a total deficit of £5857.7.2d (£5857.35) between 1871 and 1877. Two years later David MacBrayne assumed responsibility for the calls at Gairloch and Aultbea, and finally on 6 April it was announced that he had taken over the all services from Strome Ferry. The railway company retained their steamers, anticipating that David MacBrayne would wish to buy them, but this did not materialise.

Instead, it led to the amazing tale of the demise of the *Ferret*. She was chartered for a six-month cruise to the Mediterranean by a Mr Smith, ostensibly for the benefit of his invalid wife, on the recommendation of her doctor. The ship was loaded with stores, including 1,000 bottles of fine wine, from a Glasgow chandler and she set sail. Neither the Highland Railway nor the chandler ever received payment and it had to be admitted that the ship had been stolen. Information was received that the vessel had been seen passing through the Straits of Gibraltar and at Malta, to be followed shortly afterwards by news of identifiable wreckage from the *Ferret* being picked up, again in the Straits of Gibraltar. A claim for total loss of the ship was made and it was assumed that this would be the end of the saga. Three months later, however, in April 1881, a telegram was received that the *Ferret* had been detained in Melbourne and Smith and his colleagues arrested. At the ensuing trial the full story was revealed. The ship had indeed reached the Mediterranean, and had left again under cover of darkness, when the ship's gear had been jettisoned. She had then had her funnel repainted, alterations made to her superstructure, and under the new name of *Bentan* she sailed to Santos in Brazil. There she loaded a cargo of coffee and sailed back across the Atlantic Ocean to Cape Town, arriving with the name *India* painted on her sides and stern. The coffee was sold for £11,000, and Smith hoped to sell the ship as well. The latter sale did not materialise and they then sailed to Mauritius, Port Albany in Western Australia, and finally to Melbourne. Again Smith could find no purchasers. Finally the scheme came to an end when a sheet of Highland Railway notepaper was discovered in the ship's log book during a port inspection. The culprits were sentenced to between three-and-a-half and seven years imprisonment, but the railway company and the chandlers did not receive their outstanding dues. The *Ferret* was finally sold to the Australia Shipping Company and gave several years' good service along the Australian coast.

Other steamers did start to operate between Strome Ferry and Stornoway: in 1880 the *Celt*, the *Agate* and the *Stornoway* are all recorded as arriving regularly in Stornoway from the railhead. Little detail is known about the first two vessels but the last mentioned steamer had been built in 1877, and was registered in Leith, with J Blackie Jr her owner. Her tonnage was 69 and she had a crew of seven. On 30 May 1880, while on passage from Leith and Stornoway to Strome Ferry with a cargo of fish and three passengers, and in the charge of a pilot, she struck a sunken rock about a mile west of Strome Ferry and sank in eight fathoms of water. Initially she was thought to be 'all gone and broken up', and with just her masthead showing above water. On 8 June, however, she was moved to shallower water and beached with the intention of pumping her out. The *Highland News* reported that 'the steamship *Stornoway* had now been taken far enough shoreward in Fernaig Bay to enable all the patching necessary to be done to her at low ebb during a spring tide.' The report also mentioned that 'the steam tug *Knight Templar* of Liverpool – with the schooners *Regent* and *Arica* of Stornoway – (was) busy recovering the anchors of the *Stornoway* which were dropped when the vessel was about sink,' adding, 'Nautical men look upon the bringing of the vessel to anchor in such circumstances as a decided mistake, and it certainly occasioned trouble to the parties engaged in raising the sunken ship.

The recovery proved to be successful and six days later she was re-floated and taken to the Clyde for repairs. As the records show, she returned to sail between Strome Ferry and Stornoway. This was further evidence of the difficulties of negotiating the waters of Loch Carron, which were also mentioned by J and E R Pennell, who wrote in the 1880s that, for travel from the Long Island, 'the nearest way to the mainland is by Strome Ferry, where the entrance to the harbour is intricate, and so poorly lighted that once the short winter days set in, as its passage cannot be attempted after dark, traffic between the islands and the main-land is seriously interrupted'.

Chapter 8

Consolidation of Services

During the 1870s, David Hutcheson & Co. had gradually expanded their services and gained control of much of the shipping to the Western Isles. To take the place of the *Clansman* a new steamer was built on the Clyde by J & G Thomson. Launched in 1870, she was also named *Clansman* and was a worthy successor to her namesake. The bare details, stating that she was 211 feet (64m) in length, with a beam of 27 feet (8m) and a gross tonnage of around 600, do not do justice to a vessel whose design belied the fact that she was designed for everyday work between Glasgow and Stornoway, carrying passengers and all variety of cargoes. She was a development of the previous two ships built for the route and in many ways looked more like a private yacht than a commercial steamer. She had fine lines, a clipper bow with a bowsprit, beneath which was a figurehead,

The graceful lines of the second *Clansman* are shown in this drawing of her at Lochclash (drawing by the author)

while ornamental carving also decorated the graceful stern. She gained the added luxury of electric lighting when this was fitted in 1904. For the next forty years she had an uneventful career running all year round between Glasgow and Stornoway. She shared the Glasgow- Stornoway service with the *Clydesdale* until 1881, when she was joined on the run by the first *Claymore*. A sailing bill from 1870 also indicates that the *Staffa* was also sailing to Stornoway. From time to time the two regular ships on the service made calls in addition to the normal schedule, advertisements of the time listing the regular ports visited and also adding that the ships would call at 'any other places that might be agreed upon.' In 1870, for example, the *Clansman* was to make a call at Loch Carron on 11 June on her return from Stornoway to Glasgow, while both that ship and the *Clydesdale* were advertised to sail on the 13 and 16 July from Stornoway to Scrabster, with a steerage fare of 2s 6d (12p). In December 1880 the *Clansman* diverted from her normal route to pick up seventy barrels of herring from Scalpay. In the same month she was detained at Broadford for several hours due to a blinding snowstorm, consequently not arriving at her next call at Portree until six o'clock on Christmas morning.

Although David Hutcheson & Co. declined to operate the service from Strome Ferry, other routes were pioneered and developed by the company. The 'Royal Route' from Glasgow through the Crinan Canal to Oban was improved with new and bigger ships; excursion services were introduced from Oban to destinations such as Iona and Staffa; while in 1876 the service to Islay was taken over. But David Hutcheson himself was no longer a young man and in 1876, at the age of seventy-seven, he decided to retire. Such was the importance of the part he played in opening up communications to the islands that a monument to him was erected on the island of Kerrera, facing what was to become the focal point of West Coast shipping, Oban. The inscription on it reads, 'Erected by a grateful public in memory of David Hutcheson, by whose energy and enterprise the benefits of greatly improved steam communication were conferred on the West Highlands and Islands of Scotland.' Only two years later his brother, Alexander, also retired, leaving David MacBrayne as the sole partner.

Chapter 9

David MacBrayne

In June 1879 David MacBrayne changed the name of the company to reflect his position, and thereby the famous company name of David MacBrayne was created. It was one which was to become almost synonymous with West Highland shipping. He quickly imposed his own ideas on the company. He appreciated that the overland journey from the Lowlands was now much faster, and that, by developing this, traffic would increase. Accordingly, as has been mentioned, David MacBrayne took over the service from Strome Ferry to Portree in 1880. This take-over coincided with the 'fish war' involving Stornoway fishermen. Up until now the fish traffic went through Strome, within six hours' steaming distance. The opening of the railhead at Oban would involve a journey of sixteen hours and this was not considered a problem by the Highland Railway. However the fishermen were lured to Oban by the offer of a modern pier, cranes, auctioneers' stances and new offices, and in spite of the longer voyage from Stornoway, cargoes were reaching London two hours earlier than those dispatched through Strome. MacBrayne appealed to the Railway Company to provide warning lights at danger points in Loch Carron but this was not done. Eventually he agreed to supply a steamer exclusively for the Stornoway-Strome fish run from 1 May until 20 June, but this was withdrawn when it was realised that some night sailings would be involved. Fortunately the 'war' did not last long and the advantageous location of Strome brought trade back there. By 1883 navigation of Loch Carron had been made safer, with lighthouses and buoys being provided to mark islands and the most dangerous rocks.

In November of 1881, MacBrayne's control of services was further strengthened when ownership of the mail service from Stornoway to Ullapool was assumed by the Company. This had been operated until 1879 by the ageing paddle steamer *Ondine*, and then by a steamer called the *Express*. She was replaced by the *Lochiel*, a small steamer 140 feet (43m) in length, 18 feet (6m) beam and a tonnage of just over 200, which had been built in 1877 by A & J Inglis. She had sailed on a variety of routes, visiting Inverness as the Loch Ness mail steamer, then serving Loch Etive, then Islay, before operating the Strome to Portree run. Incidentally, when she was transferred to Ullapool, her place on the Portree service was taken by the *Glencoe*, which had formerly been the *Mary Jane*, Sir James Matheson's first steamer to link Stornoway and Glasgow. During May and June 1882, the *Lochiel* was replaced by the *Flying Dutchman*, while the former steamer was engaged in carrying cargoes of herring to Strome Ferry. In 1883 a similar arrangement took place, with the mail service to Ullapool being operated first by the *Flying Dutchman* and then by the *Osprey*.

The *Lochiel* was involved in an attempted rescue in Stornoway harbour in 1882. On 2 October a storm swept over the island of Lewis, reaching hurricane strength from the south-west between eight and nine o'clock at night. Several ships, including the barque *Johannes Koster* of Stralsund, and the barque *Lady Ellen* from Aberdeen, were driven ashore. The *Lady Head*, en route from Archangel to Glasgow, put in to the harbour and sheltered outside Goat Island; she dragged her anchor and became a total wreck with part of her cargo of tar and pitch being washed ashore. The barque *Rowena* of Aberdeen, sailing from Sundsvall for Greenock, had also sought shelter, and was driven a considerable distance before grounding on Goat Island. The *Lochiel*, however, did not suffer damage, but was able to go to the assistance of the *Rowena*, and attempted to tow her off the following morning, but without success. A second rescue followed in 1883. The paddle steamer *Lively*, a fast despatch vessel had been provided by the Admiralty to carry members of the Napier Commission, set up to inquire into the conditions of crofters, round the islands. On returning to Stornoway on 7 June she went aground on the Chicken Rock, just outside the Harbour. Fortunately all on board were saved, but three weeks later the vessel broke up in a gale. While parts of the deck, tables, doors and masts were washed up on the shore, the forepart of the ship was successfully floated and towed into Stornoway by the *Lochiel*. The mail steamer clearly did more than sail across to the mainland.

David MacBrayne took control of the company in 1878. He retained control until 1906 when it became a limited company

This was further illustrated in 1883 when the *Lochiel* was involved in the 'Battle of Strome Pier'. West-coast fishermen were unhappy about 'intruders' from the east coast landing and despatching their catches on a Sunday. In protest the Stornoway fishermen stayed in port on Friday 1 June. This did not deter the east coast men who landed such large catches that three ships were required to carry the herring to Strome. It was late on Saturday night when the *Lochiel*, accompanied by the *Talisman* and the *Harold* sailed from Stornoway, arriving in Loch Carron about one o'clock on Sunday morning. On tying up at Strome Ferry the ships were surrounded by small boats, while the pier was occupied by about 150 'rioters'. They put the crane out of action, repulsed an attack by police and railwaymen and continued to hold the pier until midnight, when they withdrew and allowed unloading to continue. The arrival of police and troops the following four Sundays allowed unloading of fish to proceed. One of the landings was described in the *Scotsman* on 11 June. It stated that, 'Strome Ferry … was again in the small hours of (the) morning a scene of great excitement,' adding that, 'happily … owing to the extraordinary precautions taken by the Railway Company, and the authorities, no disturbance took place.' A crowd of about 150 assembled at the pier but they, along with the fishermen in their boats, disappeared before midnight. This allowed the same three steamers to unload their cargoes of fish from Stornoway. The *Talisman* completed her discharge shortly after midnight, and the *Lochiel* arrived at 0330. 'As soon as she reached the pier, the discharge of cargo was also proceeded with. By this time it was broad daylight and there were no indications of any movement among the natives.' By 0500 the *Harold* had 'steamed up to the pier, also bringing fish from Stornoway. So as soon as the trucks were loaded, the special trains with the fish were rapidly despatched. At eight in the morning a train left for Inverness with the police, and Strome once more resumed its wonted Sunday quiet and stillness.'

A further change from the *Lochiel*'s normal routine occurred in 1884 when she was chartered and fitted out to carry 350 marines for a three-month cruise off Skye, accompanied by a troopship and two gun boats, the *Assistance*, with 350 marines and 100 bluejackets on board, and the *Bantever*, carrying sixty-five more marines, in order to suppress any possible riots in connection with land reforms. As her captain and crew were predominantly local, they refused to carry this out as their sympathies lay with the crofters and it was therefore necessary to find a new master and crew before this duty could be fulfilled. On this occasion she sailed to Uig but saw no action. A year later she was again requisitioned, and on 28 January she sailed with HMS *Assistance* to Colbost; this time 200 marines were on board the Navy ship while the *Lochiel* carried 25 policemen. All went ashore and six crofters were arrested and put aboard the *Lochiel*. They then sailed to Staffin where more prisoners, this time from Valtos in Lewis, were taken aboard. They were all landed days later at Portree, leaving the *Lochiel* to return to normal duties

Above: *Gunboats off Skye*

Above: *Sheriff Ivory, the Procurator Fiscal, and the Chief Constable approaching Portree on the steamship* Lochiel

The *Lochiel* was the mail steamer in the 1880s. She also assisted gunboats during the crofters' struggle for land on Skye in 1884, as these contemporary illustrations show: Above: the *Lochiel* (left) and two gunboats off Skye. Below: the sheriff, procurator fiscal and chief constable on board the *Lochiel* as she approaches Portree

The *Claymore* joined the *Clansman* on the Glasgow-Stornoway service in 1881. This illustration of the former vessel, from the 1883 MacBrayne's guidebook, does little to show her fine appearance

and, of much greater significance, eventually to set in motion the Napier Commission, whose report would result in much improved conditions for crofters. Four years later the *Lochiel* was again involved with land riots. In November 1887 several hundred evicted crofters in the South Lochs district of Lewis took part in a 'deer raid' on what had been their lands. The six leaders of the raid were arrested, and on 13 January 1888 a large crowd gathered on the pier at Stornoway to see the Raiders off on the *Lochiel* for their trial in the High Court in Edinburgh. Fourteen Crown witnesses and five defence witness had also been escorted on board.

As well as developing services, David MacBrayne also set about introducing new ships to the fleet. The first to be built was the *Claymore*, designed specifically for the Glasgow-Stornoway service. She was another product of J & G Thomson, evidence that that builder had given satisfaction to the company over the years, although in fact she was the second last ship to be built for MacBrayne's by that shipyard. Her launch took place on 14 July 1881, and she was ready to enter service in January of the following year. She continued the evolution of the design which had been developed from the *Clydesdale* and in particular the *Clansman*, being very similar to the latter but of slightly larger dimensions. With a gross tonnage of over 700, she had a length of 227 feet (69m) and a beam of just less than 30 feet (9m). Like the *Clansman* she had the appearance of a sleek yacht and was described at the time as 'lovely to look upon', 'a real beauty' and 'a noble craft'. The combination of long, sleek hull with curving clipper bow with bowsprit and carved figurehead, together with two masts and a tall funnel, created a vessel whose proportions seemed to be just right.

All this is perhaps surprising for a vessel whose primary duty was to carry not only passengers, but also all manner of goods and foodstuffs required by the inhabitants of the many west coast and island settlements which she visited on her outward journey, returning with her holds full of livestock, wool and all the produce from these same places to be sold at Oban or Glasgow. For this it might be thought that a much more utilitarian design of ship would have been built, especially as she was to sail all year round, in all the weather conditions the Mull of Kintyre and the Minch could throw at her. But it must be remembered that, even in those days, the tourist was an important source of income for the shipping company, and it must be assumed that a vessel with the appearance of a private yacht might well attract a greater number of discerning tourists.

For the next fifty years the *Claymore* would make the journey from Glasgow to Stornoway and back almost every week, the first twenty-eight of these in company with the *Clansman*. These two ships indeed became part of the Hebridean landscape. Almost every postcard of Stornoway harbour from these times features one or other of them. This longevity must reflect, too, on the expertise of the island crews who skilfully piloted these steamers through the restricted waters of the Western Isles, sailing in and out of rock-strewn harbours, often in darkness or in winter gales with a minimum of navigational aids but a maximum of local knowledge. The *Claymore* would leave Glasgow on a Thursday, calling at various island and west-coast ports before arriving in Stornoway on a Saturday; there she would remain on the Sabbath before returning for Glasgow on Monday mornings.

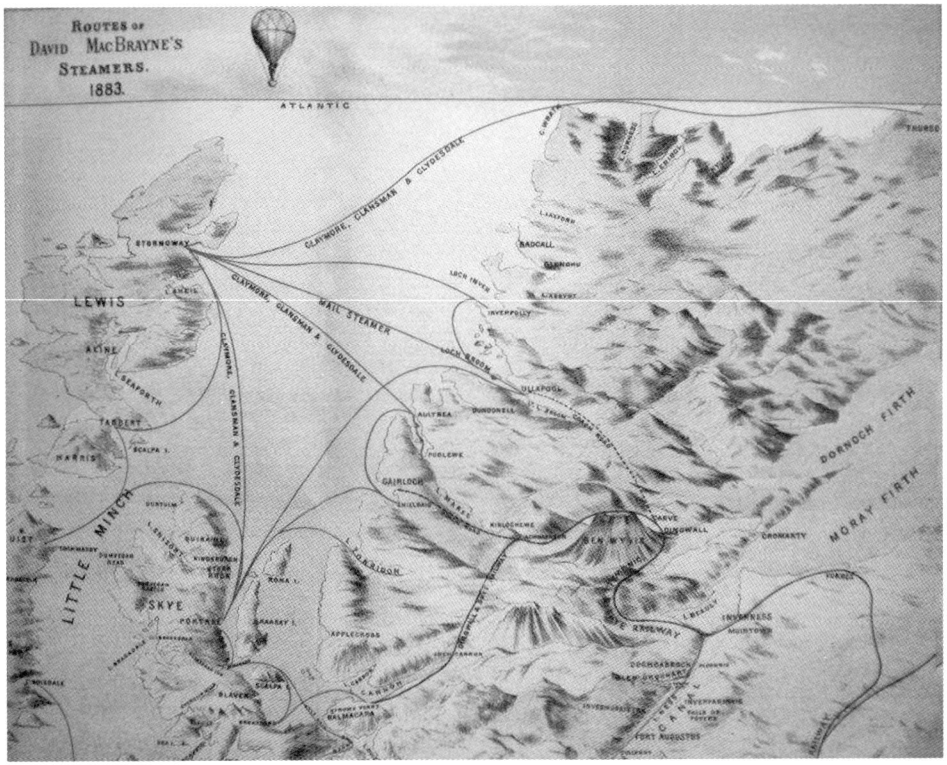

Detail of a map from the 1883 guide book shows routes operated from Stornoway by David MacBrayne

The *Clansman* performed a similar service, with departure from Glasgow on Mondays. The value of these steamers was illustrated by Captain J T Newall. who in 1889 wrote in his book, *Scottish Moors and Indian Jungles*, 'I found that by taking a deck-cabin on the *Claymore*, or one of Mr MacBrayne's other steamers from Glasgow, I got to Stornoway with far less change and worry than if travelling the same journey by land'. He further described that, 'with our servants on board, we were able to get our meals brought to our airy cabin'. This meant that 'there existed, therefore, no necessity to descend into the hot, whisky and food-stricken atmosphere of the regions below', and added that ' the beauty too of the scenery as the steamer threads its way among the various islands, repays one for the many inconveniences'.

During the 1880s it would appear that the two ships performed these services with little or no deviation, although up until the Outer Isles service was introduced in 1888, they regularly added Tarbert (Harris) to their list of calls. Some Sunday trips were made to Scrabster for herring. In September 1882, the *Claymore* brought home to Lewis 500 men and women who had been engaged in the herring fishing at Wick. An interesting aside here is

Sailing advertisement from the Inverness Advertiser published in 1885, showing that calls that were made at Tarbert in the 1880s

that another group of over 100 travelled by train to Strome Ferry, and then took the *Glencoe* to Portree in the hope of catching the *Clansman* on her regular run to Stornoway. There were delays and the connection was missed; eventually the waiting fishermen sailed home on the *Glencoe*, having paid two shillings per head to the captain to do so. In May 1887 the *Clansman* made a special Sunday trip to Strome Ferry when the steering gear of the regular fish carrying ship, the *Eleanor*, failed. The two ships also played their part in the Clearances. For example, in the spring of 1889 fifty families left on the *Claymore* on the first leg of their journey to Canada. They were mostly young, including three couples who had been married only hours before. In 1906, 148 Lewismen emigrating to Canada were transferred at the Tail of the Bank on the Clyde from the *Clansman* to the liner *Athenia*, with a piper playing them on board.

Gentry were afforded a special salute on arrival in, or departure from, Stornoway. In 1899 shots were fired in their honour as Major and Mrs Matheson left on the *Claymore*. Lady Matheson was given a spectacular welcome when she arrived on the mail boat, the *Clydesdale*, in August 1895. As soon as the steamer came in sight round the lighthouse, her arrival was signalled with the lighting of a bonfire on Goat Island, and a display of fireworks both from the steamer and from the shore. When Surgeon-Major Smith arrived back in 1900 from the war in South Africa, a large crowd gathered at the steamer wharf to watch the arrival of the *Clydesdale*. The ship was 'profusely decorated with flags', while bunting was hung from the harbour flagstaff to the fish mart.

There were also occasions when the steamers were used for charters. Between the 1890s and the 1920s, the steamers were chartered for excursions on local holidays both from and to Stornoway.

> To the average Stornowegian … the greatest event in the year's calendar is the autumn holiday … Everyone looks

forward to one day's respite, and arrangements are made long beforehand for an outing of some sort or other … The major part of the population will be satisfied with nothing less than an annual airing on the rolling deep.

The fine lines and decorated bows of the *Claymore* are clearly visible in this 1927 view of her on the Clyde

This outing, normally organised by the Lewis Pipe Band, could be arranged when the local holidays coincided with the days when the steamer lay alongside in Stornoway and would otherwise be idle. Thus the *Claymore* was used regularly, as both the Stornoway and Tarbert holidays occurred on Mondays, while the *Clansman* was used by the people of Ullapool, whose holidays fell on a Thursday. Excursions from Stornoway would go to Ullapool, Portree, Gairloch or Tarbert; the last-mentioned destination was favoured by some 'as the steamer (would) sail along the coast all the way, so that (they) need not be afraid of seasickness.' The trips had to be fitted in with the scheduled sailings from Glasgow; thus if a steamer was delayed, this in turn would affect the excursion, as happened in 1903 when 'owing to pressure of other business, the steamer was four hours late in leaving the other side (Lewis), and the excursionists (from Ullapool) only arrived in Stornoway about 4 pm.' Other steamers used included the *Chieftain*, which carried excursionists from Tarbert to Stornoway in 1910, and Stornoway Shipping Company's *Earnholm*, which was chartered for the 1916 excursion to Tarbert, including a cruise from there to Scalpay. It was not always possible to charter a steamer. In 1899 efforts had been made by the Stornoway Pipe Band to arrange terms with David MacBrayne for a trip on the *Claymore* to Gairloch, but these failed as the company was 'unable to place a steamer … on the date in question.' The same company declined to accept a charter to Ullapool in 1902, and Messrs Langlands, who were then approached, had only a cargo vessel available. The 1904 excursion from Stornoway to Ullapool was described as the first for eight years; it was suggested that the lapse was due to 'the unenviable reputation which Stornoway had made on former occasions.' Perhaps that was why the charter two years earlier had been declined.

All the excursions followed a similar pattern. This would entail an early departure, between 0700 and 1100, sometimes preceded by the Pipe Band marching to the quay playing their pipes. Between 200 and 500 locals, sometimes with the addition of up to eighty tourists, would travel, enjoying more music, dancing and singing on the crossing to whichever destination had been chosen that year. The description of the 1927 crossing to Ullapool is probably fairly typical:

> The band, in their gaily coloured uniforms, played selections at intervals, and this was enjoyed by all, especially the English tourists on board, many of whom took snapshots of the picturesque bandsmen. The lower deck, occupied mainly by the younger element, was the scene of boisterous merriment, dancing being much in evidence, while a song or chorus … was heard above the din. In the alleyways there was a continuous stream of couples arm in arm, oblivious to everything and everybody but themselves. The stewards also had a pleasant interval in the company of the Stornoway fair sex. The upper deck, on the other hand, was the favourite promenade of the seniors, and there could be seen many couples who had climbed the hill together looking as gay and spruce as on their honeymoon.

On arrival the excursionists might visit friends and relations or visit the local sights. A game of football might have been arranged, or if the trip was to Gairloch then a golf match could be played. Sometimes people went further afield, leaving insufficient time to return for the ship's departure. On the 1904 excursion to Portree 'several brakes left with excursionists for Sligachan Inn – nine miles distant – from which it (was) possible to get a good view of the Cuchullin Hills. This party delayed the return of the steamer for nearly an hour, and had a narrow chance of being left behind.' In 1927 the departure of the *Claymore* from Ullapool was 'held up for a short time for two or three who were loth (sic) to leave, and Ullapool unwilling to retain.' A year later the *Claymore* was due to return from Portree to Stornoway at 1800, and 'prompt to the minute the ship's siren summoned the company, but … Portree proved attractive, and it was fully half-an-hour later before the laggards went down the gangway, greatly to the relief of their friends, apprehensive of a temporary separation!' If the excursionists held the steamer back on those occasions, the opposite happened in 1904: all the passengers were on the pier for departing at 1500, but the steamer was aground and could not leave until well after the advertised time.

The return trip was similar to the outward one, with more dancing, singing and piping, while on one trip 'a party of tourists from the south got up an impromptu concert on deck.' The only exception to this seems to have occurred on the *Claymore* when on an excursion from Tarbert to Stornoway. Accompanied by two pipers, the crowd of about 300 islanders decided to use the deck of the steamer for dancing. The 'skirl of the pipes and the hooching of the dancers' disturbed Captain MacKechnie on the bridge and he descended to the deck, 'wrathful of such an affront to the ship'. He is reputed to have shouted above the noise of the music, 'Stop them motions. There is none of MacBrayne's boats allowed to dance!'

A detailed description of one of these excursions appeared in an article originally published in the *Stornoway Gazette* as part of a series of essays entitled 'Days of Yore' by W H MacDonald. He described the trip as 'one of the highlights of social life in Stornoway at the turn of the century'. He then proceeded to portray the day in more detail:

> This very important event generally took place in the month of July. As usual with the youngsters of the less affluent families, it was a case of saving up one's pennies to pay for the cost of the passage which was 2s 6d (12p) return. It was the old *Claymore* that generally took the excursionists across the Minch, leaving No 1 Pier at 8 o'clock on the Monday morning and arriving at Ullapool, Gairloch or Portree, as the case may be, around 10 to

10.30 am. What great excitement a steamboat trip to the mainland caused to each proud possessor of an excursion ticket! Even on the Sunday night prior to the next morning's departure, groups of small boys would be seen ogling the big "liner" as she lay serenely roped

Crowds line the quay at Stornoway to bid farewell to the excursionists leaving for a day trip to Ullapool on board the *Claymore* on 1 August 1927. This illustrates the popularity of these day trips

to her berth at No 1 Pier in anticipation of the sail across the Minch with the ultimate goal of actually landing in Scotland. Some of (them) would even go to bed much earlier than usual in order to be up early in the morning so as not to miss the boat! Some time before departure one could hear the skirl of the pipes of the Lewis Pipe Band as they marched proudly along South Beach Street towards the quay playing "Scotland the Brave" or some other such rousing tune … With all the excursionists on board, ropes would be cast off, there would be a blast of the whistle and (they) were off on (their) glorious adventure, with the Pipe Band playing "The 79th Farewell to Gibraltar", much waving of handkerchiefs and the customary farewell wishes of "Have a Good Time", "Enjoy yourselves", and facetious remarks such as "Don't Feed the Fishes Too Much" and "Don't Rock the Boat".

From a child's point of view, the writer then describes the journey across the Minch:

> Once outside the lighthouse we would start to explore the ship from bow to stern, and if we were lucky enough to get down to the engine room, we could see the intricacy of steam boilers, and watch entranced the large steel pistons moving up and down. Up on deck we could buy for a penny from the automatic vending machines which were fixed to the ship's super-structure, bars of Nestle's Swiss milk chocolate or Velina Suchard chocolate, both most tasty and sweet to the palate … The bar below did a rip-roaring trade with all the grown-ups in festive mood, determined to have a real good time and make the outing one to be forever remembered and a topic of conversation for the ceilidhs during the long winter nights at home.

He also described how the time was spent ashore once the excursion's destination had been reached:

> Once ashore the excursionists would go their various ways to explore the town, see the sights and purchase appropriate souvenirs to take back to their families in Stornoway. These were generally ceramic plaques with views of prominent places in the neighbourhood, picture postcards, decorated ornaments such as vases, jugs, plates, spoons with the town's coat-of-arms and any other nick-nacks that took their fancy. In Wester Ross towns fruit was much more plentiful than in Lewis and (they) all bought lots of gooseberries, strawberries, blackcurrants and greengages, this latter being the favourite on account of its bitter-sweet taste and lushness. And so the hours ashore passed pleasantly in sightseeing, visiting relatives … talking to the "natives" and swapping yarns about (their) home town. About 6 pm all … returned to the ship laden with purchases, gifts, perhaps even bottles of Scotch protruding from the pockets of the men passengers, to fortify them against rough weather on the homeward trip and to assist with the merriment on board. During the return voyage the adult passengers danced on the deck to the reels and strathspeys played by the Pipe Band and to the melodious strains of the accordions as they squeezed out the Merry Widow Waltz, quicksteps, polkas and other folk-dance tunes. As we approached the pier the band played a stirring tune, everyone came to the ship's rail and as a final gesture the big drummer would beat his drum so hard that he would burst the pigskin on both sides and while the seamen tied the ship up to No 1 Pier, he would proudly show the burst drum to those on shore, held high above his head and from an advantageous place near the bow-sprit, thus showing tangible proof and ample evidence that all on board had had a smashing time!

There were occasions too, when the voyages were not all plain sailing. In August 1885 the *Claymore* was involved in a mishap en route from Glasgow to Stornoway. On the night of the fourteenth, as the ship was rounding the Mull of Kintyre in foggy conditions, she ran into a small schooner, the *Maria Stewart*, of Greenock. It was thought that the latter ship was not carrying lights. Considerable damage was caused to the sailing vessel, although this could have been worse had she not altered course so that the damage occurred at the ship's stern. The *Claymore* suffered little damage, although the force of the collision awakened most of the passengers, and those who rushed on deck were alarmed by the situation. Any panic was 'quickly allayed by the business like manner in which the officials of the *Claymore* went about their work'. When it was found that the schooner, which was in ballast, was likely to remain afloat, the decision was made that the *Claymore* would tow the damaged vessel, stern first, to Campbeltown, which was reached some four hours later.

On 23 August 1888 the *Clansman* became stranded while proceeding through Pabbay Sound between Kyleakin and Broadford. It was at high water and she was travelling at a good speed when she struck a sunken reef known as Sgeir an Ròin. The occurrence was described in detail in the *Scottish Highlander* as follows:

> The *Clansman* left Glasgow with a full complement of tourists and sportsmen. All went well until soon after passing Kyleakin. The *Clansman* was then in charge of the mate, (Mr Aitchison), Captain Maccallum having gone below. There was no wind or moon, but the stars were clearly seen. At about half-past eleven the passengers, who were mostly in bed, were startled by a violent shock, rapidly followed by two others, which caused the vessel to shake from stem to stern. The scene on deck at once became one of great excitement, terrified ladies and gentlemen rushing up half-dressed, and all pouring forth hurried inquiries (sic), while some ladies were hysterically

shrieking. The captain was speedily on deck, and the engines were reversed, but failed to move the vessel. A general cry arose for the boats; but as the captain found the vessel making no water, he declared the passengers would be safer on board than ashore; but as they were eager to get ashore, he ordered the boats out. Two were filled with ladies and children, and ordered to land on the nearest point, and return. This they did with some difficulty, owing to the darkness and the rocks, the result being that the rescued passengers had to stumble about two miles over bog and rocks to Broadford. The two boats then returned, and, with others from the *Clansman* and Broadford, conveyed the remainder of the passengers to Broadford, but the vast majority had to leave their baggage on the *Clansman* until latter (sic) in the day, and pass the night as best they could on chairs in the over-crowded hotel and private houses. From Broadford the majority of passengers were brought into Portree by the *Lochiel* next evening. In the course of the day the *Glencoe*, *Lochiel*, *Handa*, and *Udea* arrived to the help of the *Clansman*, and made united efforts to tow her off the rocks, but without success.

From enquiries made at the office of the owner of the *Clansman* (Mr David MacBrayne) it appears that the steamer went stem on to the reef. All the passengers were taken on to their destination by Mr MacBrayne's other steamers which ply in that part of the Western Highlands. The disabled steamer's place was taken by the *Clydesdale*, which was lying in reserve in Queen's Dock of the Glasgow Harbour. Mr Aitchison, the first mate of the *Clansman*, who was in charge at the time the vessel struck, had been thirty years in Mr Macbrayne's services.

Five days later the *Clansman* was successfully refloated and a day after that proceeded to Glasgow for repairs. At the enquiry into the incident:

> the court found that the vessel was stranded from mismanagement of the mate in investigating the distance of the vessel from the Skye shore. Otherwise the vessel appeared to have been navigated with proper and seamanlike care. The master was in no way in default, but the mate was so far in default that he over-estimated the distance of the vessel from the Skye shore, and though the mistake might probably have been avoided had he carefully noted the bearings of Kyleakin light yet, having regard to his long and excellent services, and to the character of the mistake made on this occasion the Court thought this was no reason for dealing with his certificate.

Further accidents occurred to the steamers from time to time. In April 1898 the *Clansman* struck a rock near Badcall. While the hold remained dry, the engine room became full of water and the vessel was unable to continue on her crossing of the Minch to Stornoway. Almost exactly one year later, on a dark night with heavy showers of rain, the *Claymore* struck a sunken rock after leaving Loch Torridon on her journey south. She was able to reach Kyleakin, but it was decided not to proceed any further, with the ship's bow 'very much damaged' five feet above the waterline and also making water. In 1906 the same ship was unable to leave Glasgow on her usual weekly voyage owing to a damaged rudder. Her place was taken by the chartered steamer *Plasma*, which both arrived at and departed from Stornoway the same day, and was herself behind schedule due to severe weather conditions. These examples provide further evidence that navigating through the islands and rocks of the West Coast was no straightforward task.

Chapter 10

'A Week's Sail among the Western Isles'

Every year around the end of the nineteenth and the beginning of the twentieth centuries, David MacBrayne would publish its *Summer Tours in Scotland*, a book of some 130 pages which was both a timetable and a guide book to the steamer destinations. In it the journey from Glasgow to Stornoway was promoted as 'a week's sail among the Western Isles by the steamship *Claymore* or *Clansman*'. It then further states, 'The trip … is very pleasant. The vessels leave Glasgow every Monday and Thursday about noon … have excellent passenger accommodation, and will be found extremely comfortable by those desirous of enjoying a week's sail (sleeping on board during the night)'. Whether experienced by a tourist

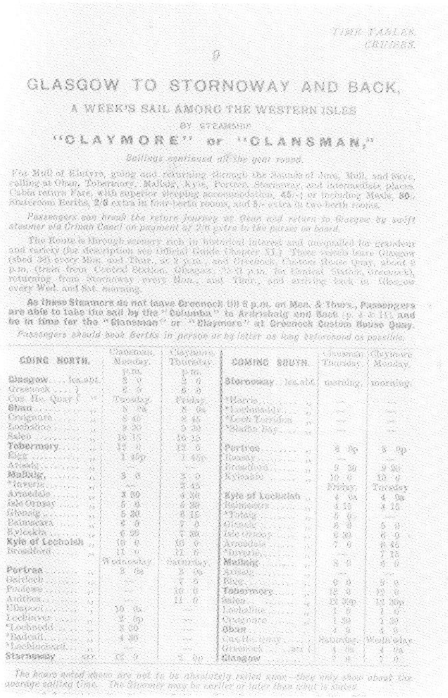

Time Tables. Cruises.

9

GLASGOW TO STORNOWAY AND BACK.

A WEEK'S SAIL AMONG THE WESTERN ISLES

BY STEAMSHIP

"CLAYMORE" or "CLANSMAN,"

Sailings continued all the year round.

Via Mull of Kintyre, going and returning through the Sounds of Jura, Mull, and Skye, calling at Oban, Tobermory, Mallaig, Kyle, Portree, Stornoway, and intermediate places. Cabin return Fare, with superior sleeping accommodation, **45/-**; or including Meals, **80/-**. Stateroom Berths, **2/6** extra in four-berth rooms, and **5/-** extra in two-berth rooms.

Passengers can break the return journey at Oban and return to Glasgow by swift steamer via Crinan Canal on payment of 2/6 extra to the purser on board.

The Route is through scenery rich in historical interest and unequalled for grandeur and variety (for description see Official Guide Chapter XI.). These vessels leave Glasgow (shed 38) every Mon. and Thur., at 2 p.m., and Greenock, Custom House Quay, about 6 p.m. (train from Central Station, Glasgow, [illegible] p.m. for Central Station, Greenock), returning from Stornoway every Mon., and Thur., and arriving back in Glasgow every Wed. and Sat. morning.

As these Steamers do not leave Greenock till 6 p.m. on Mon. & Thurs., Passengers are able to take the sail by the "Columba" to Ardrishaig and Back (p. 4 & 11), and be in time for the "Clansman" or "Claymore" at Greenock Custom House Quay.

Passengers should book Berths in person or by letter as long beforehand as possible.

GOING NORTH.	Clansman. Monday.	Claymore. Thursday.
	p.m.	p.m.
Glasgow ....lea. abt.	2 0	2 0
Greenock / Cus. Ho. Quay ,,	6 0	6 0
	Tuesday.	Friday.
Oban ,,	8 0a	8 0a
Craignure ,,	8 45	8 45
Lochaline ,,	9 30	9 30
Salen ,,	10 15	10 15
Tobermory ,,	12 0	12 0
Eigg ,,	1 45p	1 45p
Arisaig ,,	—	—
Mallaig ,,	3 0	3 0
*Inverie ,,	—	3 45
Armadale ,,	3 30	4 30
Isle Ornsay ,,	5 0	5 30
Glenelg ,,	5 30	6 15
Balmacara ,,	6 0	7 0
Kyleakin ,,	6 30	7 30
Kyle of Lochalsh ,,	10 0	10 0
Broadford ,,	11 0	11 0
	Wednesday.	Saturday.
Portree ,,	3 0a	3 0a
Gairloch ,,	—	7 0
Poolewe ,,	—	10 0
Aultbea ,,	—	11 0
Ullapool ,,	10 0a	—
Lochinver ,,	2 0p	—
*Lochnedd ,,	3 30	—
*Badcall ,,	4 30	—
*Lochinchard ,,	—	—
Stornoway arr.	12 0	2 0p

COMING SOUTH.	Clansman Thursday.	Claymore Monday.
Stornoway lea. abt.	morning.	morning.
*Harris ,,	—	—
*Lochmaddy ,,	—	—
*Loch Torridon ,,	—	—
*Staffin Bay ,,	—	—
Portree ,,	8 0p	8 0p
Raasay ,,	—	—
Broadford ,,	9 30	9 30
Kyleakin ,,	10 0	10 0
	Friday.	Tuesday
Kyle of Lochalsh ,,	4 0a	4 0a
Balmacara ,,	4 15	4 15
*Totaig ,,	5 0	—
Glenelg ,,	6 0	5 0
Isle Ornsay ,,	6 30	6 0
Armadale ,,	7 0	6 45
*Inverie ,,	—	7 15
Mallaig ,,	8 0	8 0
Arisaig ,,	—	—
Eigg ,,	9 0	9 0
Tobermory ,,	12 0	12 0
Salen ,,	12 30p	12 30p
Lochaline ,,	1 0	1 0
Craignure ,,	1 30	1 30
Oban ,,	4 0	4 0
Cus. Ho. Quay / Greenock arr.	Saturday. 4 0a	Wednesday 4 0a
Glasgow	7 0	7 0

The hours noted above are not to be absolutely relied upon—they only show about the average sailing time. The Steamer may be earlier or later than what is stated.

MacBrayne's guidebook, showing details of the weekly cruises which could be made from Glasgow to Stornoway or a Lewisman returning to his native island, the journey would be one of ever-changing sights and sounds.

The magnificence of this voyage is colourfully expressed by M J B Baddeley in his 1895 *Thorough Guide to Scotland*. He describes the journey as 'unquestionably the grandest sail to be found anywhere round our native shores,' before continuing,

> Indeed, except round the magnificent coast of Norway, it is doubtful whether there can be anywhere a voyage of similar length, capable of presenting such a succession of picturesque combinations of land and water, such a changeful, waving line of "breaking wave and broken shore," as this 40 hours' sail from the very centre of one of our greatest hives of industry, to the little sea-girt capital of the far-off "iron-grey Hebrides." Tourists who wish to see something of the inner life as well as the scenery of the people whose land they are visiting, will prefer this leisurely sail by the luggage-boat a hundredfold to the hurry-scurry scampers of the fast passenger boats through the same scenes … The longest summer day may be spent between Oban and Portree without the eye becoming wearied, or the sense of the beautiful blunted. In fact, the only disadvantage of the slow boats is that darkness often comes on before we have fairly passed the best of the scenery, but even then the blackest night can hardly dispel the feeling of keen interest which is kept alive by the consciousness that we are still steering our tortuous way through the narrow kyles and solemn hill-flanked sounds, over waters seldom flawed by aught but the passage of a steamer or two, or the wings of a seagull. If we look steadily we can always detect the line of separation between the dark sky and the still darker mountains, and at times the track of the steamer gleams with phosphorescent light. Seldom, too, is the voyage from Glasgow to Stornoway accomplished without the occurrence of some little episode, the memory of which remains fixed in our minds for years to come – some sad parting or joyous meeting of kith-and-kin – a simple picture of human interest set in Nature's choicest framework.

To reach the steamer at Glasgow, the traveller would require to have passed through one of the many sheds lining the River Clyde. Here he would have found himself in the midst of a milling mass of horses, carts and brawny stevedores, heaps of miscellaneous cargo, perhaps bags of flour, boxes of groceries, bundles of wood, and a bedstead. There might be rolls of fencing wire, bags of cement, lamp oil, farm equipment, perhaps a new kitchen range and possibly even a piano, all destined for island ports. For as well as carrying passengers, it must be remembered that the steamers were also the islands' lifelines, and all these goods would be loaded into the cargo holds to be unloaded at the various piers en route. Perhaps that explains why below the timetable it is stated that 'The hours (on the timetable) are not to be absolutely relied upon – they only show the average sailing time. The Steamer may be earlier or later than what is stated.' For who knows how slowly or quickly goods may be unloaded if the tide is low or if they have to be transferred on to one of the small boats which come out to meet the ship where there is no suitable pier suitable at which to call?

Once the traveller was through the shed, the ship would be waiting. But it would not be the only vessel to be seen, for the quays would be lined with all kinds of shipping: 'doon the watter' paddle steamers, Irish passenger and cargo boats, and ocean-going vessels, from liners to humble cargo steamers, would all be tied up, loading and unloading or making their way up or down stream, while ferry boats would be crossing the river like so many water flies. Those who had cruised on larger ships may have found the *Clansman* or *Claymore* small; in fact, to many the initial sight must have been disappointing, but this would soon have been forgotten in the activity on board and in the friendliness of the fellow-travellers. Given that the ships were of small size, and there would be only about sixty passengers, then when all were seated at the same dining-table, or were constantly meeting each other on deck, it would have unusual if friendships were not quickly established.

The actual departure has been well described by Iain F Anderson in his book *Across Hebridean Seas*:

> The first officer has taken up his position at the bow; the second officer at the stern; and preparations for casting off are complete. The captain leans over the wing of the bridge, noting with an apparently idle glance all that is taking place. Do not be deceived by his easy attitude; it is only because everything is proceeding according to strict routine that the action of casting off from the quay seems so simple. To the uninitiated it is child's play, but they are unaware that the captain has noted the rate of flow of the river, has decided whether he will have to take the ship astern before he can pull her bow out into the river, has decided whether the wind will help or hinder our gaining the centre of the river, and a host of other essentials to our safety.
>
> The captain's hand stretches out to the engine room telegraph and moves it slowly from its vertical position. A fraction of a second later two bells ring sharply on the bridge – the acknowledgment from the engine-room to the telegraph's earlier message, "Slow Astern".
>
> Looking over the ship's rail to the quay, we hear the swish of water at the stern as the propeller reverses steadily. Our bow hawsers, now cast off, let the ship edge imperceptibly out from the quay towards the centre of the river.
>
> Again the telegraph rings, the propeller stops, then recommences with a renewed vigour, and we slowly move ahead, away from the quayside … We are outward bound.

As the steamer edged its way down the river, the passenger would see the river banks lined with shipyards. At the start of the twentieth century, there were no less than twenty-nine such yards between Glasgow and Greenock. If he was eagle-eyed enough, he would be able to distinguish that of Robert Duncan & Co. Ltd at Port Glasgow, where the original *Comet* was built. Once past Dumbarton Rock, the river started to widen and the steamer followed the dredged channel across to the left bank, where she would call at Custom House Quay at Greenock. Here passengers who had travelled from Glasgow by train would join the ship, while yet more cargo for the Highlands would disappear into the capacious holds. By about six in the evening, the steamer would be under way again, passing the Cloch lighthouse, as she entered the widening waters that were now the Firth of Clyde. Perhaps a sight of Bute and the Cumbraes would be missed, as the traveller forsook the deck for the saloon on the call for dinner, but he would be up again to watch the ship passing between Ailsa Craig, about seven miles off to port, and the Island of Pladda, lying just off the bulk of Arran, to starboard. The lighthouses on both islands would provide safe guidance for the officer of the watch, as the evening light faded away.

If the weather was fair, the traveller might well stay on deck to see the steamer rounding the Mull of Kintyre. The perils of rounding of this headland in stormy conditions have already been described. Then the steamer would head up the Sound of Jura; Islay and Jura would be silhouettes to port, while the low hills of Argyll would appear as dark shadows on the starboard beam. The next morning would see the steamer heading up the Sound of Kerrera before sweeping into Oban Bay. The actual time of arrival at Oban might vary considerably. As Alexander Smith wrote in his *Summer in Skye*:

> the steamer does not always arrive at a reasonable hour. She may be detained some time in Greenock; in dirty weather she may be on the Mull of Cantyre all night, buffeted by the big Atlantic there; so he must be a bold man, or a man gifted with the second sight, who ventures anything but a vague guess as to the hour of her arrival.

Passengers could also join the steamer at Greenock, the first port of call after Glasgow, as shown in this drawing (drawing by the author)

But at whatever hour the ropes are put ashore, there was cargo to be discharged and loaded, and passengers would have an hour or two to spend ashore. They should, however, heed the comment given in MacBrayne's Guide – 'the purser of the steamer will give definite information as to the time the vessel is likely to be detained, but passengers are earnestly requested to embark when first they hear the bell'.

Scheduled to leave at eight o'clock in the morning, the steamer then headed out from Oban Bay. The route passed the southern tip of Lismore and then Lady Rock, marked by an iron beacon, where the *Clydesdale* came to a sad end in 1905. The ship then sailed up the Sound of Mull, passing Duart Castle on the first promontory on Mull, standing guard over the meeting of Loch Linnhe, the Firth of Lorn and the Sound of Mull. Although the Sound is flanked by the mountains of Mull on one side, and the hills of Morven on the other, it is not always a sheltered stretch of water:

> The Sound of Mull is fickle, ten times one can sail its length with scarcely a ripple on its surface, but one day you sail the Sound and find your ship fighting every yard in the midst of maelstrom, for the waters of the Sound flow swiftly, and the wind in counter to the current can raise a mad sea of white topped roaring overfalls that have driven many a ship helpless to the rocky shore. One cannot believe the awesome majesty of a storm in this Sound unless it is witnessed; it is a fearsome sight midst the warring of the elements.

A slightly less colourful description of the journey up the Sound of Mull appeared in J and E R Pennell's book *Our Journey to the Hebrides*. They relate that,

> Through a Scotch mist we watched Oban and its picturesque castle out of sight; through a driving rain we looked forth on the heights of Morven and of Mull. Sometimes the clouds lightened, and for a minute the nearer hills came out dark and purple against a space of whitish shining mist; but for the most part they hung heavy and black over wastes of water and wastes of land … Pleasure parties sat up on deck, wrapped in mackintoshes and huddled under umbrellas. Our time was divided between getting wet and drying off downstairs. The excitement of the voyage was the stopping of the steamer, now in mid-stream … now at rain-soaked piers … Little boats came out to meet the steamer. They lay in wait, tossing up and down on the rough waters and manned with Hamishes and Donalds. Into one stepped a real Macleod, his collie at his heels; into another, an elderly lady, who was greeted most respectfully by the Hamish as he lifted into his boat trunks (belonging to her).
>
> At the piers, groups of people, no better off for occupation than we, waited to see the passengers land. We all took an unaccountable interest in this landing. At Salen there was an intense moment when, as the steamer started, a boy on shore discovered that he had forgotten his bag. At the next pier, where a party of three got off, as their baggage was carried after them, we even went the length of counting up to forty bags and bundles, three dogs, and two maids. We left them standing there, surrounded by their property, with the rain pouring in torrents and not a house in sight. This is the way you take your pleasure in the Hebrides. We were glad to see among the boxes a case of champagne. At the last moment, one of the men, from the edge of the pier, waved a brown paper parcel, and told the captain that another like it had been left aboard. I am afraid he had forgotten something else; thence to Tobermory the captain did but revile him.

Tobermory is the main settlement of Mull, described in the MacBrayne guide book as having 'three hotels, a distillery, two banks, two churches, county buildings and a prison.' Here time would be spent handling more cargo, for goods unloaded here went to many parts of the island. A wonderful description of the *Claymore* leaving Tobermory was written by the Rev Donald Lamont from Tiree (and translated from Gaelic by Donald Meek):

> It was a fine sight to see the *Claymore* leaving Tobermory on a summer evening, resplendent in paint and every inch of her copper or brass polished as clean as a new shilling, and a row of English folk standing at her gunwale, with a telescope in the hand or at the eye of each one, gaping at the seagulls of the shoreline and other wonders which they had come to see in the Highlands. But, although the English folk were profitable to MacBrayne in the summer, the *Claymore* was not built to carry Englishmen, but to convey the people of the Islands and the West Highlands to and from Glasgow, and to transport cargo to many a township and harbour which had no other way of obtaining goods. If you have never seen one of MacBrayne's boats loading or unloading cargo, you have missed a spectacle as interesting as any in this world: bags of meal and boxes and baskets of bread, kebbucks of cheese and cement, wood and clay jars of whisky, calves and barrels of tar, all thrown on top of one another, and all the time pigs squealing so loudly and so angrily that the men pushing them cannot hear their own bad language.

As well as being extremely evocative, this account shows not only the all-important role played by MacBrayne's steamers in maintaining island life and the way in which they brought tourists and their spending power to the Western Isles, but also how much these steamers and their crews were part of the daily lives of the islanders. The arrival of the steamer was of great importance, and everyone would make their way down to the pier on her arrival, if only to see who was disembarking or leaving. This continues to the present day, although it is much less interesting to watch a string of cars pouring off a car ferry. Even in the late 1960s, the habit was so ingrained in the people of Tarbert, Harris, that several years after the change from a steamer arriving once every two days to a ferry calling twice each day, the pier would still be crowded with the local inhabitants.

By now the traveller would have become accustomed to the mountainous scenery and to the steady stream of lighthouses and ruined castles adding interest to the journey. The former were perched atop rocky outcrops, either to warn ships of the dangers, the latter to provide better defence.

Once out of Tobermory, Rudha nan Gall lighthouse heralded more open water, and then the steamer swung north past Ardnamurchan Point. Having seen the mighty cliffs of the Mull of Kintyre, Ardnamurchan might be considered a little disappointing, for it was not a rugged headland projecting into the sea, but much lower and rather more a series of rocky hillocks. But it was the most westerly point of the British mainland and worth seeing for that alone. If the weather was clear, a good view would be had of the islands of Coll, Muck, Eigg and Rhum, while ahead the Sound of Sleat opened up between Skye and the mainland. Depending on the day, a call would be made at Eigg or Arisaig, with the latter being replaced by Mallaig after the opening of the West Highland railway in 1901. From there, the steamer would head across to Armadale; here passengers would have about half an hour to stroll ashore, while cargo for the Sleat Peninsula was unloaded.

Once a week, a call would be made in Loch Duich, where the traveller would see the 'taighean dubha', or black houses, of the local inhabitants. A call would also be made at Glenelg, where the strong currents can swirl in the narrow channel between Skye and the mainland, and then as the ship swept round into Loch Alsh a glimpse would be had of the ruins of Eilean Donan Castle on an island at the entrance to Loch Duich. Further stops were made at Balmacara, Kyle of Lochalsh, Kyleakin and Broadford late on the evening of the second day. Not many would be on deck to see Portree for the call there was at three in the morning.

The *Claymore* arriving at Tobermory, after sailing up the Sound of Mull from Oban

The *Claymore* lies alongside the pier at Portree

Then it was back across to the mainland, perhaps on the *Claymore* to Gairloch. Here while cargo was being handled, the passengers might be entertained by buskers, young pipers playing to earn money to add to the Highlanders' meagre incomes. The *Clansman* would head beyond to make calls at Ullapool and Lochinver, Baddeley's Guide Book stating, 'the captain calls at which he likes first,' then sailing as far north as Badcall and Lochclash before before heading across the Minch. Both ships might add unscheduled calls if there was cargo or passengers for a particular place, such as Diabaig on the north shore of Loch Torridon, further emphasising the approximation of sailing times. The Pennells, on a similar journey, described these calls at isolated spots:

> We stopped often. At many of the landings not a house was to be seen. As a rule there was no pier. The steamer would give her shrill whistle and as it was re-echoed from the dreary hills huge black boats came sailing out to meet us … And when they had dropped their sails, and rounded her bows and brought up alongside her lower deck, there tumbled into them men and women, and loaves, and old newspapers, and bits of meat, for … there are always people on the verge of starvation.

The last leg of the journey would take the travellers across the Minch, finally passing Arnish lighthouse, to herald an entry into the sheltered harbour of Stornoway, where the ship would tie up at about midday on the third day of the journey. The Leòdhasach (native of Lewis) was finally home, but for the tourist there was a day to be passed on the island before returning to the steamer for the three day return voyage. The cost of all this would have been 45/- (£2.25) with superior accommodation, or 80/- (£4) including meals! The *Thorough Guide* adds that 'Fore Cabin tickets are issued at about half the above prices, and Deck tickets much cheaper, but few tourists will care to travel anything but "first class" on these boats. The cabin accommodation is excellent, being of the same quality as that of the fast passenger-boats belonging to the same owner.'

Unscheduled calls would be made along the West Coast if there were passengers or cargo to be shipped or landed. This is the *Claymore* at Diabaig on Loch Torridon

Buskers on board the steamer at a West Coast port. The contrast between the young pipers, hoping to earn some extra income, and the well-dressed tourists is plain to see

The *Clansman* at Stornoway. Tourists on the week's voyage would have a day to spend ashore before commencing the return trip to Glasgow

The saloon of the *Claymore*

The deck of the *Claymore*. The lack of protection for the men on the bridge of the steamer can be clearly seen

Chapter 11

A Pattern of Services

Thus was established a pattern of services which was to continue with only minor changes for almost the next eighty years. This was described in the *Gazetteer of Scotland 1882–84* as follows: 'steamers ply daily in summer from Stornoway to Ullapool and three times per week in winter; steamers sail twice weekly from Glasgow to Stornoway'. The only changes would be in frequency of sailings and in the mainland port of the 'short crossing'. The *Gazetteer* also stated that there were weekly sailings from Granton to Stornoway in summer and a year-round weekly service between Liverpool, Aberdeen and Dundee which called at Stornoway; these were not operated by David MacBrayne.

The first change to the pattern took place in 1885. Having assumed responsibility for the Portree mail service from Strome, it made sense for MacBrayne to move the Stornoway contract to that port from Ullapool. The advantages of this for accelerating the delivery of mails to Stornoway had been suggested a year earlier in the Report of the Napier Commission (a public enquiry into the condition of crofters and cottars in the Highlands and Islands) by David Cameron of Lochiel, MP. He stated that it would be advantageous to

> start the night mail from London at nine o'clock, it would arrive at Strome Ferry at half-past three … and instead of the mail passing to Ullapool, the steamer should cross direct (from Lewis) and leave immediately with the mail and light goods. Giving it six hours to arrive here (Stornoway), we would have the mail at ten or eleven o'clock at night ready to be delivered the next morning, instead of getting the letters at six or seven o'clock at night when business hours are over.

In addition, no longer would it be necessary for travellers to leave the train at Garve to endure a five hour coach trip to Ullapool; instead they could remain on the train to Strome where, as has been mentioned, they could transfer directly to the steamer on the pier. The inhabitants of Ullapool were not pleased, claiming it would set the progress of the town back by years. It was to be eighty-five years before a service from Ullapool was reinstated.

The new Strome-Stornoway mail service was inaugurated by the *Lochiel*, with the Portree run being covered by the *Glencoe*. However, it was not long before there were complaints about the former's suitability for the run. These complaints were strong enough to have reached Parliament early in 1890. On 31 March Mr Baumann, MP for Camberwell and Peckham, begged

> to ask the Postmaster General whether he is aware that the steamer *Lochiel*, which carries the mails between Strome Ferry and Stornoway, is so small that when the weather is rough she is unable to make the trip, and that she has several times during the past winter not made the voyage; whether he is aware that Mr MacBrayne, the contractor, frequently sends the *Lochiel* round by Portree, thus delaying her arrival in Stornoway till one or two in

> the morning, while the Portree steamer is sent to out of the way places to pick up sheep, cattle, and other traffic; and whether he will take some steps to provide a good and regular mail service between Strome Ferry and Stornoway?

The response from the Postmaster General was to the effect that he was aware that this was the case, and that the detour was due to rough weather, 'when a larger and more powerful vessel might have succeeded'. The deviations of the journey via Portree were apparently due to 'stress of weather'. He was 'not in a position to incur the large expense which the employment of a more powerful steamer would involve, having regard to the fact that existing arrangements already entail a very heavy loss to the revenue'.

From the end of June in the same year, the *Lochiel* started regularly diverting by Portree on both her outward and inward sailings, causing train connections to be missed at Strome and arrivals at Stornoway being anything up to three hours late. All this was caused by 'a steamer striking a rock', and to save David MacBrayne the expense of chartering a relief steamer for the Portree service. This was in spite of a promise made by Mr MacBrayne in September 1889 that 'under no circumstances would the Stornoway and Strome Ferry steamer be diverted from her course'. Only a few months later, in January of 1891 there was more discontent regarding the *Lochiel*. It was stated that the *Lochiel* was 'quite unsuited to carry the mail – owing to faulty construction, deficiency in steam power and insufficient size', and it was claimed that 'she cannot keep up to time in anything but the finest weather'. David MacBrayne stated he was not prepared to put on a bigger ship without an increase in the subsidy, which was due to be renewed in December of that year.

It is ironic, therefore, that one of the few descriptions of travelling on the *Lochiel* describes a journey to Portree, but in his writing D T Holmes has captured both her lack of stature and power.

> It is the small *Lochiel* that, in the dark days of December, bears the passengers along the chilly Sound of Sleat, and through the narrows of Raasay … At such a time there is something fearsome and weird in the aspect of the coast, as seen from the cabin window of the brave little boat as she battles and plunges along in the teeth of the north-eastern gale. Her progress is slow, for when passengers are few MacBrayne wisely economises his coal. The long-stretching hills of Raasay … are white from head to foot, and gleam through the darkness of the afternoon, vivid and ghostly. As Raasay House, with its lamp-lit windows shining in a snowy recess, is approached, the engines slow down, and through the howl of the wind can be heard the plashing of oars. The broad waves swirl and seethe cruelly round the ferry-boat and toss it about at all angles, up and down, on crest and in trough, till you fear it will end its struggles keel upwards, and send the mail bags down among the mackerel. But the boatmen know their trade, and so do the dripping, top-booted seamen of the *Lochiel*. Amid much running and shuffling and casting of ropes and much bandying of (I fear) strong expressions in Gaelic sung out upon the night, the ship's ladder is cast down and the boat tied thereto. In a few minutes the transfer of mails is over, the ladder up, and the small boat leaping back to land … A new passenger has come on board and is seen to descend the cabin stairs to unfreeze his fingers over the tiny stove. Half-an-hour's heaving still remains before Portree. A lady who has been on the borderline of squeamishness for the last hour, hurriedly leaves the cabin, probably to see if her luggage is all right.

The shortcomings of the *Lochiel* can be seen in the number of times her name appeared in the *Highland News* between November 1890 and January 1891. On 1 November it was reported that 'owing to the stormy character of the weather on Tuesday night the *Lochiel* did not leave Stornoway until Wednesday forenoon. Thus early in the season is the need for a larger boat.' Three weeks later a paragraph read, 'the *Lochiel* has again failed to run up to time, owing to stormy weather. Instead of leaving (Stornoway) at 1 am on Wednesday morning, she was not able to face the storm until four hours later.' It was only a week later that

> the *Lochiel* again failed to make her usual run on Saturday night. She left Strome at the usual hour, but had not proceeded far on her usual course when the sea became too heavy for her, and she had to put into Portree for shelter. There she remained during the night and arrived at Stornoway a little after midday on the Sunday.

It is not surprising that the following week's *Highland News* announced that 'the people of Stornoway will be gratified to learn that Dr Macdonald, their … parliamentary representative, is making a fresh effort to have the mail service between Lewis and the mainland improved.' This was of little consolation later in the month to 'several parties who had gone on board intending to spend the Christmas on the mainland.' The *Lochiel* had attempted to leave Stornoway shortly after two o'clock, but had not gone far when she was forced back. 'On the wind lowering she proceeded at half-past-seven', but the travellers 'were disappointed when they were informed there was no likelihood of her catching any of the trains that day. They preferred to spend Christmas at home rather than at Strome Ferry, and consequently came ashore again.' In the first week of 1891 the steamer was seven hours behind schedule leaving Stornoway owing to a gale which had sprung up. Before the month was out, readers of the *Highland News* would have seen the heading, 'The *Lochiel's* shortcomings', beneath which was printed the following details of yet another delayed sailing and the public's feelings about the matter:

> the gale of wind which sprung (sic) up on Thursday last continued with more or less force till Tuesday morning. On Monday the *Lochiel* left Strome about the usual time but did not arrive (at Stornoway) till after seven on Tuesday morning. She had to take shelter along the coast of Skye on Monday night. The Stornoway people are now tired of her shortcomings. This week a petition to the Postmaster-General praying for a better mail service is (sic) been signed in hundreds. In reply the Postmaster-General stated that the present contract for the mail service would expire in December next, and he was considering the advisability of throwing the contract open to competition.

That possibility did not happen, but the pressure for a change of vessel must have paid off, for in April it was announced in Parliament that 'from May 1 next a larger and more powerful vessel will be placed on the Strome Ferry and Stornoway route, which is expected to perform the voyage in six hours'. This turned out to be the *Clydesdale*, which was rendered surplus on the Glasgow to Stornoway service by the arrival of the *Claymore* in 1881, and which had now been transferred from Islay to Strome. She may have been supposed to be larger and faster, but people were quickly unhappy with her performance. Less than a month after the ship had been on the service, her failings were highlighted in the *Highland News* under the heading 'The Improved (?) Steamer Facilities'. The report described how

> on Tuesday night (28 April) the mail steamer, *Clydesdale*, did not come in sight of the harbour until after eleven o'clock, and experienced great difficulty in getting alongside the quay. Several ineffectual attempts were made, and the vessel dodged about for a considerable time before a landing was affected. An impatient crowd was gathered on the wharf, and some not very complimentary opinions were expressed as to the steamer management.

> A stiff breeze was blowing off the quay, which helped to heighten the difficulty. On Wednesday she did not turn up until midnight. She lay in the harbour until 2.30 am of Thursday, when she attempted to make the passage to Strome, but had ultimately to put back, and lay in the harbour until after nine o'clock. So far, as has yet been seen, the "acceleration of the mails" has been practically a dead letter. The old *regime* was much abused, but we question whether after all is said, the *Lochiel* did not do the work when a "better boat" would have failed.

On 23 July Dr MacDonald, the MP for Ross and Cromarty, enquired whether the Postmaster General was

> aware that the larger steamer that has been put on the Strome-Stornoway route by the mail contractor takes on average a longer time than the smaller one previously used; whether of late, the time used on the voyage has been weekly increasing; whether she is an old boat with defective boilers that cannot stand sufficient steam pressure; whether she frequently misses the 5.45 am train from Strome, and so causes serious loss to fish curers and merchants in having their fish forwarded to the southern markets; why the time of departure from Stornoway has been altered from 9 pm to 11 pm which causes the 5.45 am train to be missed; whether he knows that her being allowed to call at Portree means a loss of three hours for passengers to or from Stornoway; and whether he will put sufficient pressure on the mail contractor to induce him to give an efficient and suitable service.

The response from Mr Raikes, the Postmaster General, was suitably political and non-committal. He mentioned that he had no reason to believe that the steamer now serving Stornoway was 'inefficient either from age or imperfect condition,' and that she was larger and afforded 'improved passenger accommodation'. As regards the complaints about late arrivals and delays, he managed to spread the blame across a number of bodies. He blamed the Harbour Commission of Stornoway for not providing adequate facilities for landing the mails, though requested to do so, and missing the morning train at Strome on the late arrival of the previous day's mail train, which in turn was delayed by a previous train because the line was single track and the fish traffic heavy! The complaint about Portree was also neatly 'fudged': 'it is only on rare occasions that this steamer calls at Portree, and then only by special permission, which is not granted unless it appears necessary on public grounds'. He believed that 'no doubt passengers are delayed on such occasions', but, so far as the arrival of mails at Stornoway was concerned, 'no public convenience has arisen'. Incidentally, almost twenty years earlier, the question had been posed at the time of the Napier Commission, 'Would it suit you if the Mail (sic) were to call at Portree on the route (to Stornoway)?' The response from James McCombie, a fish curer from Peterhead who carried out business in Stornoway, was as follows: 'I do not see why it should not suit us, if they would not detain the steamer by working goods too much.' It is not recorded whether or not this was the opinion of the majority of people in Lewis, but his view would have been far from popular in the 1890s.

Chapter 12

Changes on the Short Crossing – Ships and Railheads

During the remainder of the 1890s a variety of ships served on the Strome-Stornoway service, possibly because of the complaints, and perhaps because of a general re-shuffling of steamers, as David MacBrayne steadily expanded and consolidated his services to the islands. Most of the 'new' tonnage was second-hand; this may have reflected a lack of capital or merely wise investment in proven vessels. In 1891 the *Great Western* appeared; she had belonged to the Great Western Railway, which had used her between Milford Haven and Waterford, and between Weymouth and Cherbourg. She was a two-funnelled paddle steamer, clearly designed for cross-channel duty, and as such would have been able to withstand anything the Minch might have thrown at her. She was withdrawn temporarily in 1893 for reboilering and other alterations, reappearing with standard MacBrayne paddle-boxes and a single funnel, which did not improve her appearance. She was also re-named, now being called the *Lovedale*, after a mission station in Africa, itself named after a Dr Love of Glasgow.

The paddle-steamer *Lovedale* was the first of a number of second-hand vessels to be put on the mail service in the 1890s. She is seen here dwarfed by ocean-going ships on the River Clyde

Her replacement on the mail service was the *Flowerdale*, another second-hand purchase. David MacBrayne had bought her in 1889 from the intriguingly titled Independence Marine Salvage and Steam Pump Co. Ltd of Liverpool, who had named her *Recovery*. She was a twin screw steamer, the first in the MacBrayne fleet. Most of her time was spent on the Outer Isles mail service from Oban, but she also relieved the *Clansman* and the *Claymore* on the Glasgow-Stornoway route. However, in an emergency she in turn was replaced between Strome Ferry and Stornoway by the *Lochiel*, which once again does not seem to have found favour with the travelling public. On 6 March, soon after leaving Strome Ferry in the afternoon on passage to Stornoway, 'an accident occurred to the machinery which caused great delay in delivery of mails and serious inconvenience and danger to passengers and crew'. It was suggested that 'in view of the fact that there have been other mishaps would officers of the Board of Trade use greater diligence in inspecting steamers engaged on this route', but it was pointed out that the Board of Trade had nothing to do with the mail service. As will be seen, dissatisfaction with the service provided on the 'short crossing' became the main theme for the next few years.

The rest of 1893 saw four different steamers on the mail service. The *Cavalier* replaced the *Lochiel* in March. She had been built in 1883 to operate between Glasgow and Inverness, through the Caledonian Canal. This accounted for her somewhat short appearance, for she had been designed to be the maximum size and with vertical bows to fit the locks of the canal. She was not a newcomer to Stornoway, as she was regularly used as a winter relief ship when either of the two 'all-the-way' steamers was being overhauled. She lasted until 1927, having been sold by MacBrayne in 1919 to the North of Scotland, Orkney and Shetland Steam Navigation Co. Ltd, and a year later to the Dundalk & Newry Steam Packet Company to carry cattle from Ireland to Birkenhead. In April the *Flowerdale* returned, only to be replaced during the same month by the *Clydesdale*, which was to remain on the run for the next few months, although she also had her problems, necessitating the use of other ships. In June she was laid up at Strome Ferry and the *Lovedale* carried the mails and passengers to Stornoway; the following month, while coming alongside the quay at Stornoway, the *Clydesdale* collided with the Swedish steamer *Noreg*, which was loading herring for the Baltic. She struck the Swedish ship on her port bow, piercing a hole in the hull, and in doing so her own bowsprit was carried away. A Thursday crossing to Strome Ferry was missed in August, when the *Clydesdale* was unable to sail owing to damage to her engine. On this occasion the *Clansman* deputised.

Another steamer to visit Stornoway on a regular basis that year was the *Gael*. This ship was another example of the second-hand tonnage being purchased by David MacBrayne. She had been built fully thirty years earlier for the Campbeltown & Glasgow Steam Packet Joint Stock Co. Ltd, and became an extremely popular ship. After only two years both her machinery and accommodation were modernised, but for some reason this did not improve either performance or popularity. Accordingly, she was sold in 1883 to the Great Western Railway Co. and saw service on the English and Bristol Channels, to the Channel Islands and the Isles of Scilly. In 1892 David MacBrayne brought her back to Scotland, and placed her on a service up the west coast from Oban as far as Gairloch, but she also relieved ships on other services. During the summer season of 1893, she sailed from Oban to Stornoway carrying tourists, arriving on a Saturday and departing the following Monday. The *Texa*, a small cargo steamer, was another of MacBrayne's ships to call at Stornoway that year. In January she brought coals from Glasgow, as she also did two years later, while at the start of the fishing season in April she conveyed fish-curers' equipment across the Minch to Loch Clash. During the fishing season, the 226 ton *Rossgull*, built in 1884 and chartered from the Earl of Leitrim, carried the early mails and general goods, departing for Glasgow at the end of June.

There was, however, one significant change which brought about an improvement to these services. This was the change of railhead from Strome Ferry to Kyle of Lochalsh in 1897. Six schemes to build railways to West Coast ports such as Ullapool, Aultbea and Lochinver had been proposed, and a Government Commission was set up in 1890 to decide which one would receive financial aid. The Commissioners spent a year 'perambulating the Highlands' to judge the best route. Serous consideration was given to a line from Garve with the Commission regarding Ullapool as unsuitable as a fishing port but excellent as a packet station. They visualised a train running to Ullapool, dropping its passengers there to board the Stornoway steamer, and then continuing to Lochinver for fish and general goods. Eventually in 1893 it was the Highland Railway which received Royal Assent to extend their line from Strome to its original intended terminus facing across the narrow kyle to the Isle of Skye. It took four years to build the extension, not helped by having to blast away huge quantities of rock to allow the railway to wind its way round the coast, and by crofters working on the construction who left this work to return to their homes at harvest time! Eventually on 2 November 1897 the new pier was opened and the first sailings to Portree and Stornoway took place. The honour of serving Stornoway with its first sailing fell to the paddle steamer *Gael*, at the time a relief steamer. She was dressed overall for the occasion. The timetables of the day show that there was a reduction in sailing time from seven to six hours, reflecting the shortening in the distance. The settlement of Kyle of Lochalsh prospered from the change and from being 'little more than a collection of peat huts' it grew to be a much more substantial village as the railway company provided facilities for its workers and passengers, in turn attracting further businesses and inhabitants.

It is not known what ship was on the run later in the same year, but another complaint appeared regarding the timings of sailings and their effect on the mail service, although on this occasion the complaint might be considered to be somewhat

In 1897 the railway was extended from Strome Ferry to Kyle of Lochalsh and this became the mainland port for the mail service. The steamers from Glasgow, such as the *Clansman* shown here, also called

The *Gael*, seen here at Kyle of Lochalsh, was another example of the second-hand tonnage used by David MacBrayne in the 1890s. She made the first sailing from Kyle to Stornoway in 1897

exaggerated. It was stated that the mail which left London at 2030 reached Strome at 1410 the following day, finally arriving in Stornoway 'too late in the evening to admit the business community to reply by return mail leaving an hour after midnight'. The question could be asked as to what business was being carried on in Stornoway that demanded being dealt with so speedily! It would seem that the change of railhead to Kyle of Lochalsh did little to improve matters, for the following year the people of Lewis were still demanding an earlier delivery of the mail and still not evoking a response to their liking.

With the turn of the century came another change to the 'short crossing'. In 1901 the West Highland Railway reached Mallaig. It had originally been planned to terminate the line at Roshven on Loch Ailort, where a pier for MacBrayne steamers was to be constructed. The local landlords were against this idea, and therefore Mallaig was chosen as the terminus and connecting point for the island steamers. On 1 April 1901 the *Lovedale* was serving on the Stornoway run, and it was she that made the first sailing from Stornoway to connect with the new railway. After an experimental mail service through Mallaig, the Highland Railway kept the mail contract, and postal communications were loaded at Kyle. With the opening of the route through Mallaig and Kyle of Lochalsh to Stornoway, the short crossing would now remain the same for the next seventy-two years, but it would certainly not all be plain sailing.

Mallaig also started to be used by the *Clansman* and the *Claymore*. Instead of finding their way into the narrow rocky harbour at Arisaig, a few miles to the south, it was much easier and safer to use Mallaig, although entering its harbour was by no means straightforward. The difficulties of calling at Arisaig were well described by Alexander Smith in his account of *A Summer in Skye*. He wrote:

The entrance into Arisaig is difficult and the *Clansman* was put on half steam. The gentlemen were requested to leave the hurricane-deck and there the captain stationed himself, while a couple of men were sent to the bows and three or four stationed at the wheel. Slowly the large vessel moved onward, with low black reefs of rocks on either side, like smears of dark colour, but perfectly soft and tender in outline; and every here and there we could see the dark top of a rock peering out of the dim sea like a beaver's head. From these shadowy reefs, as the vessel moved on, the sea-birds were awakened from their slumbers and strangely sweet and liquid as flute notes were their cries and signals of alarm. Every now and again, too, with a sort of weary sigh, a big wave came heaving in and broke over the dark reefs in cataracts of ghostly silver; and in the watery trouble and movement that followed, the moon became a well of moving light and the star a quivering sword-blade.

The captain stood alone on the hurricane-deck and the passengers leaned against the bulwarks watching rock and sea and listening to the call and re-call of disturbed mews, when suddenly there was a muffled shout from the out-look at the bows, the captain shouted "Port! Port! *Hard*!" and away went the wheel spinning, the stalwart fellows toiling at the spokes and the ship slowly falling off. After a little while there was another noise at the bows, the captain shouted "Starboard!" and the wheel

The mail service was extended to Mallaig after the opening of the West Highland Railway in 1901. The *Clydesdale*, in her later form with two funnels, lies alongside the pier as the mail steamer arrives from Portree

was rapidly reversed. We were now well up the difficult channel; and looking back we could see a perfect intricacy of reefs and dim single rocks behind and a fading belt of pallor wandering amongst them, which told the track of the ship – a dreadful place to be driven upon on a stormy night, when the whole coast would be like the mouth of a wounded boar – black tusks and churning foam.

After a while, however, a low line of coast became visible, then a light broke upon it; and after a few impatient turns of the paddles we beheld a dozen boats approaching, with lights at their bows. These were the Arisaig boats, laden with cargo. At the sight of them the captain left the hurricane-deck, the anchor went away with a thundering chain, the passengers went to bed and, between asleep and awake, I could hear half the night the trampling of feet, the sound of voices and the jolt of the steam cranes, as the Arisaig goods were being hoisted on deck and stowed away.

A crowded ferry transfers passengers from ship to shore at Arisaig. After the pier at Mallaig was opened, it was no longer necessary for steamers to have to negotiate the narrow, rocky harbour entrance at Arisaig, nor for passengers and cargo to be landed there by this method

Over the next few years, there was again no shortage of complaints about the ships providing the mail service, and possibly this accounted at least in part for the number of ships placed on the service. In June 1901 there was concern over poor time-keeping. Once more the responsibility fell on the Postmaster General to answer the questions 'on how many occasions between 1st April, 1901, and the 22nd June, inclusive, the Stornoway mail steamer has been late in her arrival in Stornoway and Mallaig respectively, and … how often the delay exceeded half an hour.' The response was to admit that the mail steamer frequently reached Stornoway a few minutes late, but this was often due to the late arrival of the train at Kyle of Lochalsh. During the same period the boat was more than half an hour late on twenty-nine occasions. In the reverse direction it was stated that as the mail contract service ended at Kyle of Lochalsh, that was where delays would be significant; there were only four occasions when the steamer was late, of which three were greater than thirty minutes. To appease this situation the timings of the mail steamer were accelerated, with an arrival at Stornoway fifty minutes earlier than before and a departure at 2220 instead of 2300.

In 1902 the *Clydesdale* was back on the run, but in early September she broke down. Over the next two months the mails were carried between Kyle and Stornoway by no fewer than five different ships: the *Clansman*, the *Lovedale*, the *Cavalier*, the *Glendale* and the *Gael*. The *Glendale* had come into the MacBrayne fleet only that year, but she had already had a varied career. This had commenced with her launch in 1875 at Messrs John Elder's shipyard on the Clyde, where she had been built for service on the English Channel between Newhaven and

Dieppe. Being considered too slow, she returned to the Clyde, where she was re-boilered by the Fairfield Company. She then became an excursion steamer sailing between Liverpool and North Wales, before the Hamburg-America Line bought her to sail to Heligoland. She had so far carried the names *Paris* and *Flamingo*, but after a third change, this time to *La Belgique*, she began sailing on the River Thames. At the age of twenty-seven she was finally purchased by David MacBrayne and given her fourth name, that of *Glendale*.

She arrived in Stornoway in 1902, being described as 'a large powerful paddle steamer', having done the crossing from Kyle in five hours, but 'capable of doing it in even better if required'. She was, however, not considered to be ideal for the service, and it was thought that she was to be used on the route as a temporary measure, a correspondent of the time writing, 'The *Glendale*, which is designed for a daylight service, having no sleeping accommodation for passengers, is not to be retained on the Stornoway route, and it is to be expected she will not take more than two or three trips with the Lewis mail'. This was not to be the case for in November she returned and 'is to continue the run during the winter'. She was reported to have 'been making good time on her passages'.

In January of the following year, in the Lewis Hotel, Stornoway, a presentation was made to Captain D Cowan, the master of the *Glendale*, by the people of Barra in recognition of his service on the *Staffa* sailing to the Outer Isles. In his tribute, the speaker referred to the Stornoway route as a 'vexed question', saying that 'he thought it said a good deal for Captain Cowan that his owners had taken him from the Barra route and placed him on such an important run as that to Stornoway. He had been placed in charge of a newly-purchased untried boat that had been laid up for a number of years', adding that he was pleased to say that 'Captain Cowan was making excellent runs and giving entire satisfaction to the public. So long as Captain Cowan was in command the inhabitants of Stornoway could rest assured that the mails would be delivered up to time if that were at all possible'. Having been replaced by the *Clydesdale*, she returned the following May: 'the *Glendale* resumed on the Mail route. Since last … (in Stornoway) … she has undergone extensive alterations in order to fit her for the work'. It was 'understood she will remain for at least the summer season'. Later, in October of the same year, she was reported as replacing the *Clydesdale* again when the latter ship sailed to the Clyde for her annual overhaul. The following month she suffered an accident when approaching the quay at Stornoway. Her steering gear jammed and she collided heavily with the south-west corner of King Edward's Pier, breaking the glass of one of her port lights, splitting three of the fenders, and starting a few bolts in the quay.

She served on various other routes before eventually her career came to an end on 20 July 1905, when she ran aground on rocks on Deas Point, near the Mull of Kintyre. She was en route from Greenock bound for Islay, with Captain J McKechnie, thirteen passengers and the crew on board. In thick fog she ran aground at speed on a rock and stuck fast. She was badly holed but remained upright, allowing the passengers to be taken ashore in the boats where they stayed overnight on rocks. The following morning they returned to collect their possessions and were then rowed to Southend. The *Glendale* had to be declared a total loss.

In 1902, during those two months when there was that merry-go-round of ships, the *Gael* was on the Mallaig-Stornoway run from 21 to 28 October, after which she was replaced by the *Glendale*, apart from the 30 October when the *Gael* was on the run. It was apparently this last-mentioned steamer which was the main concern, especially regarding her speed, or to be more precise, the lack of it. This was given as 15 knots by the Postmaster General in response to yet another question in Parliament by Mr Weir, the MP for Ross and Cromarty, who retorted, 'Is (the Right Hon. Gentleman) aware that her speed is not 15 knots but more likely 5?'

As mentioned above, the *Clydesdale* returned to the run in 1902, in spite of having been the cause of the Stornoway Town Council campaigning for a more satisfactory steamer the previous year, when they pressed the Government for an additional subsidy so that 'a better boat than the *Clydesdale* could be put on the mail run'. She also was a cause for complaint by Mr Weir, giving the Postmaster General more grief. In April, Mr Weir was unhappy that David MacBrayne continued to operate a forty-one year old boat which was frequently late on both the outward and inward passages. He considered that Mr MacBrayne's contract should be terminated, and tenders invited from other steamship owners to provide a faster and more suitable steamer. The Postmaster General on this occasion agreed that the service was unsatisfactory but that it would not be possible to get a better service on the same financial terms. Seven months later Mr Weir showed further discontent regarding the *Gael* and the *Glendale*, considering them to be too old and too slow, and that penalties should be imposed when the vessels failed to keep time. This was to be considered by the Postmaster General, but he stated that both steamers met the requirements of the mail contract, and as the service incurred a heavy loss, no more expenditure could be considered.

There was to be one more push for an improved mail steamer before the first decade of the century was through, and this in spite of the introduction of a new ship, as will be seen below. In 1908 a claim was made that, with a more than 100% increase in correspondence and parcels being dealt with at Stornoway during the previous ten years, a justifiable claim could be made for a faster and better steamer. Once more this was rejected, and again the reasoning was that the Post Office was still incurring a heavy loss on the service, and the increase in costs from providing a speedier service would still not be covered by any increase in revenue.

An article in the *Stornoway Gazette* in May 1933 is probably referring to this period, although the writer seems to contradict the opinions of Mr Weir, mentioned above. Under the heading 'A Wayfarer's Notebook', J N MacIver wrote:

> The MacBrayne's people were always changing their steamers in those days. I remember one very fast boat called the *Gael* which was so fast that the inhabitants of our town (Stornoway) got their mail very early in those days and I believe even got their parcels on the same day as the steamboat's arrival. She was a long rakish paddle-boat, and was an extremely fast vessel; and I believe if they had let her out to her full capacity, she would have been faster still. (She) made a great surge and fury with those two enormous paddles on either side of (her) and made such a picturesque sight on arrival or departure that it was quite a thrill to watch.

The writer also extolled the benefits of the then newly-established service to Glasgow via Mallaig over the alternative by Inverness:

> The West Highland route … necessitated a longer sea voyage, which was quite pleasant in the mornings. Lying securely in my comfortable berth, cradled by the freshly-rolling Atlantic billows, it was a delicious sensation to keep lying, and dreaming, and feeling at one with the wind and waters around me, and the two hours extra of it were very soothing, whereas Highland Railway travelling people had to get up about four in the morning.

He did state, though, that 'it was different, of course, on the return voyage, when they did not allow you to go to bed, and where two hours extra sailing before coming to the dreaded Minch, was not quite good enough'.

The unsatisfactory *Clydesdale* did not endear herself to the people of Stornoway over the years when she failed to maintain the scheduled timetable. In January 1898 she lay in Portree for four days because of storms, resulting in no mail or newspapers reaching Lewis. At the start of 1902, the steamer made no connection with Mallaig for ten days, all passengers for the south having to use the Highland Railway service via Inverness. A south-westerly gale in February 1903 caused the steamer to take fourteen hours on the crossing to Stornoway. Only a week later, heavy seas caused by another storm compelled the captain of the *Clydesdale* to put his ship into Portree for shelter. She eventually arrived in Stornoway about noon the following day.

Eventually the steamer was transferred to sail from Oban to the Outer Islands and finally came to a sad end in 1905. She had been on passage from Oban to Barra, when at 0700 on 6 January on a dark winter morning of blinding sleet and gales she went aground on Lady Rock, south of the island of Lismore. This is a rock which is visible at low tide, but the incoming waters swirl over and completely cover it. The rock was so called after an unwanted wife of a MacLean of Mull was tied there in the hope that the rising tide would drown her. The steamer's bows were left pointing skyward as the tide receded. Three hours after the grounding, the passengers were taken off by the *Carabinier* en route from Tobermory to Oban, while the *Brenda* and the *Fingal* also stood by. It was hoped that it would be possible to refloat the *Clydesdale* but like several of her predecessors she became a total wreck.

Chapter 13

Sheila and the *Chieftain*

Three years before that, in 1902, it was announced that an order had been given for a new ship, described as 'an up-to-date screw steamer fitted with electric light and all modern improvements'. Two years later the new ship appeared. This was the *Sheila*, which was to serve the Lewis people for over two decades. The choice of name is interesting: after names with Highland connections or with the suffix '-ier', there was now a steamer with a girl's simple name. The ship was appropriately named after Sheila, who was the heroine of William Black's romantic novel, *A Princess of Thule*, which is set partly in Lewis.

She was built by Inglis of Pointhouse on the Clyde and launched on 30 January 1904, taking up the Stornoway mail run in March of that year. In design she was a much more basic steamer than the likes of the *Claymore*. In place of the elegant lines, clipper bow and bowsprit, she had much more of the appearance of a workhorse than a thoroughbred, although it cannot be said that she was not pleasing to the eye, and she has been described as stately. Perhaps this was because she was designed specifically for the daily routine of the Stornoway mail steamer rather than the glamour of enticing tourists on the

A drawing of the *Sheila*, the new mail steamer built in 1904 (drawing by the author)

'all-the-way' service. When compared to the ferries of today, she seems very basic, and in fact was little more than half the length of the *Isle of Lewis*. Yet for the next 23 years, with almost no interruptions, she crossed the Minch 12 times a week in all conditions with no mishaps.

The following description of her appeared in the *Highland News* on her arrival in Stornoway on her maiden voyage:

> The vessel … is a handsome craft to outward appearance, and her inward fittings are in keeping. A special feature is the excellent quarters provided for cabin passengers. The main cabin is beautifully upholstered in crimson plush and we observed on our tour of inspection a number of cosy two-berth deck cabins and a splendidly appointed smoking room also on deck, while sheltering the main deck, and affording an excellent promenade in fine weather is a hurricane deck. The vessel is lit with electric light throughout. She is fitted with the latest type of triple-expansion engines, and has a high speed, having developed 14 knots on her trial trip. In bad weather the top hatches can be closed, and the forepart of the ship entirely covered in, which will add greatly to the comfort of the steerage passengers. Another feature is the placing of the galley on the top deck, thus removing a cause of complaint to weaker stomached passengers who used to be upset by the smell of cooking on the lower deck. Altogether the *Sheila* is a credit to her owner, and will prove a useful addition to the Macbrayne fleet. We were glad to see the cheery countenance of Captain Cameron on the bridge after an absence of two years on other steamers. As 'Colin' was recognised by the crowd gathered on Monday to see the *Sheila* come in hearty cheers were raised. We can rest assured that Captain Cameron (who has a twenty years' connection with the Stornoway route) now that he has got a first-class boat under his feet, will deliver the mails in record-breaking time. The chief officer is Mr Black, also an old friend and favourite with the Stornoway travelling public. The genial and obliging Mr Mackay, who has been purser for some time past on the *Clydesdale* and *Glendale*, fills that important office on the *Sheila*. Besides being a fast boat, the *Sheila* is also a fine sea boat, being fitted with rolling chocks to steady her in rough weather. What with a fine ship and splendid officers the public can now be sure of a comfortable trip over the Minch.

Only a few months after taking up the mail service, the *Sheila* played a part, although only a relatively minor one, in what has been described as 'one of history's most overlooked, yet significant, maritime disasters'. This was the sinking in 1904 of the Danish emigrant ship, the *Norge*, owned by the Danish-American Line. On 28 June of that year she was *en route* from Denmark and Norway to New York, when she struck a reef off the island of Rockall. She was carrying a total of 795 passengers and crew, just five short of her certificated maximum. There was lifeboat provision for only 251, within the then legal limit. Six hundred and thirty five perished, while 160 survived up to eight days in the lifeboats before being picked up by various ships. On 4 July, thirty-four of the survivors were brought to Stornoway by the passenger-cargo ship *Cevona*, which anchored off Arnish. They were then brought ashore on the steamer *Bonawe*, belonging to J Gardner & Co., which had arrived from Glasgow and was unloading coal. Later in the same day 71 more survivors, who had been picked up by the German petroleum carrying ship, *Energie*, were also landed at Stornoway. All the survivors were put up in the Lewis Hospital, Coulregrein House (the 'Poor House'), and in private houses. On 8 July, fifty-five of them, bound eventually for the United States, left on the *Sheila*. They carried canvas bags containing clothing and gifts, and were conveyed in covered cabs to the pier. Over 1,000 people stood packed on the pier and adjoining seafront, some having been there for several hours, and the cabs had difficulty in reaching the quayside. Waving and exchanging of greetings were evident as the fifty-five boarded the *Sheila*. Women and children were allowed to sit in the first-class saloon, but the men had to use the steerage accommodation. As the steamer cast off, the survivors gathered on the forecastle deck and gave three cheers for the people of Stornoway, who had treated them so well. The response from the crowd on the pier was described as 'ten times as loud'. At 0400 the *Sheila* reached Kyle, where the passengers boarded special carriages in a train which was to convey them to Liverpool. Three days later, twenty more survivors left on the *Sheila*, this time returning home to Scandinavia, followed by a further six on 15 July. The final group were carried to Liverpool on Langlands' steamer, the *Princess Victoria*. Incidentally, the *Claymore* arrived from Glasgow on the same day as the survivors were landed. The tourists on board 'had not reckoned to see survivors of an immense shipwreck and were disturbed by what they saw'. A spontaneous collection amongst the tourists raised £23, including one individual donation of £10, and this was donated to the castaways.

The *Sheila* is often remembered as the ship which ploughed her way across the Minch in all weathers, never missing a trip, and often seeming to be making no headway as she steamed her way against wind and waves. An example of both the seaworthiness of the ship and the abilities of her captain and crew was reported in the *Highland News* in December 1906. Under the headline 'Stormy Weather in the Minch – Mail Steamer Puts Back Twice', it was recorded that the *Sheila*

> encountered a terrific gale on Tuesday on the passage from Kyle, and the passengers, including about one hundred female fish workers returning from Yarmouth, had a terrible experience. When the *Sheila* left Kyle the weather was moderate, but no sooner had she gained the open (sea) than she met the full force of the gale – a north-easter, dead ahead. Most of the girls were helplessly sick, and by the orders of Captain Cameron were taken into the saloon and officers' quarters, where all possible attention was paid to them. On Wednesday the weather was still more severe. Another contingent of girls from the English fishing – numbering about 150 – was on board. After proceeding as far as Applecross, the steamer had to put about and return to Kyle. But Captain Cameron had His Majesty's mails aboard and at 8 pm he again essayed to make the passage. On again approaching Applecross the weather encountered was so terrific that the dauntless captain decided that discretion was the better part of valour, and once more put about and returned to Kyle. Most of the women had had more than enough of it by this time, and about a hundred of them went ashore, intending to wait till Thursday night, in the hope of getting a more comfortable crossing. The weather having moderated somewhat towards two am, Captain Cameron again decided to have another try, and on this occasion he was successful, and delivered the mails in time to allow of the citizens having their letters and papers at the breakfast table.

It was then mentioned that the steamer left Stornoway almost immediately, to return there at eleven o'clock that evening, having thus made up her lost time. The same storm delayed the *Clydesdale*, deputising for the *Clansman* on the service from Glasgow, by twenty-four hours.

In March 1908, the *Sheila* was again delayed by heavy weather. On this occasion a week of northerly gales created conditons which even the 'redoubtable' Captain Cameron decided were too severe to proceed beyond Applecross and he accordingly dropped anchor in the bay. Conditions improved to allow resumption of the passage at daybreak the following morning, and the steamer eventually reached Stornoway around mid-day. The gales had 'raised a mountainous sea' on the Lewis coast, also causing problems for the Langlands steamer *Princess Beatrice*; she had left Stornoway at 0100 the same day as the *Sheila*, and had had to battle against the wind and waves, managing only three miles in three hours. After anchoring in Branahuie Bay in the hope that conditions would improve, she finally returned to Stornoway at 1800. It was noted that she then 'landed a pair of horses and two cows which were in danger of being seriously injured through the excessive pitching of the vessel.' No mention was made regarding the state of any of the passengers.

The *Sheila* arriving at Kyle of Lochalsh. This photograph shows just how small a steamer she was to endure crossing the Minch twelve times a week in all weathers for almost a quarter of a century

There must also have been times when there was no wind, and the Minch like a millpond. Perhaps conditions were like that in July of the same year when the *Sheila* broke the record by arriving in Stornoway at 1910, beating the time of four hours forty-seven minutes which had been set in 1901 by the *Gael*, deputising for the *Clydesdale*. However, most of the reports on the *Sheila's* crossings of the Minch refer to times when the crossings were anything but smooth. Only two months after the record crossing, northerly gales had returned, and on 8 September the ship took ten and a half hours to cross between Kyle and Stornoway. In May 1915 a passenger described the ordeal of a crossing in extremely stormy conditions:

> Leaving Kyle at 3 pm the *Sheila* encountered a gale of hurricane force, which gradually increased in severity. Owing to the heavy seas running it was impossible to land mails at Applecross, so she continued on her course into the open Minch and there encountered the full force of a north-east hurricane. The little vessel, gallantly fighting her way in the teeth of the gale, was continually swept by tremendous seas, which practically engulfed her and sometimes laid her on her beam ends … The passengers in the smoking-room were unable to get out for some time owing to the barrels which were on deck being jammed up against the doors by the seas … Should an accident have occurred … it would certainly have been impossible to save any of those who were barricaded in the smoking-room. However, after a thrilling battle with the storm, (the *Sheila*) arrived at Stornoway … several

> hours overdue. On Saturday, 8th December, 1917, gales and a snowstorm forced the mail boat to put into Portree, and she did not arrive in Stornoway until mid-afternoon on the Sunday.

It is therefore interesting that, according to one of the few descriptions of a crossing on board her, *Travels with my Tammy*, by Cathie Lockie, the passage on the *Sheila* was uneventful:

> The "Great adventure" would begin … The 4.15 train for Mallaig arrived and with lots of other passengers and a proliferation of cases and more important things like fishing rods, we clambered aboard. Three to four hours later and half-asleep, we left the train to walk across to Mallaig harbour. There was the steamer which was to transport us north to Kyle of Lochalsh – a journey of some 2/3 hours. Warm and sunny weather and warm enough to be on deck, open up our flasks and sandwiches and have a late lunch. Sail over and we were now on the pier at Kyle. We would wait with our luggage until the *Sheila*, the Stornoway steamer, would dock. Another hour would pass as cargo and luggage preceded the passengers and rucksacked tourists were allowed on board. The sea breeze had become a stiffening wind by this time, threatening to "de-tammy" me. I have this memory of great anxiety about this. The Minch is well known for its turbulence and the cause of much seasickness. Indeed, stretcher cases have been known to be taken off at Stornoway, but steamers are much better equipped with stabilisers now. My father, a soft spoken Highland gentleman, but a strict disciplinarian had one answer to this, "Take the travelling rugs, get up to the top deck, fill your lungs with good fresh air – and don't DARE to be sick!" And, you know, we weren't! Three hours on, past the Shiant Isles, known for its teeming bird life covering the rocks and once owned by Compton Mackenzie the novelist and celebrated author of "Whisky Galore", who lived on Barra. Four hours pass and the houses of Stornoway have come into view and the decks are lined with passengers, binoculars at the ready. The Stornoway pier was packed with townsfolk, as in these days, that was the event of the day.

A second description, by W H MacDonald, gives a less pleasant description of travelling on board the *Sheila*:

> It was quite an experience to cross the Minch from Stornoway to Kyle and vice-versa on the old mailboat the *Sheila*. For travellers undertaking the voyage, a strong mind, a steady nerve and a near-iron constitution were required if one were to triumph over the many hazards and discomforts. Many … who could not afford to pay for travelling astern of the sign on board which read – "Passengers abaft this cabin pay full fare" – were relegated to the forward part of the ship, known in seaman's jargon as the "steerage". This part of the ship was shared by passengers and animals. The livestock, usually cattle and sheep, naturally fared better being less sensitive to their surroundings. But the real "fun" on board only began when the ship approached the Shiants and the ground swell increased causing her to perform a nightmarish dance of rolling, pitching, plunging and a corkscrew type of lunging at the waves. This was the accepted signal for many of the passengers to assume a woebegone appearance, their faces changing to a yellowish-blue colour, prior to their making a frantic rush to the rails to feed the "fishes". Down in the steerage proper, the hardy souls who were not afflicted by the dreaded seasickness endeavoured to keep their spirits up by singing Gaelic "porsts" to the accompaniment of a melodeon or mouth-organ. However, once the beams of the Stornoway lighthouse were sighted, magically everybody cheered up,

When the *Chieftain* was launched in 1907 she was the largest steamer yet to serve Stornoway. Both her size and the development of the classic 'yacht' lines are evident

> the vessel soon tied up to No 1 Pier and passengers once again became human beings as soon as their feet stood on terra firma. The voyage was over, passengers were greeted and welcomed by their families and friends, with warm handshakes and oft times tears.' In the article there are also 'a few words about the ship's company'.

There was 'old "Lachie" the Purser, who used to chase from bow to stern demanding of passengers – "*Tickarts please, tickarts please*" ', while he paid 'tribute to the Master … the late Captain Colin Cameron. He was a great seaman of the old school, a fine navigator and above all a fearless mariner who, in all kinds of weather and rough seas, braved the fury of the elements to bring his ship, passengers and cargo safely across the legendary Minch.'

Annual excursions along similar lines to those described earlier were also part of the *Sheila*'s duties. The minutes of the Stornoway YMCA of July 1924 reported the arrangements for an excursion to Portree. The boat was to leave Stornoway at 0700 and start the return journey at 1800 with the Sea Cadet Band, and a police constable to travel with the party. The duties of the police constable were not clarified. At the next meeting of the YMCA it was reported that the excursion had made a profit of £73/4/6d (£73.22).

A second new ship to serve Stornoway was introduced in 1907. While smaller, more economical motor vessels had been built for other routes, the development of the Glasgow to Stornoway service for tourists prompted MacBrayne's to build their largest ship yet. A combination of the realisation of the growing potential of the West Coast tourist trade and an attempt to beat off opposition from shipping companies such as M Langlands & Son, which had introduced cruises in 1892 with their *Princess Victoria*, followed by *Princess Maud* in 1902, led to the ordering and building of the *Chieftain* by the Ailsa Shipbuilding Co., at Troon. Much has been written about this steamer, which at 241 feet (74m) in length, 33 feet (10m) in breadth, and the first

MacBrayne ship to have a gross tonnage of over 1,000, was by far the largest in the fleet to that date. These figures do little to explain the impact she made on her appearance on the West Coast. The classic 'yacht' design developed through the previous 'all the way' steamers was taken to new heights. She had the same basic design of clipper bow and decorated bowsprit, sweeping lines with an elegant sheer ending in a graceful counter stern, topped by two masts and a tall funnel. Whereas on the previous ships the sleeping accommodation opened off the after saloon, where both officers and crew dined at a long table, the *Chieftain* had a new layout with a dining saloon forward on the shelter deck, aft of which was an entrance hall and then staterooms. There was electric lighting, and bells were fitted throughout the ship. She had drawing rooms and smoking rooms, and electric winches to handle cargo quietly without disturbing the tourists' slumbers. All this was detailed on advertising handbills, which stated that the ship was 'specially built for the West Highland Tourist Trade and is more like a Yacht than a Tourist Steamer'. She has been described as 'like a millionaire's yacht', a 'noble ship', 'the Hebridean and Edwardian equivalent of *Queen Elizabeth 2*'. She definitely secured both her own and MacBrayne's position as leader of the Western Isles tourist trade.

Unfortunately, the other word which has been used on a number of occasions to describe the *Chieftain* is 'anachronistic'. To begin with, she was extremely popular, and satisfied tourists were making repeat bookings for the following seasons. But she suffered from a number of disadvantages. She was heavy on fuel, and her slightly under-powered engines meant she struggled to maintain some parts of her schedules. The design of both her cargo holds and her cranes and winches increased the time she had to spend at piers, while she proved unsuitable for carrying sheep and cattle, an essential part of the west coast trade. Added to this was the fact that she operated only during the summer months, spending the winter laid up on the Clyde, earning nothing.

During the summer months, the *Chieftain* had replaced the ageing *Clansman*, and joined the *Claymore* in providing a twice-weekly service from Glasgow to Stornoway. In the winter the new steamer's place was taken, initially, by the *Clansman*, until she reached the end of her useful life, and was withdrawn and broken up in 1909, and then by the *Cavalier*. In January 1910, the *Chieftain* had to be hurriedly made ready for service during

The main purpose of the *Chieftain* was as a cruise ship

the winter to cover for the *Claymore*, which had gone aground at Broadford. In August that year, the *Chieftain* herself had to be relieved when she went on to rocks on Raasay.

As the onset of the First World War approached, the steamer services to Stornoway seemed to be fairly settled. For most of the time the Glasgow route was operated by the *Claymore* and the *Chieftain*, while the *Sheila* maintained the mail service. However, only six years after last-mentioned vessel had been introduced on the mail service, the dissatisfaction regarding both the ship and the service, which had started during the days of the *Lochiel* and continued when the *Clydesdale* was the mail steamer, re-appeared. While criticism was levelled at the size of the ship, her speed, and the excessive charges for both passengers and cargo, on all occasions nothing but praise was reserved for the captain, officers and crew of the *Sheila*. The following extracts from letters can be taken as a typical of the high esteem in which the ship's company was held. 'The Captain and crew of the *Sheila* lie altogether outside the question of the adequacy or inadequacy of that boat for her present route. No-one who deserves the least consideration doubts the prowess of her Captain or the crew.' 'Were it not for the undaunted bravery of the captain and crew of the *Sheila* the vessel on many occasions would not be able to make the passage.'

Some of the complaints about the *Sheila*, often taking the form of letters to the press, were made by individuals. In 1910 a letter, signed 'Sigma', was printed in the *Highland News*, strongly criticising both David MacBrayne and the *Sheila*. It pointed out that

> As long as the MacBraynes (sic) have a monopoly of that route, one may rest assured that nothing will be altered for the better, except under the strongest compulsion, either by a rival Company or by pressure brought to bear on the owners by the Government through the Postmaster-General. That the boat on the route is not paying is simply absurd. Does anyone in his senses believe that the boat is run by the MacBrayne at a loss, and therefore as a charity? It is absolutely useless for the Stornoway people to advertise the town as a summer resort until the means of transport are rendered safer, speedier and less costly.
>
> The boat now on the route is not much larger than an ordinary steam trawler, and it says a good deal for the skill of the officers navigating her that there has not been considerable loss of life already. It is unreasonable to have a mail boat on such a route with a less speed (sic) than 15 knots at the very least.

The writer then proceeds to criticise the vessel's accommodation, stating,

> The last time I crossed … the deck allocated to cabin passengers was so congested with returned empties, mostly from Billingsgate, that there was no proper space to walk on, and presumably this is of frequent occurrence. Now, if cabin passengers are deprived of the means of enjoying the sea breezes, what becomes of the steerage passengers?

Somewhat grudgingly, he did offer some praise for the catering. He had to pay 6/- (30p) for 'the privilege of occupying the saloon' for thirty minutes while taking his tea, for which he was charged 2/- (10p). This latter charge, he said, was 'perfectly fair and reasonable under the circumstances, even if margarine be supplied instead of butter.'

Later the same year, a second letter appeared, signed 'Lewisman', written by an emigrant returning home to his native island. Having safely crossed the Atlantic from Quebec to Liverpool, he had thought the worst was over when he went aboard the *Sheila* to cross to Stornoway on the final leg of his journey. He wrote,

> But alas! The worst was yet to come. I will not in a hurry forget Wednesday, 16th November, in that wretched little boat. The night was bad, but what made it a thousand times worse was that there was no accommodation whatever for third class passengers … It is a disgrace to have such a slow, miserable little boat running to an important town like Stornoway.

In 1910 the 'agitation for an improved mail steamer service' had resulted in correspondence being carried on between Stornoway Town Council, David MacBrayne, the Board of Trade and Mr Weir, MP, consequent to a visit by a deputation sent by the Town Council to Westminster. The dispute concerned a number of issues. Firstly, the standard of accommodation, particularly as regards third-class passengers, was not of an acceptable standard, the Town Council claiming that 'the discomforts suffered by many deck passengers have [en]gendered disease which has sent many of them to an early grave', while they held that 'Messrs Macbrayne cannot close their eyes to the fact that deck passengers aboard the mail boat have no better treatment, as regards accommodation and comfort, than the brute beast'. Secondly, the freight rates from Stornoway were higher than from other places in the Highlands, thereby 'hampering the island and the industry on which it depends', and resulting in the fish curers chartering an extra steamer to carry fish to the mainland for transfer by rail to Billingsgate market in London. A third complaint was that of the steamer's late arrivals in Stornoway. The Council related these complaints to the report of a Committee appointed by the Postmaster-General in 1898 to enquire into mail steamer services on the north and west Coasts of Scotland, which laid down 'that mail steamers on the West Coast of Scotland should provide for not only carrying mails, but have suitable accommodation for passengers, and that trade requirements should be considered'. The Lewis District Council, less vociferously than their urban counterparts, entered the dispute in 1911, when they pressed for a larger and swifter steamer.

A complaint about a different matter arose in 1912. This concerned the state of the pier at Stornoway, both on the arrival and departure of the *Sheila* or whatever steamer was on the mail service. 'Crowds of people of all ages and sizes, females in particular, (would) rush to the pier as if their very life depended upon seeing the steamer arrive, and what is worse, they collect(ed) in large numbers round the gangway, (so) that passengers (had) difficulty in getting off and finding their way to the street.' The same applied when the steamer was departing, with intending travellers being heard to ask, 'Where is the gangway?' as they could not see it for the assembled crowds. The police were there, but their powers on the pier seemed to be limited. It was considered that it was 'worse than a stormy passage on the Minch to come to Stornoway and have to meet the inquisitive gaze of the people on the pier.' It was further thought that it was no wonder that 'newly married couples betake themselves by motor to Harris'. An exiled Lewisman living in Alexandria, Egypt, was motivated to respond to this by writing to the *Highland News*, suggesting that if the situation did not improve, there should be a return to the methods used in the 1860s. Then, he wrote,

> the landing of passengers was splendidly managed … There was a barricade at the north end of the wharf, and adjoining were two higher gates … There were two policemen, one of them named Kenny, and the other a ginger-headed one. When they would see a steamer at the lighthouse they would go about the wharf. Boys playing and people found gallivanting about the wharf were chased through the gates, and the gates closed till all the people had landed. To get through the gates was out of the question, because Kenny was foxy and wicked … and he would have no "shinanegan".

The writer considered that the situation did not occur 'in any other part of the world' and that in 'Portree and Oban the people there take no more notice of a mail steamer than they do of the fifth wheel of a coach'.

Dissatisfaction with the *Sheila* and the mail service reached such a pitch that in 1913 what was described as a Public Indignation Meeeting was held in Stornoway Town Hall. It was organised by the Town Council and chaired by Provost Mackenzie. The strength of feeling can be judged by the fact that it was attended not only by members of the general public, but also by traders from other places doing business in Stornoway, such as East Coast fish curers and their agents, as well as a considerable number of female fish workers, in whose interest much of the fight for more comfort and accommodation was being pursued. A deputation had been sent to various relevant Government departments, but time had slipped by without anything happening. The poor timekeeping of the mail boat was illustrated: she had been late during October on twenty-three occasions, representing a loss of nineteen hours twenty minutes; in November she was late twenty-three times, representing twenty-seven hours fifty-five minutes; in December twenty-six times, twenty-five hours fifteen minutes; and in January twenty-seven times, thirty-one hours six minutes. This made a total of 101 times late, representing an aggregate time of 103 hours thirty-five minutes. While it was accepted that some of the delays could be attributed to trains arriving late at Kyle of Lochalsh, it was considered that a larger and faster vessel could make up some of the time on the sea passage. The chairman then referred to the condition of the *Sheila*, stating that she was not in a fit condition to cope with the current amount of passenger traffic, and he considered that the conditions under which the fish workers had to travel was a disgrace to humanity. Perhaps with a degree of exaggeration, he went on to say 'without fear or contradiction that some of the Lewis girls were now in asylums through nervous shock received on board the mail steamer, and some of them were in premature graves owing to the usage they received crossing the Minch.'

Ex-Provost Anderson took a less extreme view, stating that 'as a town and island they were entitled to a better steamer service than the present one.' Rather compromisingly, he then considered the *Sheila* to be a 'wonderful boat', and 'although he had crossed the Minch in her very frequently he was never afraid but once.' He then stated:

> there was really no accommodation provided for steerage passengers, and even that provided for those who paid the excess cabin fare was very unsatisfactory. The present steamer service was quite inadequate for an important community like theirs, and the time had come when they must put their foot down and demand their rights.

A resolution was then passed

> That this public meeting of the inhabitants of Stornoway and the Lewis, including traders from other districts doing business in Stornoway, do emphatically protest against the continued unsatisfactory mail service between Stornoway and the mainland, and now calls upon H.M. Government to give immediate effect to the representations made to them on former occasions, by deputation and otherwise, for a swifter and larger mail steamer than the one presently on the route.

Copies were sent to the Prime Minister, the Chancellor of the Exchequer, the Postmaster General, the President of the Board of Trade and Mr Macpherson, MP for Ross and Cromarty.

A year later the situation had not improved and memorials were signed by 'traders and the general public' in Stornoway and by 'the 2,500 female workers and 1,500 hired fishermen who went to the herring fishings in Shetland, the East Coast of Scotland, and in England'. It was the fisher girls in particular who were subjected to the lack of suitable accommodation on the *Sheila* when they travelled to and from work on the mainland. Examples of the numbers that travelled can be seen in the following statistics. During two weeks in 1906, between 100 and 300 were carried daily by the mail steamer, with the *Staffa*, relieving on the Glasgow service, being called upon to make an extra crossing one week, while the *Clansman* was used the other week one night when over 500 crossed the Minch. In 1910 the number of fish workers returning to the island was so great that the *Handa*, a small steamer built in 1878 and used mainly for carrying cargo, was put on to convey passengers' luggage to Stornoway. In April a deputation visited London to meet a member of the Treasury, the President of the Board of Trade and the Postmaster General, to whom they 'stated briefly and forcibly the great inconvenience suffered by merchants and traders, especially during the fishing season, owing to the inadequacy and irregularity of the mail services, and the sufferings of the fisher girls and others owing to the lack of accommodation on the mail steamer for such a passage as the Minch'. It was then stated that 'promises were made that the matter would be looked into immediately'. The intervention of the First World War is probably the reason why nothing more seems to have been heard regarding the issue until 1919.

The Member of Parliament for Ross and Cromarty found the performance of *Sheila* unsatisfactory. He stated, 'she is constantly late in her arrival in Stornoway', and he wondered why the inhabitants of Lewis should not be provided with a similar service to that to the Isle of Man, where the contract stipulated a speed of fourteen knots as against the eleven in the Stornoway contract. Once again he did not receive satisfaction, the response being that:

A humorous postcard dating from just before the start of the First World War. In spite of all the complaints about the service at the time it shows the affection with which the steamers were held by the people of Lewis

> the *Sheila* fulfils the contract requirement that the steamer employed shall perform the service at a speed of 11 sea miles an hour, and shall maintain the scheduled hours unless prevented by bad weather. Her speed according to Lloyd's List is 14 miles an hour, and her normal speed is 12 miles an hour. The unpunctuality in her arrival is chiefly due to the late running of trains from the south, in connection with which the steamer works. Little time is lost on the voyage between Kyle and Stornoway; and that loss being in every case due to bad weather.

A concern of a different kind, but again liable to affect the *Sheila*, occurred in May 1914. It started as a rumour, 'apparently well-founded', that the Post Office authorities were considering sending the mails from Achnasheen to Gairloch and thence by a motor boat to Stornoway. The proposal was considered to be totally impractical on a number of grounds. Of greatest concern was the fact that there would be great difficulty in carrying the mails, weighing anything up to three or four tons, on a small motor boat in winter conditions, and that Stornoway would be left without mails on many days. Concern was raised that, if the subsidy was withdrawn from the existing route, then in all likelihood it would be an excuse to reduce the present passenger service (and there was no mention of passenger provision in the new proposal), and 'that would be the last straw in an already unsatisfactory state of affairs'. It was thought that the official who conceived the idea could have had no idea of what crossing the Minch in a north-easterly gale incurred. Fortunately, nothing further was heard of the proposals and the mails continued to be carried by the *Sheila*.

There were some who praised the little ship and her crew, although these would appear to have been few and far between. One admirer of the *Sheila* wrote that he had 'no hesitation in saying that a more beautiful or better equipped vessel never sailed the sea'. He went on to say that, were he a poet, 'he would sing of the *Sheila* as the Harris bard sang of her famous predecessor on the Minch:

'Hurrah! Hurrah! for the bold *Lochiel*,
With her gallant crew so brave;
She ploughs the ocean like a seal
In spite of wind and wave.'

He further praised the ship, writing, 'The *Sheila* still shines brightly, and sails sweetly to and fro across the Minch … A more splendid craft will never be seen conveying the Lewis mails.'

For the next couple of years all seems to have been peaceful, only for a disagreement to have arisen between MacBrayne's and the Stornoway Pier and Harbour Commission over berthing dues. This was not the first time this had happened, for in the 1880s the Commission discussed the fact that David MacBrayne was every year in arrears with 'payment for his ships and rents', and concluded that the company 'should be called upon to avoid this in future'. In 1912 it was discovered that dues had been charged for the *Chieftain* based on a tonnage of 306, which should have been 604! This left an outstanding balance due of £803/17/6 (£803.87) and an invoice was duly sent to the MacBrayne's agent. He returned this to the Commission, who then sent it to MacBrayne's Head Office in Hope Street, Glasgow. Even with the sum reduced to £368 MacBraynes withheld payment. The tussle went on until 1914, when the Commission asked David MacBrayne to pay weekly as they had received nothing for two years!

Chapter 14

The First World War

It was some time after the start of the First World War before there was any significant effect on the services to Stornoway. While tourist numbers had been on the decline before 1914, there was always the need for supplies to be carried to the island, and local produce to be brought back to the mainland. At the outbreak of the First World War the fishing industry became paralysed, and on one night the *Sheila* brought home to Lewis 200 fishermen while MacBrayne's had to send the *Gael* and the *Chieftain* to assist in carrying over 1000 fishermen another night. Within a year, however, economies were starting to be made, and services were being reduced to a minimum. The effect on Lewis was that the mail service was reduced from six to three crossings each week, as the *Sheila* combined the Stornoway and Portree mail services, sailing to the two ports on alternate days; this was to cause dissatisfaction for a considerable number of years. One result of the reduction in services was that mail and newspapers were carried on only three days each week; this situation was resolved by the local postmaster in Stornoway agreeing to allow the mail to be carried by any suitable ship, as happened in March 1915 when the steamers *Lady Tennant* and the *Kimberley* both carried out this duty. This practice of using an additional boat to carry the early mails was continued after the war; it would seem that any suitable vessel might be used for this purpose, as the following incident, which occurred in February 1919, and was recorded in the *Highland News*, shows:

> When leaving Stornoway harbour for Kyle, H.M. Drifter *John Watt*, with mails, and leave men returning to duty, on board, collided with a coal hulk, and was so badly damaged that she had to put back to port, and was safely berthed. It did not take long to find another boat, in which mails and passengers were taken to the steamer terminus.

There had been no steamer named *Clansman* sailing to Stornoway since 1909 when the worthy veteran of that name was withdrawn. But in 1915 a third *Clansman* appeared for a short time on the Glasgow-Stornoway service. Built in 1880, she originally carried the name *Ethel*, under Northern Irish ownership; she was then briefly registered under the French flag as *Obokh*, before reverting to her original name and as such entered the MacBrayne fleet in 1885, operating originally between Glasgow and Inverness, then to Islay and finally relieving on a number of routes. She became the *Clansman* in 1910, in all probability to enable the company to retain the right to use the name on a more prestigious ship in the future. Thus under this name she appeared for a short time sailing into Stornoway. It was after a voyage from Stornoway to Fecamp in France, with a cargo of salt herring, that she was sold to a Glasgow shipping company. Finally, after two more changes of ownership, she was lost at sea in 1924.

In 1916 there was further disagreement with the Stornoway Pier and Harbour Commission, firstly over increased water charges and then about lack of storage facilities. In the first case, MacBrayne's refused to pay the new charges. As regards the problems of storage, MacBrayne's claimed the *Sheila* was unable to discharge all her cargo. Worried Stornoway locals thought the inhabitants of the town might be starved if a solution was not reached, but Baillie Smith responded that 'the government will not allow the inhabitants of the Isle of Lewis to be starved, whatever MacBraynes or any other carriers might do'. Another concern arose the same year, when it was claimed that the Highland Railway was refusing to grant cheap rates as it did to David MacBrayne for goods carried by the Stornoway Shipping Co. Ltd. This company then contemplated legal proceedings, but nothing further was heard about the problem. It was not all moans and complaints, however, for on the bright side it was reported that in Stornoway the YMCA would provide 'comfort facilities to meet demand for the duration of War at various times from 6 pm onwards, including the time from 11 pm to 3 am on the nights the mail steamer sailed'. In 1917 it was decided to import American mines into the country using Kyle of Lochalsh as the point of entry. Accordingly, the Admiralty requisitioned the pier and transport facilities there. While sailings were not unduly interrupted, restrictions were placed on the movements of goods. Notices announced that, regarding traffic for Lewis, the only traffic available through Kyle of Lochalsh was passengers' personal luggage, mails, perishable traffic, 'in lots not exceeding 1 cwt.', and Government stores. The routes through Mallaig and Oban were similarly not available, and all other traffic for Lewis had to be conveyed via Glasgow. Thus it can be seen that, apart from a reduction in services, the First World War had relatively little significant effect on Stornoway's shipping. One minor detail which can be added is that after the steamer *Plover* was involved in an incident with a German submarine off Tiree, the *Claymore* was painted in camouflage colours. This occurred only four months before the end of hostilities, and as a result, she was the only member of the MacBrayne fleet to be so treated. It is to be wondered how the inhabitants of Stornoway took to 'their' steamer being painted in this way.

Chapter 15

The *Iolaire* and Hard Times

The time after the Great War was not good either for the people of Lewis or for MacBrayne's. In particular, the year 1919 saw a number of happenings which did little to help the immediate post-war circumstances.

The first of these was the terrible tragedy of the *Iolaire*. It was one of the most poignant catastrophes in the annals of the British Navy and in the history of the Isle of Lewis. The vessel was built in 1881 for the Duke of Westminster as the luxury sailing yacht *Amalthaea*, later sailing under various owners with the names *Iolanthe* and *Rione*. In 1915, she was requisitioned for war service from her then owner, Mr Duff Assheton Smith (later Sir Michael Duff). Although converted and used for anti-submarine warfare and patrol work, much evidence of her pre-war style was retained (although boarded over for protection). Her name was changed again and she became HMS *Iolaire*, serving as the naval base ship at Stornoway.

On 31 December 1918 she happened to be in Kyle of Lochalsh when large numbers of soldiers and sailors were returning home to Lewis after serving in the Great War. There were too many to be accommodated on the *Sheila*; so over 300 were put aboard the *Iolaire*. No-one is absolutely certain about the reason, but she went off course, and struck the rocks known as the Beasts of Holm, literally within sight of Stornoway. Over 200 servicemen lost their lives, and there was not a village on the island which did not lose someone. One survivor was found clinging to the rigging the following morning; six others doing the same thing had not survived the night. Today, cemeteries on the island provide a moving reminder of the impact of the disaster.

Originally published in the *Stornoway Gazette*, 10 August 1956, the following is a graphic description of the voyage and the disaster, written by one of the few survivors:

> Early in the morning of the 31st, Jack informed me that he had received his discharge and beamingly remarked: "It's me too for the Road to the Isles." By 10 am, I was on my first lap homeward, crossed the treacherous Pentland Firth on a Naval boat, and landed in Scrabster terminus in the north of Scotland. I took the train immediately to Kyle of Lochalsh via Inverness and arrived in Kyle at about 6pm. Upon arriving in Kyle, I noticed that the sleepy little town was swarming with sailors, soldiers, civilians and munitions workers, carpenters and engineers from the Clyde, kilted soldiers from the Highland Regiments and sailors from various ports. I could hear Broad Scotch and English, but mostly Gaelic, the last my mother tongue which I loved so much. Their sad and bitter memories were now submerged, anticipating meeting their beloved ones. The Isle was the Isle of the Blessed to them, a haven of peace and rest. Word went around that there were over two hundred passengers more than the mail boat could accommodate. Wireless was sent to Stornoway, and it was decided that the mail boat would convey the soldiers and civilians and an Admiralty boat would convey the sailors.

It was not a passenger boat nor did it resemble one. It was different from any we ever had the pleasure to sail on. It was a beautiful 900 ton steam yacht which belonged to a rich Clyde ship owner. It was now commandeered by the Government for patrol and submarine scouting. Here it was with little alteration, with the exception of a coat of slate grey on its hull and tall masts and an 18 pounder on a high stern platform surrounded by numerous depth charges. It was called the *Iolaire*. I felt rather honoured being conveyed on my last lap homeward on a millionaire's yacht. Once aboard an Officer shouted, "Make yourselves comfortable". Some went into the fo'c'sle, a number to the saloon, most of them remained on deck. I with twelve others found a cosy spot in the Chart house. In half an hour we shoved off.

Soon the Inner Isles were fading behind, rugged rock Rona and misty Isle of Skye were vanishing on the port quarter. Now with a pitch and roll we were in the open sea. The night was cold and threatening with a stiff breeze from the south-east hurling us along as if conscious of the fact we wished to be on "Terra Firma" to hear New Year's chimes and foot our Hogmanay. Meantime I made myself comfortable, stretched out on the floor with my kit-bag for pillow; the kit-bag with my good sword inside, harmless and dormant, wrapped in a blanket. Sleep would not come my way. I got up, walked around and noted the wind stiffening to a gale. I heard no loud talk, no celebrations. Everything was serene. I again returned to my temporary shake-down, told an acquaintance to wake me when nearing the lighthouse a mile from the pier. I fell into a restless sleep. I had a horrid dream. I saw my father talking to me. I could feel his breath, his torpedo beard touching my cheek. "Don, be careful", he said. With those words ringing in my ears, I woke up with a terrible foreboding.

The naval vessel *Iolaire*, which ran aground with the loss of over 200 lives just outside Stornoway on the night of 31 December 1918

Just then a scraping heaving of the boat rolled me across the floor. I got up, spruced myself, heaved my kit-bag on my shoulder shouting to Jack "We are alongside the pier". The refrain was taken up by the remainder. I caught the doorknob on the wind, then came a louder scraping vibrating noise and a terrible impact – simultaneously the boat lurched at an awful angle, catapulting us mercilessly against the lee-side of the chart-house. This was certainly not the pier. The doors were closed. I could not see. Instinctively, we clambered to the door on the wind side. As we opened the door, the lighthouse flashed its blessed beam – on mountainous waves relentlessly lashing against over-towering cliffs with narrow ledges and jagged crags. The waves descended in a mighty cataract into the boiling and spuming depths below. We were parallel to the cliffs and a stone's throw from it. The scene was terrible to behold. We were used to mines, torpedoes and shell fire, but this struck fear in our hearts. We knew we were trapped, as no lifeboat could live in that maelstrom. The most powerful swimmer would be a toy. We would be dashed to pieces, quartered and torn asunder by the piercing knife-like crags. We struck a submerged reef, came to a standstill twenty yards from the cliff, a mile from the pier and our destination Stornoway. I spoke to Jack. "This is a wooden boat. No provisions made for passengers and not enough lifeboats or lifebelts. Minutes count. I am off for a lifebelt. Good-bye, Jack and God bless you". I threw my kit-bag down, threw my heavy overcoat away. With the aid of a flashlight I groped my way amidships. By now the lights were out. Rockets were fired from the bridge and the Captain shouted "Every man for himself". In the rockets' flare, I could see sailors everywhere, single and in groups. Pieces of the lifeboats on the wind side were being hurled over our heads. Some sailors were trying to get two boats out on the lee side. Some were climbing the tall masts, fearing being washed overboard. Most of them were on the gun platform aft. I managed to get to the lee side of the galley. While contemplating what to do I noticed a sailor with a big round cork lifebelt around his shoulders. As I jumped up to him I noticed he had a cork jacket as well. "Please give me one of those lifebelts." He gazed at me. I put my arm under the lifebelt and pulled it over his head. He still gazed not uttering a word. Now I felt safer and descended to the bulwarks to jump into one of the boats. Thank goodness, I missed it by seconds. It was loaded. I watched it churning and whirling and in an instant down it went. I could see little black specks in the foaming froth. Something deterred me from jumping into the second boat. I gazed at it as it shoved off, then a mighty back wash wave seemed to fill the boat. It seemed to glide up to their shoulders, their heads – and then no more. I could not see any survivors from either of the boats.

I managed to climb a davit, twisted a leg around it, the other leg resting on a cross-pin and my head under a narrow platform. This platform helped to break the walloping waves. I was hardly in this position when one of the boilers exploded. Large sheets of flames with forked fingers were bellowing from the galley and tucking at my back. The aftermast snapped and bodies came plummeting down around me. Looking down into the boiling cauldron below me, there were scores of bodies rolling, appearing, tumbling and disappearing. I prayed "Oh Mighty Sea, roll them ashore, Roll them ashore". Now I thought I could hear far away voices from the shore. It turned out that a sailor with a heaving line jumped from the gun's platform, was hurled by an incoming wave to a ledge. He pulled a hawser ashore. A number managed to make shore hand over hand on this rope. I felt that I should get at this rope, but it was impossible. The boat was awash. Fire, steam and lashing waves prevented me. Oh! What eerie noises and sounds – the swirling water, the pounding waves, roaring fires, screams of the burned and the dying and above all the chimes of the bridge bell as if tolling our knell! The yacht's keel was by now well broken up. The boat was sliding backwards into deeper waters. Finally, I found myself opposite where the rope was tied ashore. There were sailors below me, trying to grasp the rope, wading to their shoulders.

My position was fearful in front and frightful behind. I must jump over the heads of those below me to grab the rope. I braced myself for a good long leap – a leap of death, I thought. Something caught me by the arm. I turned round and found another sailor had hooked his arm through my lifebelt. This was serious. My last deed was going to be a good one, so I took off my lifebelt and handed it to him, saying "Take it and good luck".

I jumped and caught the rope. One, two heaves shoreward then my legs went round my head. I felt myself carried forward, I hit the crags. I was numb. I rolled like a football down the jagged rocks. The backwash hurled we outwards. Now I was dancing with the dead, seized one, spun around and lost him. Another (was washed) to me. I'd hug him, make a few grotesque whirls and then lose my grasp. It happened that some of the sailors who had managed ashore on the rope had enough strength left to be able to run back and fro with the waves, hauling ashore the dead and the living. One of them hauled me to a ledge.

Next morning, I woke up in Sick Bay in Stornoway, my father was sitting by my bedside. He informed me that over 200 perished below the cliff. Some sailors were washed ashore a few yards from their home cemetery as if to say "This is your final resting place". Only three of the yacht's crew were saved. The Captain was found mangled amongst the rocks. By noon, all that was left of HMS *Iolaire* was a fathom of the foremast, pointing like

'By noon all that was left of the *Iolaire* was a fathom of the foremast.' Taken early on 1 January 1919, this photograph shows how close to the shore the ship was when she foundered

> a long accusing finger at the cliff. Nobody could throw any light on this mysterious disaster, half a mile from the lighthouse at the harbour's mouth.
>
> Jack did not answer the roll call.
> Somewhere, some place, someone blundered.

A two-day public enquiry was held in February at Stornoway at which evidence was taken from survivors, the shore staff at Kyle of Lochalsh, the master of the *Sheila*, the skipper of an East Coast fishing boat which was near the scene of the disaster, and the Stornoway coast guard. The jury returned a unanimous verdict that the wreck of the *Iolaire* resulted in the death of 205 men; that the officers in charge did not exercise sufficient prudence in approaching the harbour; that the boat did not slow down, and that a look-out was not on duty at the time of the accident. It was further reported that there were insufficient lifebelts, boats and rafts for the number of people carried, that no orders were given by the ship's officers regarding saving lives, while the time between distress signals being seen and the arrival of life-saving apparatus was considered to be too long. Today, a monument on the shore above the cliffs at Holm commemorates the disaster, while the wreck still lies below. Divers confirmed in the 1970s and 1980s that the remains of the vessel are lying badly broken among rock outcrops in between twelve and twenty-three metres of water. A large boiler, three metres in diameter, and two propellers are all that remain of the vessel, while shells and cordite lie around the wreckage.

A second impending disaster facing the inhabitants of Lewis was a shortage of food. Although in the rural parts of the island people were to a certain extent self-sufficient, for those living in Stornoway it was necessary to import much of the basic foodstuffs, while all luxury foods had to be brought in for the whole island. The problem of a shortage of food had started earlier during the War when the cargo services from Liverpool and Aberdeen were withdrawn, and was exacerbated by the reduction of *Sheila's* calls to three per week. The return of servicemen at the end of the War further increased the problem. It was noted that one hundred gallons of milk had been sent daily to Stornoway, whereas they were now receiving only half that amount. At Westminster it was pointed out that 'since the Armistice was signed communication between Glasgow and Greenock and Lewis has been so defective as to result in acute distress amongst the inhabitants' and that the shortage during May was due to 'a certain large contractor' building houses whose materials took up cargo space that was required for food.

In December 1919, there was considerable discussion in Westminster regarding the reduced service and its effect on the people of Lewis. Dr Murray MP asked the Prime Minister

> whether he has received communications from public bodies in Stornoway and Lewis protesting against the recent reduction of the steamer mail services to one-half what there have been for over thirty years; whether he is aware of the injury which this step is certain to cause to the economic life of the Island of Lewis, with its population of 30,000; whether he is aware that the island is dependent for over 75 per cent. of its food supply and for all its passenger traffic upon transport by the mail steamer, and that the food supply of the people is thus seriously imperilled; and whether the Government will take immediate steps, through the various Departments concerned, to restore these services to their pre-war level?

The Financial Secretary to the Treasury, Mr Baldwin, replied:

> The mail boat services for the winter months have been fixed at three calls a week for Stornoway. These services, though less frequent than those enjoyed before the War, are nevertheless, only being maintained with the aid of a heavy Exchequer subsidy. It has, however, been represented to me that the great reduction of frequency …

> causes considerable hardship, and after consultation with my right Hon. Friend the Secretary for Scotland I am giving directions for the restoration … of the service temporarily adopted in September last.

Dr Murray was not to be fobbed off with this, and he continued, 'While thanking the Hon. Gentleman for his concession, may I ask if he is aware that the question of a daily service is a matter practically of life and death to Stornoway and Lewis?'

The same Member of Parliament later continued in similar vein, stating:

> I wish to raise a matter that concerns the third largest island in the United Kingdom. My complaint is that the communication between the Island of Lewis and the mainland has been cut down, owing to the action of the Treasury, to one half of what it has been during the last thirty years. It is difficult for people who live upon the mainland and under the fine social conditions in which you live in London to understand what that means to a population of 30,000 living on an island 70 miles away from the railway terminus. This is not a mere matter of inconvenience to the people in those parts, but a matter of life and death. It affects their trade, industry, commerce and social life generally, and their food supply. Even thirty years ago, when the population was much less than it is to-day, their commerce and industry was one fourth, the passenger traffic was only one-sixth and the postal traffic probably about one-tenth, it was found necessary by the Government of that day to institute a daily service between the island and the mainland. The island during that period was such that even before the War, although there was a steamer service from Liverpool and Aberdeen by which supplies, food and other necessaries of life were carried, it has been stopped by the War, consequently the pressure put upon the little mail boat was very greatly increased. In spite of that the service has now been reduced from six to three days a week through the action of the Treasury. The Secretary for Scotland, who knows the conditions and requirements of those parts, with the best intention in the world appointed a Committee some time ago, in pursuance of the policy of reconstruction initiated by the Prime Minister, to inquire into the transport of these ports. This Committee drew up an excellent Report which said, "We feel that the Lewis people have a very distinct grievance in respect of the great physical inconvenience they suffer at the present time owing to inadequate transport accommodation. That was when there was a mail service six times a week". The Committee made several recommendations. They recommended an improved mail service and a larger steamer; also coastal traffic along the whole coast of these islands. While this was being dangled before the expectant eyes of the people the Treasury comes along and takes away half the existing service. Their motto seems to be: "Unto those that hath shall be given, and from those that hath not shall be taken away even that which they have".
>
> I am acquainted with every detail of the fishing industry and other industries in that island, and they are essentially dependent upon an efficient daily service with the mainland. The food of the people is also involved. Many times last winter food was lost on these islands because of the want of transport. The Chancellor of the Exchequer said to-day that the people there could get plenty of work if they wanted it. Is it the policy of the Government to make the conditions such that the people cannot live on the island, and to compel them to go into the cities? That is what the Chancellor means; if they cannot get work there they can get it in the slums of Glasgow. The War has proved that it is necessary to keep a population of this kind on the soil. An

> essential condition of doing that is there should be facilities for the transport of fish, cattle, and sheep, and other foods to market, and a full service for passengers. I think it is a disgrace at this time, that in a big fishing industry of that sort a daily passenger service should not be provided. I hope I shall have a sympathetic and practical reply from the Government. I am sorry that there is not a representative of the Treasury present. The Treasury is the enemy.

On this occasion it was the Secretary for Scotland, Mr Munro, who responded, saying,

> I would congratulate my Hon. Friend on the vigilance which he always displays about any matter which affects his Constituency. He need offer no apology for bringing forward this matter, the importance of which I, as a Highlander, recognise. I am rather doubtful whether I am the proper Minister to reply. The Post Office is interested; in fact, it is upon the Post Office Vote that the cost of this steamer service rests, and, as he knows, the winter fishing is approaching and during the next two or three months it will be in full swing. During that time there will be arrangements for the special carriage of the fish to the mainland. In that regard it is unimportant whether the steamer service is one on three days of the week or six days.

Dr Murray commented, 'It is supplemental to the steamer,' to which Mr Munro concluded the discussion with, 'The special carriage will carry all the fish which may be caught during those months, and whether the steamer service is on three days or six is absolutely immaterial from that point of view'.

Only four days later the subject was raised yet again. Dr Murray asked the Minister of Transport:

> whether he is aware that, even when there was a daily service between Stornoway and the mainland, numerous complaints as to the insufficiency and inefficiency of the service were made by public bodies and by representatives of the trading and travelling public; that now, since the services have been reduced by one-half, there is a real danger of the necessaries of life being short during the winter, as well as the business and trade of the port and island being seriously hampered; whether he is aware that, owing to the invariably crowded state of the mail boat, travelling by this service, which is a night service, is always uncomfortable and often dangerous; whether he is aware that over 200 women returning from the English fishing were held up recently at Kyle for two days with little food or shelter; and whether he will induce the Highland Railway Company to exercise their powers to maintain an efficient daily service between Kyle and Stornoway, or in any other way to take steps to restore a daily and efficient service?

It was the Financial Secretary to the Treasury, Mr Baldwin, who replied:

> I have been asked to answer this question. While I regret that it is not possible to restore the pre-war mail-boat service to Stornoway, I am advised that the present service, coupled with other steamer facilities, is adequate both for the supply of food and for necessary trade purposes. The regrettable incident referred to in the latter part of the question was, I believe, the result of the women missing the mail-boat connection by about two hours. It is, of course, impossible to guarantee that a small steamer is not at times rather crowded when the traffic is subject to great variations of this kind, but I do not gather that this is a normal state of affairs. So far as I am aware, the Highland Railway Company have no powers to maintain the present service from Kyle, but in any case they would not be likely to undertake it, still less to increase it, without a subsidy from the State.

Dr Murray was still not satisfied, and persisted, 'Is the Hon. Gentleman aware that the Transport Committee appointed by the Government when the War was going on reported that even when there was a daily service between Lewis and the mainland it was inadequate, and recommended an extra steamer?'

While this was being discussed at Westminster, MacBrayne's were still responsible for providing their services, both from Kyle of Lochalsh and from Glasgow. During the war, several ships from the fleet had been lost on active duty, but these had not included those used on the Stornoway services. As we have seen, however, services had been pruned, largely due to the general economic difficulty which had resulted in a downturn in traffic; this has been aptly described as a 'loss of money coming up the gangplank'. The Glasgow run had been cut from twice weekly to once every week, and this had meant that the uneconomic *Chieftain* was no longer required. Opinion on the reason for her sale seems to vary. Although she was only twelve years old she was considered by some as no longer being a useful member of the fleet. On the other hand the ship was also described as the company's best asset and that she was only sold to provide necessary capital for MacBraynes. Initially she was purchased in June 1919 by the North of Scotland & Orkney & Shetland Steam Navigation Co. Ltd and renamed *St Margaret.* After six seasons sailing to the Northern Isles, she was purchased by the Canadian National Steamship Co. Ltd, who took her across to the Pacific Ocean to trade from Prince Rupert, B.C. At this point she lost much of her good looks, for the clipper bow and bowsprit were replaced with a much more functional slanting stem, while various other alterations were made to her superstructure. In 1940 she came under the ownership of Union Steamships Ltd of Vancouver and for five years continued to sail on the Pacific Coast, now with the name *Camosun.* Another crossing of the Atlantic followed when she was bought by the Oriental Navigation Co. Ltd of Tel Aviv. Under yet another name, *Cairo*, she commenced trade in the Mediterranean. Yet another change of ownership saw her registered under the Panamanian flag and the ownership of Zarati S.S. Co.; she still traded in the Mediterranean, but now between Marseille and Beira. In 1948 she made yet another crossing of the Atlantic on voyage to the West Indies, but by now her career was drawing to a close, and in 1950 she was laid up at Marseille, finally ending her career two years later in a shipbreakers at Spezia. All this indicates a soundly built and reliable ship, and it would be interesting to speculate just how long she might have graced the Minch and Stornoway, had conditions been different after the War.

Her departure in 1919 left only the ageing *Claymore* on the run from Glasgow and to accommodate this, the service was reduced from weekly to once every ten days, and only a year later it was cut again, this time to once every fortnight. This prompted Dr Murray to bring the impending plight of the Lewis people to the attention of Parliament yet again, using very similar arguments and receiving a like response. He asked the Minister of Transport if he knew:

> whether Messrs MacBrayne have reduced the sailings of their cargo boat between Glasgow and Stornoway to one trip in 14 days; whether he is aware that this service is the chief means of transport for food and other necessaries to a population of 30,000; that during the winter the population is increased by several thousands in connection with the winter herring fishing; and what steps (does) the Ministry propose to take in order to secure regular food supplies to the people of Stornoway and Lewis?

To this Sir W Mitchell-Thomson replied

> The answer to the first part of the question is in the affirmative. I am informed that the fortnightly service between Glasgow and Stornoway will be maintained by larger boats, and that there is no reason to fear any

> immediate shortage of supplies at the latter place. If, when the herring fishing starts, the present service threatens to prove insufficient, the matter will be reconsidered.

The year 1919 also saw the publication of a government report by the Rural Transport (Scotland) Committee. This considered all forms of transport in the country areas of Scotland, and included specific references to shipping services in Lewis. Had some of the proposals been put into operation, they would have led to some interesting services from Stornoway. The authors of the Report considered that there was 'no communication save by a very mountainous road' between Stornoway and Tarbert, and that 'some of the villages on the coast have no connection with the main road system and are obligated to bring supplies from Stornoway by boat – (which was) often an impossibility during winter'. They therefore advocated the introduction of a 'small, stout steamer capable of carrying between fifty and seventy tons, with accommodation for twenty, plying between Stornoway and Tarbert'. The vessel, which would have been of a type similar to a drifter, was to carry mails and call at the townships of Grimshader, Crossbost, Leurbost, Balallan, Laxay, Keose, Cromore, Marvig, Gravir, Leiravaggh (sic), Eisgin, Aline, Maaruig, Rainingadale (sic), Molinginish and Scalpay. A glance at a map of Lewis and Harris would show that this was an extremely convoluted journey, sailing to the heads of the long sea lochs which penetrate the coast. It was estimated that a nine-knot boat would take about twelve hours to accomplish this, and the vessel would lie in Tarbert overnight before returning to Stornoway the following day. On its southward run it would take fish and other produce collected in the Lewis townships to Tarbert for the 'Southern Hebrides mail-boat'; returning northwards it would carry similar cargoes to be sent south the same night by the Stornoway mail-boat. Passengers could also avail themselves of either of the mail steamers to the mainland.

It was also considered that an additional service would be required to serve the Bays district of Harris and the west side of Lewis. This would again require 'a stout 9-knot steamer of some 70 tons, capable of standing the stiff seas of the Atlantic Coast'. It was proposed that the vessel, based at Stornoway, would proceed to Tarbert and then call at Scalpay, Grosebay, Stockinish, Manish, Finsbay, Rodill, Obbe (now Leverburgh), Taransay, Avansuidhe (sic), Scarp, Breidhnis (sic), Miavaig, Bernera and Carloway. The trip would occupy some fourteen hours. The boat would lie overnight at Carloway then, having received on board the previous day's mails collected overland, it would make the return journey to Stornoway, travelling 'express from Tarbert'. The members of the Committee considered that 'this would afford a very good passenger service between Harris and Stornoway. (They) anticipated that at an early stage these services would pay their way, and they would add materially to the cargoes of the main mail-boats'. Had either of these services materialised, the benefits would indeed have been felt by the inhabitants of the isolated townships, while for intrepid tourists it would have been an exciting, if somewhat primitive, excursion. Rather than introduce these services, however, roads were gradually constructed to lessen the isolation of the islanders.

The Report also looked at the provision of 'Coasting Steamer Services'. In considering circumstances at the time, it stated:

> in dealing with passenger traffic from the island to the mainland, distinction must be made between two directions in which the main currents of such traffic flow, viz.: (1) to and from Glasgow, (2) to and from Dingwall and Inverness. It seems that the majority of the inhabitants of the islands and their relatives travel between these districts and the Glasgow area, and that for this reason they attach great importance to a connection with Mallaig. A smaller section of the communities is

> interested in communication with Inverness and Dingwall for stock sales, county business, etc., and for this a connection with Kyle is desired.

The Committee members then went on to consider other mainland ports, but under the heading 'Improvements of Mail Steamer Service to Stornoway', they opted for the status quo, and suggested that of more importance was the provision of a better steamer for the service. It was accepted that the people of Lewis were almost unanimously in favour of a service to the port nearest Glasgow, that being Mallaig. There was therefore reason to doubt that a service to Lochinver (which under the proposals was to be served by a railway) would be acceptable, even though it would be a shorter sea route and fares would be similar. Members were 'disposed to think that the steerage passengers would prefer the Lochinver or Ullapool route, which would probably not involve an overnight journey', but this did not sway the decision. The main demand was for an improved steamer, the Report stating that 'a 15 knot boat with adequate accommodation for 200 passengers is necessary'. There was sympathy for the islanders as the Committee members concluded, 'We feel the Lewis people have a very distinct grievance in respect of the great physical inconvenience they suffer at the present time owing to the inadequate accommodation of the mail boat'.

The conclusions reached in the above Report are remarkably similar to the conclusion reached by the Walpole Commission, which presented its findings to the Marquis of Lothian, Secretary of State for Scotland, in 1890. It argued that improved communications with markets in the south would aid the fishing industry of Lewis. It considered that on the west coast of Scotland, the sea was 'the natural highway,' and amongst other things suggested that some new inter-island services be introduced. Two of these routes would be centred on Stornoway. The first would be to Tarbert, with stops at Grimshader, Liurbost, Keose, Ballalan, Cromore, Mariveg, Calbost, Gravir and Lemreway. It would operate thrice weekly, operated by a steamer 'whose speed need not exceed eight and a half knots,' although 'the vessel used must be of the best seaworthy qualities and good power.' The second route would use the same vessel on alternate days and sail to Ness, with stops on the inward route at Skigersta, Tolsta, Gress, Portnuguiran, Bayble and Knock. Both routes were to be organised to link in with the mail steamer to Strome Ferry. It must be assumed by the similarity between the two Reports that little had been put into place in the intervening thirty years.

The argument mentioned earlier between Dr Murray and Mr Munro was still being continued eleven months later! It had now been established that during the War the service had been supplemented by an Admiralty boat, which ran on the other three days of the week, but this had been discontinued after the Armistice. The Rural Transport Committee, which reported in 1919, had included as one of its recommendations that the six-day service to Stornoway should be restored. In 1920, a deputation from Lewis presented itself to the Secretary of State for Scotland, and must have suitably impressed the politician, for in June the daily service was restored. Part of the fight had been won, but the six days' service was to be resumed only during the summer months. The Secretary of State for Scotland, having consulted with the Postmaster General, considered that there was not sufficient justification for an extra expenditure of £7,000, neither from the postal point of view nor from the public interest, to provide a six-day service in winter. A concession of extending the summer season slightly beyond its end date of 30 September was granted. A second piece of good news in the Report was a recommendation that a better steamer service be established with the provision of a fifteen-knot vessel with accommodation for 200 passengers. The *Highland News* greeted this news with the comment, 'No more lying on deck exposed to the elements! "Speed Bonny Boat"!' It would, however, be ten years before the new ship appeared.

The three-fold criticism of the mail service which existed before the First World War reared its head again in 1921, perhaps not surprisingly in the light of how little had changed. At a meeting of the leading businessmen in Stornoway, the matter was described as 'desperate'. A new four-year mail contract had just been awarded, and it was felt that the action of the Government in 'binding the island to a mail, passenger and traffic service on the (existing) lines … would prove destructive to the island's trade and commerces (sic) … it would be utterly impossible to trade with the Southern markets, and it would result in the ruin of the fishing industry of the island'. As far as the fishing trade was concerned, there was only one suitable boat each week on which to export fish. 'By the present arrangement the boat left Stornoway on Monday night when there were no fish. On Friday night it was too late to send fish as it would be useless before reaching London so that only Wednesday was available.' Yet another deputation was to set out for London, to be followed a year later by still another. The problem was highlighted again 1922, this time with added comments about the fares and the state of the steamers, although the *Gael* must have been on the mail run, for it was she who came in for criticism. 'Why should the fares be so high? Is the comfort of the journey so overwhelmingly great? Is the accommodation of the boats so princely? No! The vessels running on the Stornoway-Kyle route are NOT models of comfort and convenience. One of them runs till it breaks down, and then the other takes its place till it, too, gets done up, for the time being; and so the merry game goes on.' A Board of Health Inspector was to travel on the *Gael* to test her sea-going properties. Unfortunately for the people of Lewis, he did not cross the Minch in stormy weather, 'when the boat rolled, and the waves broke on deck with a noise like thunder.' He did not 'feel the awful sickening jerk when paddle or propeller left the water.' Nor did he 'try to sleep on the narrow berths surrounding the saloon, out of which one was ignominiously chucked every time the boat rolled.' Instead 'he travelled on a fine day, with all the comforts that obsequiousness could shower upon him, and then he certified the *Gael* a good sea boat!'

The *Lochiel*, formerly the *Devonia*, was acquired from the Admiralty in 1919 and worked on the Glasgow to Stornoway service until 1927

The problem of an unsuitable steamer was to remain for a number of years, but the shortage of ships was to some extent solved when, as compensation for the war losses, the second *Lochiel* was acquired from the Admiralty, and she was put on to the Glasgow service. Although originally built in 1906 by Scott of Kinghorn, Ltd, Fife, for service to the Channel Islands under the ownership of the Anglo-French Steamship Co. Ltd of Devenport with the name *Devonia*, she bore more than a passing resemblance to a number of MacBrayne steamers, such as the *Clydesdale*, and to the casual observer might always have been one of the fleet. She was given the name *Lochiel* and was put on to the Glasgow-Stornoway service late in 1919. From this time, the *Claymore* was now making only irregular calls at Stornoway, following a schedule which restricted her mainly to mainland west coast piers. The *Lochiel* remained in the MacBrayne fleet until 1937, serving Stornoway until 1927 when she was transferred to the Islay run. She then returned to the Channel Islands, now renamed *Isle of Alderney*, saw war service on the Clyde, and then ended up in the Mediterranean under the names *Annoula* and *Monte Lirio*.

Of a much more mundane nature, but adding to the problems of 1919, there was a concern about the restricted amount of office space available in Stornoway. At one point David MacBrayne wrote to Lord Leverhulme, now the owner of the Lewis, to complain that he had six clerks working in a space suitable for only two.

Amidst all the serious discussion of the state of the mail service, an article about the *Sheila* in a much lighter vein appeared in the *Highland News* in 1921. The article quoted and discussed a poem, described as 'doggerel of the very worst type'.

The *Sheila* is a gallant ship, which ploughs the ocean main –
Her funnel is a vivid red, the badge of D. MacBrayne,
Her hull is black and battered, rather the worse for wear,
And her smell of grease and varnish rather contaminates
the air.
But oh! she is a gallant ship, and rides the fiercest gale,
Then let us drink to her success in ammunition ale.

The meals the steward gives you are not in great demand,
The food would taste delicious if eaten on dry land;
But when the waves run mountain high, the human
appetite
Is very hard to tickle, you can hardly eat a bite.
At meal times they should land you on some friendly shore,
Then you would do them justice, and keep on asking more.

Look twice at meat or broth, I pray, before you eat thereof,
A bit of toast is safer, or common baker's loaf.
Beware of ham or bacon, for danger there resides,
And kippers on the ocean are poison for insides.
'Tis best to eat of nothing upon the sad sea waves,
For he who does not eat at all his three-and-sixpence saves.

Behold the wretch who rashly eats of kippers Kilty Brand –
Go through his aftermath of woe, and on the bulwarks
stand,
Leaning o'er the vessel's side – but no! we cannot gaze
Upon a sight so sad, so terrible a case.
But he who eats no kippers, nor looks at bacon's wiles,
Enjoys the cool sea breezes, sits on deck and smiles.

His three-and-six is quite intact, and peace reigns in his
breast,
Because he left the kippers – wise man! – unto the rest,
The other foolish passengers, who will not take a hint,
But gorge themselves with ham and eggs and kippers
without stint.
But if I give advice like this, the firm of D. MacBrayne
Will think I'm trying to rob them of commissariat gain.

In commenting on the above lines, the writer considers the benefits of eating on dry land rather than on a heaving and pitching mail boat. He suggests, no doubt with tongue in cheek, that for this purpose 'there is a beautiful place, especially provided by Nature, for the purpose, namely the Shiant Islands. The largest of these, "Eilean Mhor" (sic) … would make a most excellent stopping place for passengers to dine … We would all enjoy our luncheons and teas under these conditions, and MacBrayne's' stewards would reap a golden harvest in tips from gratified travellers, who now loath the sight of both food and stewards.' He then proceeds to endorse the poet's praise of the *Sheila*. While acknowledging that the steamer has 'some smells about her that do not sweeten her, he is captivated by her red funnel, 'as it would enrapture anybody.' He also agrees on her sea-going qualities, writing, 'The *Sheila* is a magnificent sea-boat. She has encountered the fiercest Atlantic gales, and has weathered them like the brave staunch ship she is.' Finally he asks why the poet has not mentioned the 'braw new jerseys the crew are wearing', pointing out that 'these sons of Neptune look like yachtsmen … The word 'Sheila' is written on their smart caps, and in red lettering on their new jerseys … One of them has several red words on his jersey, and he looks like the king of them all. The words are: "In charge of passengers' luggage".'

After these upheavals, the steamers on the two services became settled for the next few years. The *Lochiel* and the *Claymore* covered the service from Glasgow while the mail service to Kyle and Mallaig was operated by the *Sheila*, apart from during 1921 when she operated the Outer Islands service to Harris, the Uists and the Small Isles from Kyle and Mallaig. Her place was taken by the *Gael*, which was also on the run along with the *Sheila* the following year. It would appear that the two steamers may not have been in the best of condition, as in April 1922 a letter to the *Scotsman* complained that the *Gael* had broken down for two hours during a crossing, while the previous week the *Sheila*'s pumps had refused to work, and the vessel had to return 'partially submerged'.

As well as serving Stornoway from Mallaig and Kyle, the mail steamer also called at the remote settlement of Applecross, from where a small ferry would make its way out to lie alongside the steamer while goods and passengers were transferred. Alistair Alpin MacGregor, in his book *Behold the Hebrides*, evocatively describes the *Sheila* calling there in the 1920s, and the skills of the local boatmen in carrying out their at times difficult task:

> As we sailed past the mouth of Loch Carron and the Crowlin Islands, old Cailein Cameron, our venerable captain, sounded the steamer's shrill whistle to warn the ferryman that the *Sheila* would soon be rounding the headland and gliding into Applecross Bay. There, to be sure, the ferryboat awaited, and as the steamer moved slowly by, the accustomed rope was thrown to Murchadh, who lashed it to the seat below him with such an agility and dexterity that in an instant we were alongside. Just think of it! He has been doing this, day in and day out, for more than thirty years, while his comrade has manipulated the oars to keep the ferryboat erect, and its bow to the proper direction.
>
> Never once in more than twenty years have Murchadh MacRath and another Murdo, his life-long companion in oars, failed to meet the mail steamer. And during all these years what stormy seas have they experienced together in that old, frail craft!
>
> You really cannot imagine what skill and strength are entailed in getting alongside, when on dark, winter evenings and mornings the sea is rough, and the position of the ferryboat is indicated only by an oil lantern that at the stern bobs up and down as the boat is being rocked by heavy seas and howling winds.

> It was with bated breath and with suppressed excitement that I stood aside until the mails were safely lowered by an overhanging derrick, and until the little rope-ladder was slung over the wale of the steamer that I might descend into the ferryboat.

He also briefly describes two other experiences of travelling on the *Sheila*. The first shows how a peaceful crossing was possible, as he describes an arrival at Applecross: 'One Autumn morning as the *Sheila* sailed quietly into the inky black bay I was awakened from my sea-sleep to find that the Minch had been crossed during the night.' The second extract shows the importance of the mail steamer to the people of Stornoway, for he claims:

> Stornoway does not really begin to wake up until about 10.30 pm, at which hour the mail steamer is due to arrive from Kyle and Applecross. Having seen the green and yellow lights, that bobbed and flickered far out at sea, we hurried to the harbour to welcome the incoming mail steamer which had just crossed the Minch in a storm which would have bent and broken in smithereens the largest and strongest trans-Atlantic liner.

A further romantic view of the Stornoway mail steamer was penned by H V Morton in his book, *In Search of Scotland*, describing a journey from Mallaig to Kyle of Lochalsh:

> I lean over the deck of the Stornoway boat with a greater feeling of adventure than I have felt when bound for the ends of the earth … I look out to the misty headlands, grey in a drizzle, and down into the clear, bottle-green depths where small fish swim; and all around me is the exciting bustle of departure. We are a varied crowd. There is a beautiful, long-legged girl in Harris tweed with a queer yellow mastiff-like dog in leash, and a pile of luggage which contains golf-clubs and fishing-rods. She is, perhaps, the daughter of some clan chieftain going home to a castle on a rock.
>
> There is a fat-faced young man wearing a religious hat of black velour, and a pair of dove-grey spats. In Ireland he would be a priest: here he is a son of the manse or a son destined for the manse. A governess sits out of the wind with four small boys, all in new suits. Her luggage contains wooden boxes of provisions. She has made a raid on civilisation for clothes and for those epicurean refinements not sold on her particular mountain-top. A commercial traveller comes aboard preceded by a pyramid of goods tied in black oilskin; artificial stockings perhaps, civilisation's inevitable gift to the Hebrides!
>
> Shaggy islanders walk the forecastle wearing plus fours and unpolishable boots, whose tags stick out behind against their fluffy homespun stockings. They lean on long sticks, almost crooks, and talk in Gaelic about the price of sheep. Black and white sheep dogs, frantic with anxiety, run all over the ship in search of shepherds who are below having a drink. There is a great commotion as a wild and unwilling black horse is led and pushed aboard.
>
> The little ship is drenched in all those smells which women try to forget as they run down to Dover in the Continental Boat Express: pea-soup, fat mutton, batter pudding. The cook's galley is on deck. He emerges in a rich, composite cloud of smell, his sleeves rolled above his elbows, saying something in Gaelic to a steward, who picks up a bell and goes noisily round the ship.
>
> Bells sound from the other little ships around us. Rival whiffs of pea-soup fight their way sturdily to us from our companion vessels. Passengers exactly like ourselves gaze at us from other decks and know that we, too, are going out into remote blueness; that we, too, carry a black horse,

many shepherds, and a lovely girl in Harris tweed; that we, too, are about to eat pea-soup, fat mutton, and batter pudding drenched in treacle.

The ship is steaming up the Sound of Sleat between mountains vague in rain. The grey mists steal stealthily down their great brown flanks: their heads are lost in ragged cloud edges. Each new vista is one of hills behind hills, dim, remote. The clouds move slowly, and the sun, finding a way through a rent in them, sends a momentary golden haze into a valley or lights up, alone in all the wild, dark, landscape, a mile or two of heather, and a small, white farm.

Suddenly the engines stop. Away over the desolate, green waters of the sound two men pull lustily at a clumsy boat. As they come alongside with Gaelic shouts and greetings the governess, the children, and the boxes are lowered into the boat …

A bell rings and we steam on towards the mountains that close in on the Kyle of Lochalsh. We tie up to a wooden jetty covered with pink sea-anemones.

Unfortunately, the career of the *Sheila* came to a sudden and untimely end early on the morning of 1 January 1927. Captain Cameron, her regular skipper, was on leave; so the ship was under the command of another officer. On passage from Stornoway to Kyle, possibly through wrongly identifying a light instead of heading for Applecross Bay, she ran aground in darkness in Cuaig Bay just south of Loch Torridon. Fortunately there was no loss of life, all the passengers and crew being safely lowered over the ship's side on to the beach, but shortly after the ship slipped into deep water, all hopes of refloating her were abandoned and she was declared a total loss. A contemporary report of the stranding described how 'the vessel did not strike with a fierce jar but glided gently up a shore which at low tide is strewn with small boulders'. The six passengers and some of the crew were put in a small boat and rowed clear of the *Sheila* till daylight. They were then taken aboard again and had breakfast, 'but with the ship lying at an awful angle'. The reporter then continued, 'On the side of the ship where I was it was hardly necessary to chew your food; it just slipped down with the slope of the boat'. Meantime the radio officer was busy, his messages being picked up eventually by Malin Head Radio and an American steamer off Barra Head. The passengers were later safely taken off by the *Plover*.

Judging by the reminiscence penned thirty-three years later in the Stornoway Gazette it would appear to have been one of the most relaxed shipwrecks to have happened:

It was a New Year's morning that we sailed along on waters as tranquil as a summer sea and I, who had been sleeping in the saloon, felt a jarring bump and the ship gave a shudder. I awoke and murmured to myself 'That's

The remains of the *Sheila*, high and dry on the shore in Cuaig Bay, after running aground in the early hours of 1 January 1927

the wee boat coming alongside at Applecross,' and went off to sleep again, but not for long.

A steward came and shook my shoulder saying, "Come on lad we're on the rocks." We got up and were ordered to don life-jackets, but I had a look out at the calm sea and the land looming ahead and decided I wouldn't bother.

Some time later we were ordered into one of the ship's boats and about eight passengers, a few of the crew, and an officer went for a sail round Loch Torridon for that's where we were; mine the pleasant task of comforting a young lady with auburn hair from North Tolsta.

When daylight came properly, we were summoned back to the ship which was now high and dry on the shore of the loch. On our return to the ship we were invited down to breakfast in the saloon, and there we were sitting enjoying the repast when the ship slipped and fell a good many feet.

That's when they say, she broke her back, and put an end to the sailing days of the "old lady" who, for some unknown reason, kept straight on instead of taking the turn for Applecross.

We picked ourselves up after the jolt and I, for one, finished my breakfast. When we got on deck everyone was standing seemingly waiting for something; the only one who seemed to be busy was Mr Adams, the Radio Officer.

Jimmy Sneddon, the cook, announced that there was no more food on board, and it was apparent that most of the men aboard were running out of smokes. I suddenly remembered that I had a half-box of cigars in my bag, a Christmas gift, and they were duly issued and set alight, while Jimmy Sneddon, puffing away, stood in the door of the galley and said, "Aye, aye, smoking cigars and there's no meat in the house."

Just then the ship's cat prowled and Jimmy said, "Thomas, you may land in the pot yet tonight." But the fate of the passengers was better than that, because we were eventually taken ashore, via a ladder from the bows to the rocky beach below and billeted out in the houses of the nearby village of Cuaig.

It was my good fortune to have landed in the home to two old men who had been in service on yachts in their day, and I received a very good supper (lunch had been missed) and through time was shown to a very comfortable bedroom with instructions "Not to be in a hurry in the morning. Tomorrow is Sunday and you can rest there as long as you like, and when you feel like your breakfast just give a tap on the floor and it will be brought up to you."

Well on into the morning I did as instructed and up came one of my friends with a tray on which was a lovely breakfast and, besides my "New Year". "Oh yes! You'll be the better of that wee drop after yesterday's happenings," said he and I didn't disagree.

That day was spent in reading and eating until a sailor came to the door to say the *Plover* had arrived to take the passengers to Kyle of Lochalsh.

We got down to the shore and ultimately aboard the *Plover* and as we steamed out of the loch, little did I think that I was saying goodbye to the ship that had been my dream-boat in my childhood; on which I had experienced with much pleasure, the kindly ministrations of Mrs McCabe, stewardess in charge of women and children, received the bluff and hearty greeting, many a time, from Captain Cameron of "Well boy, had you a good crossing?"; listened to the yarns and received much kindness at the hands of Mr Leitch, the Mate, and been

> taken into the cabin of "Colin Crae", the purser, to be initiated into the mysteries of how tickets were dealt with.
>
> A good ship was gone! Many a Lewis man and woman had harrowing and hazardous passages on her, but she always got there until that New Year's morning when the call that used to be made at Stornoway pier by Roddie Mackenzie, (known locally as) "Flemmon", was made for the last time, "All Ashore! Going ashore!"

An interview with another passenger on the *Sheila* contains both corroboration and some contradictions of the events of that fateful night. It was claimed that eighteen year old Annie MacIver had carved herself 'a small niche in nautical history' as the only female passenger on the mail boat. She described how the events unfolded:

> My mother had told me before I left to be sure and have a cabin on the ship, so I did, and I found out I was sharing the cabin with a stewardess. There were two single beds or bunks in the cabin and I didn't give her any rest all night asking when we were going to reach Kyle. It was a dreadfully rough night and I couldn't sleep – so finally the crash came. We knew something had happened. Everything above my cabin crashed into the next cabin. And the next thing we heard was "everybody is wanted on board". So I was fortunate that I had my coat and clothes and everything beside me. I donned all that and somebody met me at the top of the stair and took me on deck.
>
> The lifeboats were out and I was helped into the lifeboat and we cruised around there for hours in the darkness and the storm, frightened that the boat might top over at any time. They had been trying to contact some place. And the first place they contacted was Mallin (sic) Head in Ireland. In the meantime, when the tide went out, the *Sheila* was on the rocks, wedged between the rocks. And the people of Cuaig realised there must have been something wrong. They all came down to the ship and took all the passengers to their homes, gave us a meal and wanted us to stay for the night, which we did. In the morning the *Plover* came and we were taken to Kyle. By the time the people came, morning had come and we managed to get out of the small boats on to the shore. We got back later to the *Sheila* and retrieved all our possessions.

On being asked why the ship went on the rocks, Miss MacIver said it was the Captain's first Christmas off in twenty-four years, and that 'the new skipper went off course'. She also said she had seen no evidence of drink – 'I was in my bunk'.

Not surprisingly, the members of Stornoway Town Council took advantage of the sinking of the *Sheila* to make 'strong representation to the authorities with a view to getting a much better and larger boat for the route'. They did admit that it was 'fortunate that there was no loss of life', with one councillor adding that he 'could picture what might have happened had there at the time been, as so often there were, two or three hundred women on board', but they then went on to say that 'when the *Sheila* first came on the route over twenty years ago (she) was regarded as inadequate to the requirements of the community'. A demand was made for a larger and faster ship, which would be capable of meeting the morning train at Kyle of Lochalsh and doing the journey in four and a half hours. One councillor, Mrs Fraser, did give credit to the sterling service which the *Sheila* had given, saying, 'I think one of us should pay a tribute to the *Sheila*'. She went on to say:

> I have crossed and recrossed in her over and over again in the last seven years and I have been in her when it was so strong that … one of her boats was washed off the davits. Every wave that struck her it seemed would break her, but

> I comforted myself that being the *Sheila* she would arrive all right. Many a time I have been on the *Sheila* when it was very stormy, but I have never felt the least bit afraid as to her ability to stand the sea and make the journey. The *Sheila* is gone. You may get a bigger boat but you won't get a safer one.

It was a fitting tribute to a steamer which had served the people of Stornoway and Lewis faithfully for almost a quarter of a century.

The loss of the *Sheila* led to some re-shuffling of ships. The *Claymore* was in the vicinity at the time, and she took up the mail service before being replaced in turn for the next two and a half years by the *Clydesdale*. This ship had been built by Scott & Sons of Bowling. She was launched on 28 May 1905, being named by Miss Evelyn MacBrayne and was, in fact, the last steamer built for David MacBrayne before he died in 1907. She was designed to operate on the Glasgow-Inverness route, and accordingly had a stumpy appearance similar to the *Cavalier*. However, she was destined to visit Inverness on only two or three occasions, being transferred to serve Islay before replacing the *Sheila* as the Stornoway mail steamer, pending the arrival of a new steamer. Like the *Sheila*, she too had to endure severe weather conditions. At the end of January 1927, sailing into the teeth of a gale, she left Kyle on time, and reached Applecross an hour later, but then ran back to Broadford for shelter, where she remained at anchor until 2345, by which time conditions had improved enough for her to continue her voyage, finally reaching Stornoway at 0500. She served the West Coast ports for many years, and in 1946 visited Stornoway as a relief cargo ship. In spite of being described as a less than able substitute for the *Sheila*, she was apparently a good sea boat.

It was not long before it was announced that a new boat was to be built to replace the *Sheila*. However, at one point a rumour was heard that the *Clydesdale* was to be fitted with extra cabins to be used as the mail boat. When the Provost of Stornoway heard this, he immediately pointed out that this would 'not be suitable at all.' Mr Mackenzie Livingstone, MP for the Western Isles, at once put down a question in Parliament on the subject, to be told that if he repeated the question in a week's time the Secretary for Scotland would be in a position to answer. The following week he received the reply which had also appeared in the press to the effect that three new boats were to be built for the west coast mail services, one of them a larger boat than the *Sheila* for the Stornoway run. Details of the vessel as announced by the Lord Advocate were initially vague, especially as regards speed and dimensions, resulting in the Town Council impressing on Mr Mackenzie Livingstone that he should persuade the Board of Trade that the new ship should be capable of doing the passage in five hours, an hour faster than the *Sheila*; that ample accommodation be provided for passengers, especially those in steerage; that there should be a reduction of freight charges in both directions; and that passenger fares should be reduced by twenty-five per cent. Councillor John Kennedy thought that 'the Council should get in touch with Messrs MacBrayne before the actual design of the new boat was fixed and bring before them economical facts regarding the trade of the island which perhaps they might be overlooking. He knew from experience with crossing with the fisher girls the hardships they had endured on the Minch after a two days' journey from the South,' adding that 'the accommodation in the past for fishworkers was of such a nature as would not be given to workers of any kind in any other part of the British Isles or the British Empire.' It was, however, considered that this would not be the proper thing to do and that an approach should be made instead to the appropriate Government departments.

At the same time, a replacement was needed for the Islay service, and this took the form of the *Lochiel*, which had been carrying out the Glasgow-Stornoway cargo service. To fill the gap there, MacBrayne's were forced to charter cargo steamers, one of which was the *Cameo*, dating from as far back as 1883. She does not appear to have been the most reliable of vessels, for in 1928 she ended up at the mercy of the weather just off Corryvreckan, where she drifted helplessly for twelve hours, dragging her anchor in the process for seven miles. Other ships were also chartered to cover the service from Glasgow; in 1922 the *Royal Firth* is recorded as operating for David MacBrayne, followed by the *Slateford* in 1924, while the *Welshman* carried cargoes over a four-year period from 1925.

Chapter 16

1928 AND AFTER

DURING 1927 MacBrayne's lost two more of their ships. Added to this much of their fleet was becoming elderly, and the depressed economic situation of the 1920s meant a continuing lack of both passengers and cargo. The situation was not a good one for the people of Lewis, and indeed all the Western Isles, and during the next two years more discussion ensued at Westminster as the time for a new mail contract grew near. Amongst considerations was a proposal to nationalise the shipping services rather than put the mail contract out to private enterprise. In fact, it had been recommended in 1919 that the steamer services of David MacBrayne & Co. Ltd be taken over by the State on equitable terms, presumably on account of trading difficulties and the number of complaints regarding the provision and quality of services, but after consideration this plan was rejected. Furthermore, after a public announcement, described as 'open to the whole world', no interest was expressed by any concern in taking over the services, should they be put out for competition. It was pointed out that it was the lack of freight and passengers that was at the root of the trouble. The discussion broadened into a number of other concerns regarding steamer services to Stornoway.

The MP for Dundee, Mr Johnston, clearly had little affection for the *Sheila* when he stated, 'The old *Sheila*, praise be, is now at the bottom of the Minch, although I am told that her rudder has been carefully lifted and very appropriately presented to the museum of antiquities, where it lies along with the relics of Bonnie Prince Charlie'. He then went on to complain about the cost of travel, quoting a letter from a Portree man to point out that, 'The cabin fare (to Stornoway) is 38s 2d (£1.91), and this does not entitle one to a bed. If you have a bed you must pay 5s (25p) extra. I understand it is the only service where one has to pay over and above the cabin fare for the privilege of having a bed.'

This seemed to open a flow of 'MacBrayne bashing' There were vague comments such as 'Anyone who attempts to cross the Minch must be a man with a solid stomach and strong nerves to go through with it without feeling that it is a grave ordeal in windy weather'. Others were more specific:

> When the fisher lassies have to come across the seas they have to cross in MacBrayne's boats. These Scotch fisher lassies, some of the finest looking women the sun ever shone on, are the daughters of the Highlanders, not the daughters of landowners, or of MacBrayne's. They have to stand in all kinds of weathers on deck. No passenger accommodation is provided for them, no sleeping accommodation; and they have to cross one of the stormiest seas in the world, the Minch. None but the women drawn from the hardiest and most intelligent race could stand it.

Emmanuel Shinwell went on to state:

> Much has been said about the facilities for passengers, and something has been said about the facilities for cattle, but

> I have not heard a single word said about the facilities for the crews; and those who are acquainted with the crews' quarters on MacBrayne's vessels – I can hardly think of one exception, for all their vessels are alike in this respect – must admit that the accommodation provided for the crews is the worst to be found in the shipping services of this country. The crew's quarters are absolutely vile, and it is paying mere lip service to the qualities, the admitted qualities, of the crews on board the MacBrayne ships.

There was clearly concern for the condition of passengers, cargo and the ships' crews. It was also considered that the state of the Hebrides and its inhabitants was closely linked to the quality of its shipping services. It was stated in Parliament that 'The question of MacBrayne's contract goes right to the roots of the evil which besets the Islands of Scotland … The government have suggested that the only alternative to starvation is emigration; but (it is considered) that this MacBrayne contract is one way in which we can change all this.'

Finally, it was agreed that a new contract be offered from the Postmaster General to MacBrayne's, including maintenance of the cargo and passenger services between the mainland and Stornoway. The contract included an increased subsidy of £50,000 per annum, and the construction of four new vessels within two years. However, as has been hinted previously, David MacBrayne & Co. Ltd was on the brink of insolvency, and would have been unable to finance the building of fleet replacements as the contract stipulated. Accordingly, they declined to tender for it. No other organisation was willing to take it over. The situation was aptly summed up in the House of Lords by the Marquis of Salisbury when he stated:

> There was a service of boats in the Highlands and Islands of Scotland, and owing to a certain amount of friction … the service of boats was suddenly put to an end. The inhabitants of that area … within a very brief time were put in the position of losing this necessary means of communication, and it was necessary for the Government to intervene.'

The initial reaction of the Government was that their only option was to ask David MacBrayne to agree to a more favourable subsidy, while the Scottish Office was said to be 'afraid of MacBrayne's'. A Select Committee appointed by the House of Commons decided to consider other sources. Initially it held discussions with Sir Josiah (later Lord) Stamp, president of the LMS Railway, and Mr J Calder, general manager of the LNE Railway. Coast Lines, under the chairmanship of Sir Alfred Read, was then brought into the discussion. The LNER were not interested, and finally a new company was established, with Coast Lines and the LMSR taking over the whole stock, assets and goodwill of Messrs MacBrayne Ltd. The new company was entitled David MacBrayne (1928) Ltd; David Hope MacBrayne, son of David, retired and for the first time in seventy-seven years there was now no MacBrayne at the helm. But the name MacBrayne was still there, and, more importantly for the sake of the islanders, services continued.

As mentioned above, part of the agreement stipulated that four new ships had to be built within two years, and the people of Lewis were to benefit from this. The first new vessel to be built was specifically designed for the Stornoway-Kyle-Mallaig route. This was the *Lochness*, built by Harland & Wolff Ltd at their Govan shipyard. The choice of name for the ship was interesting; although there had been other ships with 'loch' names, this was the first to have the name spelled as one word, a nomenclature system that was to be used for all new ships until a two word 'loch' appeared in 1947. The contract had specified a vessel 'having a speed of not less than twelve knots in moderately bad weather and with a length of 175 feet'. When this news got abroad, there was what has been described as a 'perfect deluge of telegraphic and other protests from the outer Islands', including

The *Lochness*, with the grey hull in which she initially appeared, passing Kyle lighthouse (drawing by the author)

comment from the Stornoway Town Council that the people of the Lewis wanted no less than fourteen knots and 250 feet. Further discussion took place about this, with one comment in favour of the larger dimensions stating, 'Why should we provide small-sized boats for this rough Atlantic journey?' What resulted was somewhere in between.

The *Lochness* was launched on 6 June 1929, and the following week the *Stornoway Gazette* provided the people of Lewis with details of their new ship, stating:

> The stately appearance of this new MacBrayne liner bespeaks seaworthiness and comfort and it is confidently expected the vessel will quickly establish herself as a prime favourite with travellers between the mainland and the Isle of Lewis.

The newspaper then went on to describe her in more prosaic terms:

> The vessel is a twin screw passenger and cargo steamer, 208 feet (63m) in length, 34 feet (10m) in moulded breadth, 14 foot 6 inches (5m) in depth moulded to main deck, of 830 tons gross and 14 knots speed. She is of the open shelter deck type, with cruiser stern, complete main and shelter deck, boat deck, focsle deck and lower deck, and is subdivided by seven complete watertight bulkheads, with double bottom under the engines for the carriage of feed water. There will be accommodation for 428 passengers. For the first class passengers there will be nine deck cabins and five state rooms, a finely furnished dining saloon, a smoking-room and a lounge, as well as a spacious shelter deck and promenading space on the boat

> deck. The third class will have special accommodation with every possible comfort and convenience, a fine dining room, a smoking-room, ladies and gentlemen's sitting-rooms and ample promenading spaces. The propelling machinery, provided by Messrs John G Kincaid and Company Limited, Greenock, will consist of two sets of triple-expansion engines obtaining steam from two oil-fired multi-tubular boilers fitted with Howden's system of forced draught. The deck machinery will include a steam windlass, a steam capstan, a steam winch for the rapid handling of cargo by a three ton derrick on each mast, and steam steering gear controlled from the wheelhouse by telemotor. The vessel, which has been built to the classification of the British Corporation Register, will expedite the route by an early arrival at Stornoway and will make possible southwards connections with the early morning trains from Kyle of Lochalsh and Mallaig.

The launching ceremony was performed by Mrs H T Leith, wife of MacBrayne's General Manager. At the luncheon after the launch, Mr Dudding (manager of the shipyard) presided, and in proposing 'Success to the *Lochness*', said his firm 'laid the keel of the vessel in March and she had been launched three months and one day later. They would do their best to have her ready for the Glasgow Fair Holidays.'

The *Lochness* was actually the last steam ship built for the Stornoway run. She was a huge improvement on the *Sheila*, being a third as long again and nearly three times the tonnage. Compared to the previous ships, she could be considered a miniature liner, especially in her first three seasons when her hull was painted grey, later reverting to black. Her accommodation was also greatly superior, although it has been said that she was furnished to a much lower standard than cross-channel ships of the same period. The first class lounge was described as 'pretty', being decorated in yellow with imitation windows on which were hung dainty curtains. It was furnished with comfortable settees and there was a 'neat' writing desk. The smoke room was finished to resemble an old country inn, while the dining room, painted a shade of green, had small tables for four rather than the traditional long dining table of earlier vessels. It could not be said that she had the classic lines of previous ships such as the *Clansman* or *Claymore*. Her hull was of a fairly utilitarian shape with bluff bows and a cruiser stern, reflecting her role as an everyday passenger, mail and cargo ship, rather than having any illusions of being a cruise ship.

Harland & Wolff did have her fitted out by the date they had anticipated, and her first duty was a service to Tarbert, Loch Fyne, on Glasgow Fair Saturday. The eager anticipation with which the people of Stornoway awaited the arrival of the new ship can be seen in comments in three consecutive editions of the *Highland News* in July. Initially it stated, 'Stornoway's new mail boat, the *Lochness*, is due to take the place of the *Clydesdale* at the end of this week. Justice to a long-suffering travelling public has at last been done … Success to the newcomer and prosperity to the owners. If half as commodious as broadcast, all grousing (will be) forever banished!' The following week it stated that it was 'disappointing the new mail boat has not put in an appearance; several people have been delaying their holiday to cross the Minch in a luxurious cabin.' By the third week in July doubt was creeping in that the ship would arrive at all – 'much concern is expressed at the non-arrival of the new boat. Some say that she was not big enough, and some that a more lucrative run had presented itself.' Those who 'maintained that the old things were the best' and presumably happy crossing the Minch on board the *Sheila* or the *Clydesdale*, were considered to be 'all off the deep end'. The *Lochness* took up her intended role as Stornoway mail steamer on 1 August of that year, replacing the *Clydesdale* which returned to the Islay run. Her arrival at Stornoway on that evening was eloquently described in the *Highland News*:

> The arrival of Stornoway's new mail and passenger boat … caused not a little stir in the community. The importunity of a long-suffering travelling public for over a quarter of a century had at long last been rewarded by the acquisition of a ship which has surpassed the dreams of the most sanguine. The firing of a salute of rockets announced the approach, and soon the pier was crowded, all eager to catch a glimpse of the new ship. "A miniature ocean liner" was the universal comment. As soon as the passengers, which (sic) were picked up at Mallaig and Kyle, landed, a deputation of the Town Council – Provost Bain, Baillie H M Matheson, and ex-Provost R Smith, members of the Harbour Commission, and public officials – were invited and entertained on board by representatives of the owners, including Mr Leith, general manager, Captain Pell, marine manager, Mr Macdonald, local agent, and Captain MacArthur, of the *Lochness*.
>
> Mr Leith, in welcoming the deputation, thanked them for their presence and said he was sure the ship would meet with their approval and would prove most suitable for the service. The Company had chosen the name "Loch" as an index for their ships, and as Ness was an important part of Lewis, the name of the vessel was quite appropriate.
>
> Provost Bain, in proposing success to the *Lochness*, spoke of the necessity for such a vessel which, replete with everything for the comfort of the passengers, was only what they had been asking for for years, and he did not think the new vessel was, as some people thought, too good for the Minch.
>
> Baillie Matheson and ex-Provost Smith also spoke, and emphasised the necessity of having a fast boat on the run. They also commented on the fine accommodation and the beautiful equipment of the vessel, and congratulated the designer and the builders.
>
> Captain MacArthur said he was proud to be in command of such a fine ship, and was sure she would give satisfaction to the travelling public.
>
> The guests were afterwards shown over the ship, and expressed gratification with all the departments. The cabin passengers have every comfort – a large lounge (luxuriously upholstered), a ladies' boudoir, a smoke-room for gentlemen, 14 two-roomed state rooms, a dining hall with tables for four persons, bathrooms (hot and cold sea water), and ample seating accommodation on the decks. All the rooms are tastefully decorated with panels showing Highland scenes, and amber-coloured electric light. The most noteworthy feature, however, is the up-to-dateness of the third class passenger apartments – a spacious lounge with cushioned seats, a ladies' room, a smoke-room for men, a dining hall, a wet canteen, and deck accommodation, while aft, behind the cabin, there is further seating below the deck. This additional space will be very serviceable when the ship, during the fishing season, will be crowded with workers going and returning from the various East Coast and English ports.

The *Lochness* quickly settled into the routine of the service, satisfying the people of the Stornoway, who considered her a vast improvement on both the *Sheila* and the *Clydesdale*. Her arrival on the service enabled alterations to be made to the timetable. Going south, it became possible to meet the morning trains at both Kyle of Lochalsh and Mallaig; this meant that travellers could now arrive in Glasgow just before two o'clock. This was achieved by advancing the departure time to 2300 at Stornoway and a general speeding up of the service. Travelling north, it now meant that the arrival time at Stornoway was two hours earlier, at 1930 rather than 2130.

Two weeks into her service, she had the misfortune to run down a small boat in Stornoway harbour, while in January of the following year she ran aground on Goat Island, the result of avoiding colliding with two trawlers. In the summer of 1930 MacBrayne's had to complain to the Stornoway Pier and Harbour Commission that they had to stop discharge of the mail boat's cargo due to the impossibility of getting trucks through the crowds assembled on the pier. The *Stornoway Gazette* responded that 'In our town at this time of the year the daily tonic of seeing the mail steamer come in is much greater and more effective than at any other time'. MacBrayne's wanted more effective control by the Commission, suggesting for departure that a constable and two crew be posted at the entrance to the gangway half-an-hour before sailing time to direct passengers and assist with controlling the crowds. Apart from these rather minor problems things seem to have run fairly smoothly for the next few years.

One of the few mishaps to occur happened not to the *Lochness* but to the vessel which was relieving her, while she had gone south for her annual overhaul. On 21 March 1931 the *Lochearn*, a motor vessel built in 1930 and normally serving the Outer Islands from Oban, was on passage from Stornoway to Kyle of Lochalsh. She was running late, having been delayed by dense fog on her previous crossing to Stornoway. The fog was still very thick, and this was probably what caused her to run aground about four o'clock in the morning at Lonbane, near Applecross. This was very near the spot where the *Sheila* had foundered three years previously. This time the grounding was much less severe, and Captain Macdonald immediately gave orders to reverse the engines, and the ship was successfully backed off the rocks. However, it was discovered that one of the propellers was broken, the steering gear was damaged and she was slightly holed. A wireless message was sent out and her sister ship, the *Lochmor*, which was proceeding to Mallaig at the time, came to her assistance.

There are few descriptions of voyages on the *Lochness*. With brevity of words, Robert Atkinson, in his book *Island Going*, described the sort of crossing which must have been familiar to many travellers to Stornoway, writing:

> Mallaig; the third-class quarters of the *Lochness*; the Minch suitably grey and heaving under a uniform grey sky … the bone-seeking breeze after a usual unslept day and night of travel from the south … The cliffs of Shiant showed faint to the south, the, ahead and all on one bow, the grey teeth of Lewis appeared like some uncharted archipelago where a ship could enter and be lot in rocks and seaweed and northern birds … The crowd to meet the steamer, the fish-market, the waterfront hotel, the line of bruised buses.

He also captured the atmosphere of the 'nightly event of the town, (the) departure of (the) mailboat … the singing and waving and bagpipes and evidence of whisky, the good-sized steamer sliding out astern and taking away the lights, the crowd on the dark quay struggling home to bed.' This was after he had earlier driven the car 'alongside the *Lochness* to be, as they say, "uplifted" … The usual few anxious motorists watched their cars swung on board in the black-and-white glare of the ship's floodlights; another summer's long light evenings were gone.' The hour of departure came, and:

> the ropes splashed into the gap of black water, and the ship began to slide out astern. The water was so calm within the harbour that he mirror image of the moon was whole and flawless. Stornoway Castle withdrew, Scottish baronial against the steely night sky. The surprising skyline of real trees growing from the Castle grounds was tinged above with orange, the last of the west. The moon was full

sized … At first the ship steamed plumb along the moon-track as she might have been a car driving down a straight road. She cut through a school of porpoises whose wet hides glistened with moonlight, and whose revolutions swirled up phosphorescence in the shadow side.

It was with a sense of anti-climax that he finally mentioned, 'The *Lochness* got to Mallaig at eight o'clock in the morning, as usual.'

A second description describes a smooth crossing of the Minch, and it also shows the importance of the mail steamer to the people of Stornoway. In *The Isles of Sunset*, published in 1931, W A Mursel wrote:

> The new Stornoway boat *Loch Ness* (sic) was getting up steam and loading merchandise at the Kyle of Lochalsh pier. She is a handsome vessel, a vast improvement on her predecessors, with the appearance and comfort of a pocket liner … The dreaded Minch was on its best behaviour; I do not think the *Loch Ness* gave a single heave or roll … We did get a glimpse of Applecross … a ferry boat came out to meet the steamer, and we dumped one lady passenger, four boxes of goods and some mail bags for Applecross. I should have mentioned the lady passenger last. Baggage and mails are the most important items when these ferries come out; it is a matter of "goods and mail bags first" and passengers nowhere …
>
> The arrival of the steamer (at Stornoway) is the event of the day. Half Stornoway seemed to be on the pier. A representation of the Police Force, two strong, was parading on the pier, keeping a space clear through the crowd for passengers. It was rather embarrassing, not to say intimidating, to land beneath such a battery of curious eyes, and to run the gauntlet clutching ones' suitcase through a lane of girls and youths with a sparkling of old salts hovering in the background. I half

A car is swung on board the *Lochness*. This method of loading cars continued until the coming of the car ferries

> expected to be smacked on the back with a strap or a knotted handkerchief or a rope's end as I threaded my way through the lane. They were all there with peaceable intent, eager to meet friends, curious to see what sort of strangers were invading their island solitude.

In another article, published in the *Journal of the Stornoway Historical Society* in 2000, Janet C Macleod further describes how during the 1930s the arrival of the mail steamer played such a prominent part in the daily lives of the Stornoway people:

> One of the main events of our day was the arrival of the *Lochness*. This was especially interesting at the time of the Glasgow Fair when the boat was packed with passengers, most of them dressed in their "Sunday best".
>
> Whenever the *Lochness* rounded Arnish Point, crowds of people advanced on the quay. There was a lot of friendly banter among the waiting throng. One character called "Lightfoot" kept the chit-chat going with his jokes. He acted as porter in one of the hotels, and collected the luggage of their guests.
>
> In no time at all the boat was alongside the pier. Captain Macarthur checked from up aloft that all was well at the gangway; he blew a signal on a small whistle, then the exodus of passengers began, led always by the wireless-operator, Mr Adams, and the purser, Mr Campbell.
>
> We stood and stared at the interesting passengers – such bad manners! The daily papers were unloaded and whisked away to the paper shops on barrows. There was always a line of waiting buses from all over Lewis and Harris, lined up opposite the Caledonian Hotel. In a short time, the travellers found their transport and the quay was quiet again.

In a second retrospective article, which appeared in the *Stornoway Gazette* in 1973, nostalgic memories of the *Lochness* are described by 'Nighean Chalum Choinneach Iain' (her Gaelic family name):

> When we arrived at Kyle, we would not go aboard the steamer until we saw our trunks (usually two huge ones) loaded into the luggage net and swung down into the hold. Once on board, in all weathers, we had to stand on the deck of the *Loch Ness* (sic) until the Applecross passengers had embarked. We envied them the journey in the small rowing boat which rather reminded us of Jonah and the Whale, when the passengers stepped into the bowels of the steamer while we looked down from above. There were no sophisticated lounges, T.V. sets or cocktail bars, but we had great fun watching our elders making their own entertainment. The boat seemed crowded with young girls and there seemed to be a wonderful spirit of camaraderie among the passengers ... My father (a piper) would be asked to strike up a tune and there would soon be an Eightsome Reel on the deck. Later on, someone would start singing – and we would listen, enthralled ... while the singers sang hauntingly of their love for a sweet young maiden, or the love of an exile for the Isle of the Heather. We might see an occasional drunk (who usually just slept peacefully through all the proceedings), but the *Loch Ness* passengers of those bygone days did not need the stimulus of alcohol to show their "Joie de vivre".

A fourth writer, the anonymous JB, was moved in the mid-1930s to write a poem entitled 'The Lewis Mail', praising both the steamer *Lochness* and her crew. This light-hearted verse indicates the significance of the steamers and the affection which locals had for them.

Come join us in another song, its theme you'll quickly guess,
We'll journey o'er the famous Minch' in Norman's brig 'Lochness';
We'll leave the Lewis Capital, when chimes the midnight hour,
Then land you on the pier at Kyle, just as the clock strikes fower.

The men who take the Lewis Mail are seldom long in bed,
But you've got to see the way the steward has got the table spread;
Good ham and egg, then eggs and ham, for dinner broth and meat,
The Minch gives them that appetite, when any food is sweet.

The Captain's from the Misty Isle, its stories he can tell,
His wife, sweet Tobermory Maid, from Mary's Dainty Dell;
He loves the life, adores his wife, and worships his wee daughter;
Great service marks his duty here, each night upon the water.

The mate is called Calum Black, from Muileach's Sunny Isle,
The weather never counts with him, he greets it with a smile;
Then Jura claims the second mate, son of a worthy squire,
Land of the Paps, the Shaws, the Macs, all men of fame and fire.

The lads that tend the 'Coffee Mill' you're safe to call them Mac,
All proud to serve their noble chief, who's only lately back
From far away and distant lands where once he wandered free,
But now the homeland charms his heart and home he'll ever be.

First Angus takes the wheel awhile, then Calum does his spell,
Don looks the compass in his face, for each one knows it well;
They joined the 'Lochness' when she was new, and though the work is hard
Are proud to take this Lewis Mail and get the rich reward.

When Sandy's gangway doors are tight, the Captain rings 'standby,'
With Finlay at the furrid rope, then Neilly must look spry;
The wind is blowing fresh tonight and as we pass the Crowlin,
Donald he gives Chips a hand, sou-west the gale is howlin'.

We're sailing now before the wind, and steam is blowing off,
For Johnnie Green's on duty now, the sea is rather rough;
Wee John is sitting down below, while Dan is snug in bed,
For Arnott has the throttle closed, just as the Chief has said.

Now Ronnie, give that rod some oil, and keep her running sweet,
We'll need our time when running south, when sea and wind we meet;
Tell Ramage to be handy when we're coming near the light
And Stachie keep the burners clean for running south tonight.

Another writer, S P B Mais, should have crossed to Stornoway on the *Lochness*, but as his writing describes, he travelled on a different steamer from Kyle of Lochalsh:

> For the greater part of the day … Kyle sleeps, but at luncheon time there is a scurrying to and fro from the quay and the platform to meet the slender paddle

steamer *Fusilier* on its way to Broadford and Portree, and the stouter *Lochness* wich has to sail over the Minch to Stornoway

The *Lochness* was in dock getting herself painted up for the summer season, so we had to be content with the *Lochmor*, a smaller but equally comfortable and seaworthy vessel, her only handicap being her lack of speed.

The weather now had become wild, with rain sweeping on us from the north-west. But the hills of Skye behind Raasay were looking magnificent. They are at their best in a storm. At Applecross a motor boat came out to pick up mails and we headed for the open sea. It got rough, and people lay down. The line of the mainland grew fainter and Skye was at last left far behind.

We passed close to the Shiants, but not close enough to see any of the sea birds, and the high hills of Harris were very indistinct. Lewis lay low straight ahead.

I strode round and round the decks admiring the notice amidships which read: "Deck forward is certified for 84 passengers when not occupied by cattle, animals, cargo or other encumbrance". On this day there were neither cattle nor encumbrances, so I was free to roam in the blinding rain for some seven hours at the end of which we steamed into the wide bay of Stornoway …

When we drew into the quay I was struck as much by the silence as by the size of the crowd that met the boat. There were a number of redheads among the girls, and the voices of those who spoke at all were very soft. It was like being in a foreign country, for the men were all speaking Gaelic.

While the mail service had taken on a settled pattern, the 'all-the-way' steamers saw a number of changes. The first change came in 1931, when the *Claymore* came to the end of her long career. In fact, she had not been a true 'Stornoway steamer' since about 1926, when through a rearrangement of services she was mostly restricted to calling at mainland ports as far as Lochinver or Loch Inchard, with the journey across the Minch removed from the schedule. Having safely sailed for all these years with only one serious mishap, when she ran aground off Pabbay, near Broadford, and did not return to service for six months, she finally came to the end of her useful life when it became uneconomic to fit new boilers. There was a scheme to convert her into a floating hotel to be located on a Highland loch, but like a number of these plans it did not come to fruition, and

The *Claymore* was finally withdrawn from service in 1931. Her fine lines could still be appreciated as she lay waiting to be broken up at Bo'ness on the Firth of Forth

finally she was sold on 5 May for the sum of £75, to be broken up at Bo'ness on the Firth of Forth. Even when beached at Bo'ness before being broken up, it was possible to appreciate just how fine were her lines, perhaps even more so with the whole of her graceful hull exposed. She had lasted fifty years, not as a summer passenger steamer sailing on sheltered waters but as a ship working all year round in exposed waters and calling in at all sorts of rock-strewn inlets to carry passengers, cargo and livestock to numerous West Highland settlements. Perhaps part of her longevity could be put down to the fact that her hull was built of iron, while it also says something that in all those years she was powered by the same two-cylinder compound engine and pair of single-ended Scotch boilers. So revered was she on the west coast that the panelling from her saloon was removed to grace the municipal buildings in Oban, her figurehead ended up in an Angus garden (and is now in the Scottish Maritime Museum in Irvine), and three feet of her main waste steam pipe became a lacquered umbrella stand.

The *Claymore*'s replacement was the *Lochbroom*, an even older ship. She had been built in 1871, designed for the Aberdeen-London service. Her boilers were in better condition than those of her predecessor, which explains the purchase of a ship of her vintage. Some of the space designed to carry cargo was converted to make additional passenger accommodation, enabling her to carry up to eighty passengers; nearly fifty of these could be accommodated for meals at the traditional long table in her saloon. She took over the West Highland cruising, leaving Glasgow every ten days during the summer, but, as in the later days of the *Claymore*, her duties did not take her across the Minch to Stornoway on a regular basis. A booklet titled *Good Cruising*, published in the mid-1930s, carried an advertisement for the '*Lochbroom* Cruise'. It describes how 'There is a glamour about the Western Highlands and Islands – a lure of tradition and romance – of dancing seas and towering bens – that calls to the heart at the mere mention'. It goes on to state that passengers 'find themselves find themselves transported through scenes of delightful interest' and that they could not 'travel under more charming auspices than by the "LOCHBROOM" Cruise'. The steamer is described as 'an established favourite with many in Scotland and England. She is fully equipped with single-berth, two-berth and four-berth cabins, hot salt water baths, large dining saloon, music saloon and smoke room, while electric light is installed throughout.' Details of the ports visited and their attractions are mentioned, the booklet stating that 'on certain trips Loch Inchard is ... visited and on occasion a crossing is made to Stornoway'. Intending travellers are also informed that 'At most ports of call the vessel generally discharges cargo and there is usually time to visit the various places of interest in the vicinity. The purser of the steamer can always give definite information as to the period the vessel is likely to be detained at the different ports'. A final paragraph mentions, 'The rates (inclusive of meals) for the cruise are approximately from £6 10s. 0d. (£6.50) to £11 0s. 0d. (£11). To encourage extension of the Highland Season a rebate of 20 per cent is allowed "LOCHBROOM" Cruise Passengers, except during June, July, August and early September'. One of the crossings to Stornoway was in August of 1931 when she was to make a Bank Holiday excursion to Kyle, leaving at seven in the morning. Unfortunately for her passengers, she was back alongside in Stornoway an hour later, having hit Holm Point. Happily, there were no injuries and the newspaper article of the day adds, almost as a postscript, 'the sea was calm but there was dense fog'. She also visited Stornoway when acting as the relief mail steamer in August 1935, when that duty was also carried out by the *Lochearn*. The *Lochbroom* continued her summer-only cruises until 1937, when she, like a number of MacBrayne's ships, was broken up at Port Glasgow.

The continuing success of these summer cruises prompted David MacBrayne to replace the *Lochbroom* with another second-hand vessel, which was renamed the *Lochgarry*. When launched in 1898, she had initially carried the name *Vulture*, serving the Burns fleet between Ardrossan and Belfast. In 1929, now under the ownership of Burns & Laird Lines Ltd, she was renamed *Lairdsrock*, and it was under this name that she was chartered by David MacBrayne in 1936. She became a MacBrayne steamer the following year, having undergone considerable changes to adapt her for cruising purposes. This involved building a completely new dining saloon and shade deck, and refurbishing the interior to a high standard. There were six single cabins and forty two-berth cabins, all with hot and cold running water, and salt and fresh water baths and showers were provided. A large smoking room, painted blue, was fitted with a cocktail bar, ice-making equipment and facilities for making tea and coffee. There was a large dining room, with tables to seat ten passengers at each, a spacious writing room and a sports deck. She was described as 'complete with everything that matters on a sea holiday'.

Although now principally a cruise ship, it must not be forgotten that she still provided an essential lifeline, carrying cargo to the isolated west coast communities. She sailed to Stornoway on a number of occasions, in particular when she relieved the *Lochness* on the mail run, between January and April in 1938, for example, and a year later during the months from February to May. The onset of World War Two meant an immediate cessation of the cruises, and the *Lochgarry* was requisitioned in 1940. She took part in the evacuation of Dunkirk in that year and was later converted to serve as a transport ship. On the night of 20 January 1942, while she was on a passage from Glasgow to Oban to collect soldiers bound for the Faroe Islands, she struck rocks off the Mull of Kintyre. With her engines crippled she drifted off course in gale force winds and eventually sank off Torr Point on Rathlin Island. Of the forty-two on board only twenty survived.

Returning to the service from Glasgow, at the start of the 1930s this was being maintained by chartered vessels. To resolve this unsatisfactory arrangement, a permanent replacement appeared in 1931. This was a ship which was new to MacBrayne's, but had been built as many as forty years earlier. She had been built for Messrs J & G Burns as the *Grouse*, to trade between Greenock and Ireland, before being renamed *Kelvindale* when she passed to the ownership of Grahamston Shipping Co. Ltd, who used her to carry cargo between Glasgow and Stranraer. She was sold to Burns & Laird Lines Ltd, and was then transferred to Coast Lines. As they were now co-owners of David MacBrayne, it became relatively straightforward for her to be put under the ownership of the West Highland Company and she was duly renamed yet again, this time becoming the *Lochdunvegan*. She was a fairly typical Irish Sea cargo steamer of her time, 175 feet long and with engines amidships. She was to be a good servant for MacBraynes, although sailing only to Stornoway for six years. Whilst the *Lochdunvegan* did not often appear in the news, she did feature in an unusual incident which was reported in a national newspaper over seventy years after she had ceased to sail to Stornoway. On 10 March, 2011, while fishing for scallops in the Sound of Mull, a crew member of a fishing boat found a bottle amongst its catch. The bottle contained a message signed by a twenty-one-year old seaman, Kenny Gunn, mentioning that it had been thrown from the *Lochdunvegan*. The message also contained the date it had been dropped – 10 March, 1935 – seventy-six years to the day before it was found. Kenny Gunn died in 1987, but his daughter from Oban said, 'It's a strange feeling – quite emotional', while the fisherman commented, 'It is a bit spooky that the message should be found on the same day, 76 years apart'.

After serving on a variety of cargo runs the *Lochdunvegan* was finally withdrawn and scrapped on the Gareloch in 1948. She was replaced in 1936 on the Glasgow to Stornoway service by another second-hand vessel, transferred from Burns & Laird Lines Ltd. She had been built in 1896 as the *Lily*, then renamed *Lairdspool*. Initially she was chartered by David MacBrayne, sailing to Stornoway under the latter name, before being

The *Lochdunvegan*, an ex-Irish Sea steamer which operated the Glasgow-Stornoway service in the 1930s

transferred to MacBrayne ownership and renamed *Lochgorm* early in 1937. Although essentially a cargo ship, she began to carry a few passengers in the summer of 1938.

In spite of her being considered such an improvement, the *Lochness* was soon reckoned by some to be inadequate for her duties. The two main complaints were her speed, or rather the lack of it, and the poor standard of her accommodation, which had been so fulsomely praised at the time of her launch. By 1937 questions had been raised in parliament about both these things. In Stornoway Baillie Steven asked for a reduction in fares and a faster boat. He went on to complain:

> This is the slowest crossing in the whole of Great Britain, where a mail service is concerned, with the exception of other services operated by the same company. The *Lochness* was heralded to cross in four and a half hours, but never to my knowledge, has she done this in less than five and a quarter and usually five and a half. This is no real improvement on the *Sheila*, which is frequently the same time and always less than six hours.

Baillie Mackenzie calculated that 'the call at Applecross added half an hour, the sailing was often delayed by the train at Kyle and that the ship could manage an extra two knots'. MacBrayne's retorted that doing that would be too expensive! Baillie Steven further recalled that the *Gael* in 1913 or 14 did the crossing in four and a half hours. 'I think the skipper got into trouble because he had to fire the second boiler and he never did it again'. Reference was also made to the *Clydesdale* arriving at one o'clock, and the *Gael* even later at half-past-six the following morning, neither strictly relevant to the plight of the *Lochness*. Councillor Gunn quoted a notice on some ships: 'This deck has

The *Lochness* approaches Stornoway. By 1936 she was considered inadequate for the mail service, although she was only seven years old

accommodation for so many passengers when not occupied by cattle, sheep or other encumbrances. If the community was trying to attract tourists to Lewis, there must be a good ship and attractive fares'.

The Stornoway Pier and Harbour Commission took up the case against the *Lochness*. In January 1938 they asked the Town Council to raise with the Postmaster General the question of improving the mail and passenger service, stating, 'The goods service by the Coast boat from Glasgow is quite all right but our passenger service is very far behind'.

The Town Council also took up the question of unsatisfactory accommodation, writing to the Minister of Transport with particular reference to that provided for steerage passengers and the inadequate conditions under which Lewis fishing girls had to travel. His response at the end of June stated, 'Although no sleeping accommodation is provided for this class of passengers, the accommodation available is large and airy, and on the main deck, and a ladies' room is provided. The dining room is placed amidships and half the amidships shelter has been allocated to third class passengers.' He further mentioned that the numbers carried were below the certified number 'so it would not appear that the accommodation is inadequate'.

Councillor Morison responded that things were different:

> On one occasion they saw a crowd of fisher-girls being treated worse than cattle. When we ship cattle from Lewis to the sales on the mainland, we give them a covered space so that the rain and the sea spray won't get at them, but when we ship fisher-girls across we crowd them in such a manner they cannot get protection.

He described how on one occasion, when there were 250 to 300 girls crossing, when he 'looked down on the main deck, the hatches were one mass of human bodies packed in such a way that one could not get a foot between them'. He continued,

'Surely the Minister of Transport could not maintain that it was humane treatment of the fisher-girls that they should lie packed together on the decks.' David MacBrayne (1928) Ltd had entered the discussion by saying that seating accommodation was provided for all passengers, but Councillor Morison refuted this as 'utter nonsense', and further suggested that a special boat be provided when the fisher girls were travelling. He further pointed out that it was wrong to state that food was provided on board. 'When so many fisher girls are crossing, they could not be catered for and had to carry their own food.'

The problems did not end there. In November of the same year the *Stornoway Gazette's* headline announced 'Another round in Stornoway's agitation for an improved service'. It gave details of a further letter to the Minister of Transport, listing a series of complaints and suggestions. These included a plan to have the Applecross call taken over by the Portree steamer; this was turned down on the grounds that it was not geographically suitable, and that it would delay the arrival of mail in Portree. There was a further plea for:

> improved and more commodious accommodation, especially for third class passengers. The (present) steerage accommodation is far from what is desired, being, in fact, primitive, lacking in ordinary comforts and far below present-day standards. Except for additional space it is really little better than what existed in the steamer which preceded the present vessel.

It was further pointed out that:

> sleeping facilities are not available, which compels many who can ill afford it to pay first class fare, and others, especially children and invalids, to suffer hardship, having to make the journey under conditions which do not exist in any other steamer service in the Kingdom. On certain occasions even shelter and sitting room is not available for all third-class passengers, many of them, both male and female, having as a result to spend the five or six hours which the journey normally takes on the open deck.

The first class accommodation also came in for criticism, as it was considered that 'the public rooms [were] ridiculously small in a ship certified for fifty first class passengers'. 'There are times', it was stated, 'when first class passengers have difficulty in obtaining a seat'. Councillor Lees complained about the difficulty he had in obtaining sleeping accommodation. 'I have had experience of having to sit cheek by jowl with other passengers, with not enough space to lie down. We have a long journey in front of us when we get off at Mallaig, and one feels very unfit physically and mentally to undertake it after such an experience'. He went on to add that 'third class passengers are as much entitled to better conditions as first class passengers'.

The Council agreed 'it was pegging away at the question like an aunt sally, but every time it came up again. They had to keep at it until they knocked it down.' Whether or not all the complaints were fully justified, they must have had some effect, for late in 1938 the commissioning of a replacement was made part of the new mail contract. It was stated that 'she will be faster than the present vessel and will have sleeping accommodation, both first-class and third-class, and the accommodation generally will be much improved'. However Malcolm MacMillan, MP for the Western Isles, was still concerned about the speed of the new vessel, asking the Minister of Transport, 'Can the Right Hon. Gentleman give us a rough indication of what the speed of the new Stornoway boat will be?' The answer demonstrated that attention was being given to the running as well as the building costs, and that nothing firm had yet been decided:

> As that is a matter of detail and as the plans are not yet finally determined, perhaps the Hon. Member will allow me to make some inquiries. I should imagine it will be 14 knots or over, but I am imagining when I say that.

> The Hon. Member will appreciate the fact that speed and planning must be combined and that speed and cost are very relevant factors. The driving of a vessel through the water at a knot or two above a given figure may multiply the cost, instead of merely adding to it. That is a general reflection which I seem to have carried over from my Board of Trade days, but I hope the Hon. Member will not seek to pin me down to a definite statement of the actual number of knots of this new vessel. I hope, as the members of the travelling public do, that the new vessel will be an improvement on the old one.

This was clearly an unsatisfactory response, for Mr MacMillan went on to say:

> The *Loch Ness* (sic) is put down as capable of 13 knots: it does 11 knots. We have been promised that the new boat will do 14 knots. I can assure the Minister that this will not at all satisfy the people in the Lewis district. They will not be satisfied with a boat which is going to do the journey in just a little less time than the present boat. They have asked for a 20 knot boat, hoped for a 17 knot boat, and will be dismayed at getting a 14 knot boat. Fourteen knots is not a modern speed for such boats. I hope the Minister will insist on a boat of higher speed and that he will carefully consider the specifications. Seventeen knots is not too high a speed to ask for, and I hope the Minister will not think they are unreasonable in asking for this.

The final outcome of this debate will never be known. The Mail Contract stipulated that David MacBrayne was required to provide a new vessel before the end of 1940, but as late as July of the previous year plans for the new steamer were still under consideration. However, before the building of the new ship could be started, the Second World War unfortunately intervened.

Chapter 17

The Second World War

Once again, services were restricted and MacBrayne ships were requisitioned by the Admiralty. Initially the effect on the Isle of Lewis services was minimal. The *Lochness* continued her daily run, and in the late summer of 1939, immediately after the outbreak of war, was very busy with visitors from sporting estates and other holiday-makers cutting short their annual breaks, and she also carried large numbers of reservists as they were called up. A moving scene was witnessed one night in September when several hundred sailors of the RNR filed on board the steamer at No 1 quay on the Sunday night of their departure for active service. The 'touching and memorable' part of the proceedings came as the *Lochness* cast off. The dense crowd on the quay 'spontaneously joined in singing the Gaelic Psalm forty-six to the tune "Stroudwater", and the RNR contingent lining the rails of the mailboat joined fervently with them, the strains floating towards each other over the calm water until the ship rounded the head of Goat Island and was lost to sight.'

By December there was concern that there would be alterations to sailing times and curtailment of services, as was happening elsewhere and at the start of the following year Stornoway Town Council protested about a rumour that the mail boat would call three times a week at Portree and Raasay, considering that this would add three hours to the journey, but they were optimistic that it would not happen. From 1940 the *Lochness* did call three days a week at Raasay rather than Applecross, while Mallaig was not visited, as there was a boom across the water at Kylerhea. Scheduled sailing times were altered, with the departure from Stornoway put back to 0300, although frequently the steamer did not sail until 0700, with the result that train connections were missed, and a 'wearisome wait for trains was added to the night-long vigil at Stornoway'.

German submarines regularly patrolled the waters of the Minch, but fortunately they never regarded the mail steamer as a legitimate target. There was one incident, however, which indirectly involved the *Lochness*. On the afternoon of 27 September 1940 word spread round Kyle of Lochalsh that the cargo ship *Port Napier* was on fire. Earlier in the week she had left Kyle of Lochalsh for sea, but a hawser had fouled the propeller and she had been forced to return to her base there. She had been refuelled, and was ready for sea again when the fire on board had been discovered. The seriousness of the situation became apparent when it was realised that she was carrying 500 mines on board, and could blow up at any moment. Immediately the area was cleared. This included evacuating MacBrayne's shipping office, while the two mail steamers tied alongside the pier, the *Lochness* and the *Lochnevis*, were instructed to sail at full speed beyond the lighthouse. Captain MacArthur on the *Lochness* described hearing seven tremendous explosions, the first as he hurried his ship out to sea, and as a column of flame shot sixty metres into the air. 'The plates of the vessel,' he stated, 'were "playing likkan-lokkan" (a local phrase for skimming stones) for a mile across the loch.' The officers and crew of the *Port Napier* abandoned ship, by boats, rafts and by swimming to safety. The ship continued to burn until, in the gathering dusk of the evening, two huge explosions occurred, echoing and re-echoing round the hills. All night the ship burned, lighting up the mountainsides in the darkness. At daybreak all that remained was the burnt-out hull.

The biggest protest came as a result of MacBrayne's using the *Clydesdale* as a relief steamer on the Glasgow run. The Glasgow cargo service had been operated from 1937 by the *Lochgorm*, but as she was required elsewhere, the *Clydesdale* returned at the ripe old age of thirty-five. In September 1940 conditions on board her were described in vigorous language by councillors in a letter to the Minister of War Transport:

> This vessel is so lacking in passenger accommodation that she is operated as third class only. The passenger accommodation consists of a so-called lounge of very limited dimensions aft, which serves as the sitting room, dining room, etc, for both sexes, and is often so crowded that some passengers are constrained to spend the journey of six hours on the deck which is wholly unsuited. In severe weather men, women and children are compelled to remain in the apartment, congested and uncomfortable, in conditions which are definitely unhealthy, as such accommodation as there is, is cheerless and forbidding, and its atmosphere is permanently pervaded by an odour which seems to come from the cattle space. The sanitary arrangements are inadequate and outdated and it is no exaggeration to say that the conditions are not only appalling but degrading.

They also mentioned that servicemen would stay on deck to leave the cabin to others, adding that 'naval men inured to vigorous seafaring described conditions as "tough" '.

The *Clydesdale* of 1905 returned to Stornoway during the Second World War as relief ship for both mail service and the Glasgow run. She was unpopular with the people of Lewis because of the inadequacy of her accommodation. It is unlikely that this picture would have been taken during the War as she only had a certificate for 168 passengers at that time

All this had no effect, for in May 1941 the *Clydesdale* again appeared, this time as relief mail steamer. Her condition was such that the steerage and deck cabins were now occupied by the crew, bringing into question whether or not she could safely carry the 168 passengers (contingent on the deck space not being otherwise occupied) allowed by her certificate. After only a month, the local Member of Parliament, Mr Malcolm MacMillan, asked in Parliament that note be taken of the representations which had been put forward for the past seven years about the use of this steamer, which he claimed, 'is in a state of senility'. At the same time a petition was raised which 'hoped to ensure that she (the *Clydesdale*) will never again be used as a passenger vessel on the Minch'.

MacBrayne's response was that they could not provide another vessel, nor could they put temporary accommodation on deck, as the space was needed for cargo and cattle. On returning from a Council meeting at Dingwall, councillors were forced to endure a crossing on the *Clydesdale* and clearly found little to their satisfaction. Provost Mackenzie said, 'Fortunately for the eighty passengers on board, it was one of the finest nights I have known, but otherwise conditions would have been not only degrading but revolting. They could hardly get food, and as for the lifebelts, I did not know where they were or how they would have been available, if the crash came'. Baillie Mrs Fraser was equally vehement in her comments, saying 'The ship has degenerated since previously on the Stornoway run; I could go so far as to say that on a stormy night there might have been deaths through conditions on board'. She had never sat in a 'more filthy atmosphere'. The steward had very kindly offered her a bed, but she could not have stayed in the cabin with the awful smell of paraffin. Ex-Baillie Tolmie claimed, 'if one hundred and eighty six passengers (the total allowable) were on board, conditions would be no better than on a slave-dhow'.

The situation rumbled on through the year. In August the Ministry of Transport stated they were looking for a vessel other than the *Clydesdale* to relieve the *Lochness*. In October the Council was once more in a panic over a rumour that the *Clydesdale* was to be used again. Ex-Baillie Tolmie claimed, 'The Company's cry was they could not get a better vessel than the *Clydesdale* to relieve the *Lochness*', to which comment Mrs Fraser quipped, 'They certainly couldn't get a worse one'. Finally in November, the matter was raised in Parliament. Mr Malcolm MacMillan asked the Minister of Transport,

> whether he is aware that the S.S. *Clydesdale*, which was recently put on the subsidised service between Stornoway and Kyle of Lochalsh by the MacBrayne Company, is unfit for the accommodation of humans, is not equipped with reasonable sanitary conveniences, has only room by Board of Trade standards for a small number of persons; if he will seek an assurance from the MacBrayne Company, under Clause 26 of the subsidy contract, that this vessel will not again be used on that run; and that, against such an emergency recurring, one of the other better vessels belonging to the company will be sent?

Mr Montague, the Minister, replied,

> The *Clydesdale* was put on this service for two periods of about a fortnight each recently to replace the regular vessel, which had to be withdrawn suddenly for repair; the company had no other suitable vessel available for this purpose. While I agree that the *Clydesdale* is not up to the normal peace-time standard of comfort and convenience, she has a passenger certificate for 168 persons and I cannot accept as accurate my Hon. Friend's description of her deficiencies. The company have assured me that if the necessity for a substitute for the regular boat arises again, they will provide the best vessel available, but I am afraid that in present circumstances it is not possible to give an undertaking that the *Clydesdale* will not be used.

Meanwhile the cargo service from Glasgow was being maintained by a variety of steamers. In 1940 the *Lochshiel*, a small motor coaster built in 1929, carried out the service during February, followed at various times throughout the year by the *Clydesdale*, the *Lochdunvegan*, the *Lochgorm* and the chartered *Cragsman*. The following year, the *Lochgorm* appeared back on the service, but for the last four years of the war a number of chartered ships carried out the duty. These included the *Ulster Star*, built in 1904 for the Aberdeen, Leith & Moray Firth Steam Sipping Co. Ltd, but now owned by the Belfast Steamship Co. Ltd, J & A Gardner Ltd's *St Bedan* and *St Rule*, the *Snowcrete*, and finally the *Hebrides*, owned by McCallum, Orme & Co. Ltd, and well known throughout the west coast, having served the Outer Islands and St Kilda since being launched in 1898.

Chapter 18

The Post-War Years

At the end of the war, the *Lochness* was still soldiering on across the Minch. It was reported that on the evening peace was announced, while the rest of the islanders celebrated:

> the dockers on number one wharf in Stornoway went solidly on with their work of loading the *Lochness* whilst most of the passengers stood patiently and undemonstrably on the deck, finding the hours of waiting just as wearisome as on any other night; quite a number of passengers, especially servicemen and women, took their luggage and went ashore again. Almost the only sign of excitement at the mailboat quay was provided by a cow which broke loose and had to be rounded up.

No sooner had the Second World War ended than more complaints started to be made about the inadequacies of the mail service and its steamer. The *Stornoway Gazette* noted that a rival company was considering running a thrice-weekly service to Ullapool, using a vessel that could cover the journey in two-and-a-half hours, a journey time that is faster than at the present day. Nothing more was heard of this venture. In 1945 it was reported that cockroaches had been found on board the *Lochness*; the explanation for their appearance being that they must have escaped from parcels of presents sent from members of the forces abroad! MacBraynes were concerned about the cleanliness of the ship, admitting that after six years of war the previous standards had slipped, which was not surprising considering that she had carried about 2000 passengers per week during that time. Stornoway Town Council strongly criticised the condition of the *Lochness*: there was overcrowding, with sometimes no room for passengers to sit, forcing them to wander round the deck all night; also the food, the state of the cabins and the sanitary arrangements all came under fire. Baillie Tolmie said, 'The lavatories are in a terrible state. Ladies are sick before the boat leaves the quay.' Councillor MacNeill understood that there was no stewardess. He felt it was not right that there should be no stewardess when so many women travelled. He had heard complaints about the bedding in the cabins. 'People finding soiled pillowcases had turned them round, and found that they had been turned already. After all, people paid 6s (30p) for a berth, and the Company was taking advantage of them. People going on a long journey should not have to plead with the steward for a berth.' Councillor Newall, supporting the complaints about the bedding, said he had found the sheets full of blood on one occasion. Ballie Tolmie said visitors had declared they would never return to Lewis because of the conditions on the *Lochness*. There had been numerous complaints about the food. 'People had to go ashore and get their breakfast in the Kyle Hotel. Why was there not enough food available on the *Lochness*? If the Company hadn't food for the passengers they should not carry them.' He continued, 'From the treatment the passengers get, you would think this service wasn't paying them. Instead of that, it's the top notch boat in the fleet, and it's paying them hand over fist.' The Council unanimously agreed to make a strong protest to the Company, and to ask the Secretary of State for Scotland to 'expedite the construction' of the new steamer provided for in the 1938 contract.

It was pointed out that the *Lochnevis* was being used as a 'pleasure boat' sailing between Oban and Fort William, while the *Lochness* still had to serve Portree three days a week; this was solved in 1946 when the former vessel returned to resume her work as the Portree mail steamer, and a six-day service returned to Stornoway.

The Stornoway Town Council still saw major problems and posed three questions – what had happened to the new ship, why had the service to Mallaig not reopened, and what about conditions on the *Lochness*? Provost Mackenzie declared 'We in the islands should demand immediate freedom from the monopolistic masters of the Minch. We must tear asunder the terrific transport tentacles which are slowly but surely strangling our future prospects.' The Council pointed out that the naval restrictions preventing the mail steamer sailing to Mallaig had been lifted the previous March, but nothing had been done to resume the service there. In spite of MacBrayne's assertion that the complaints about the sanitary conditions on board the *Lochness* were 'unreasonable and unfounded if prevailing conditions are recognised', the Council refused to withdraw their previous complaints concerning the state of the steamer, further adding the additional charges that the ship was so infested with rats that the mail bags were being attacked, and parcels containing edibles were being damaged, while cabins were infested with beetles or cockroaches which 'swarm over the walls and bedding'. The Council stated, 'These conditions are well known to the public, may be confirmed by examination of the ship, and are such that their remedying demands immediate attention.' Baillie Tolmie said that four people had complained to him that, after crossing the Minch, their travelling bags were full of cockroaches, and that one of the four, a sea captain, who was travelling to Harris would return by the *Lochmor* rather than cross again on the *Lochness*.

BACK FROM HER OVERHAUL.

"It's disgusting, Oscar Dear. She's spotless—come on back to the Burgh Dump."

There were many complaints about the condition of the *Lochness* at the end of the Second World War. These included the presence of rats on board! The cartoon from the Stornoway Gazette indicates the improvements that had been made when she returned from her first post-war overhaul

A further complaint was that the steamer company was accepting first class fares while allowing third class passengers to encroach on the first class accommodation. Ex-Provost Smith said, 'That was one of the worst features of the situation', with Councillor MacNeill speaking strongly on the same point, saying that there was 'now no examination of tickets on the crossing, and people who had paid first-class fare had to stand on deck all night while the Company did nothing to find out whether the people in the first-class accommodation had paid first-class fare or not.' It was clear that anything which would further the cause of a replacement for the *Lochness* was going to be brought up with the Council. Baillie Tolmie complained that, at times, when the boat was very crowded, only one gangway had been used, with the result that it had taken as long as one hour and twenty minutes for the passengers to disembark. 'There was no excuse for herding people like cattle in that way,' agreed Councillor MacNeill.

In September 1945 the Council complained again about the relief ship for the *Lochness*. This time it was not the *Clydesdale* but the *Hebrides*, a steamer built in 1898 for Messrs McCallum's West Highland services and on charter to David MacBrayne. The Council did not consider her appropriate – her accommodation was unsuitable and out-of-date, and the vessel would take seven hours on the crossing, causing train connections to be regularly missed. Instead, they wanted the *Lochfyne*, a diesel-electric powered ship built in 1931, capable of sixteen knots but with no cargo holds and designed for cruising out of Oban. MacBrayne's apparently offered the *Lochnevis*, the Portree mail steamer, but this was not suitable. In October the Ministry of Transport had examined 'all the captured German tonnage available' to see if a more suitable ship than the *Hebrides* could be obtained to relieve the *Lochness* on her annual overhaul, but had been unsuccessful in their search. This problem was further exacerbated when the *Lochness* returned from her overhaul on 20 November, but suffered boiler trouble on reaching Kyle of Lochalsh, and had to return to the Clyde, leaving the *Hebrides* to maintain the mail service for another three weeks.

The much-maligned *Clydesdale* finally departed the scene in October 1946, moving to Oban and Glasgow, from where she operated cargo-only and sheep-ferrying services to various islands and west coast ports. She was finally sold for scrap at Port Glasgow in 1953. Her replacement was the *Lochgorm*, returned from the Ministry of War Transport, and resuming her pre-war duties on the Glasgow to Stornoway weekly service, until in 1951 she was withdrawn and broken up, also at Port Glasgow. In 1949 and 1950 an additional cargo service was operated between Stornoway and Mallaig, carrying mainly fish to the mainland. For this run, two ships, the *Lothdale* and the *Rimsdale*, were chartered from Charles B Simpson of Helmsdale.

Chapter 19

The *Loch Seaforth* – 'The People of Lewis Would Never be Satisfied'

At Westminster the Member of Parliament representing Lewis, Malcolm MacMillan, continued to try to obtain the best for his constituents. In February 1946 he asked the Minister of War Transport:

> if he is aware that the estimated time to be taken for the construction of the new mail steamer, now on contract, to replace the *Lochness* on the Kyle—Stornoway service is 18 months; and whether he will ensure that she is ready before next winter, in view of the overcrowding and discomfort suffered, especially in winter months by passengers on this State-subsidised service.

The reply was, 'The estimated time to be taken for the construction of this vessel from date of keel laying to completion is 12 months. As the keel will not be laid for some months yet, there is no possibility of her being in service next winter. She should, however, be ready for the winter 1947–48.' In June Mr MacMillan pointed out the difficulties experienced in travelling to the island by suggesting,

> Let a leading Cabinet Minister come along, if that is conceivable. Let him leave Glasgow at 10 o'clock at night, or preferably at 5 o'clock in the morning, on the Highland train, setting out for the wilds of Perthshire. He would go through Inverness town and through Inverness-shire itself. He would try for hours to get a cup of tea in the morning at Inverness station if he went on the 10 pm train. He would come up by Dingwall, through Ross and Cromarty to the coast. He would reach the Stornoway steamer at Kyle. If Hon. Members cared to go by road they would go through all those places which, to English Members and certain Lowland Members generally, are so romantic. They would see the beauties of the Perthshire Highlands and the unmatched majesty of the hills and lochs of Ross and Cromarty. On board the steamer they would see a brass plate, which ought to interest all members of the Cabinet, and especially the Minister of Agriculture. On this little brass plate are these words: The deck forward from this mark X on both sides to the forward screen bulkhead, contains 801 square feet and is certified to accommodate 89 passengers, when not occupied by cattle, animals, cargoes or other encumbrances. The "other encumbrances" are not specifically mentioned, but I wondered whether it might apply to the late famous cockroaches. The logic of the notice is that if there are sufficient cattle, animals and encumbrances to make the voyage profitable, no human beings are permitted there at all. They are allowed only 800 odd square feet by this standard where these things nevertheless take priority. To a large extent that has expressed the attitude of the company to the people of the Western Islands and the North-West coast and their problems.

Eventually the Provost of Stornoway announced that he had seen draft plans of the new ship, to be named the *Loch Seaforth*, and the other councillors were suitably impressed by his description. The order to build had been placed with Wm. Denny & Co. Ltd of Dumbarton before the end of 1945, but with post-war shortages of materials, construction of the new vessel was delayed. Malcolm MacMillan continued to be concerned about this delay, stating that the ship had originally been promised in 1938, and suggesting that a switch to a less busy shipyard might expedite matters:

> Why is it necessary for the new Stornoway, I should say the foreshadowed and still very shadowy Stornoway steamer, to take 18 months to complete? Why did MacBrayne's place that contract with Denny's Yard, already cluttered up with so many other orders? Why, since they were supposed to build the ship in 1939 did it take them until this year even to complete the arrangements for placing the order? The people of the Outer Hebrides will have to wait for another year before she is on the water. I want the Minister to answer that, and tell me whether it is still possible for that contract to be switched over to a yard which will be able to undertake the work and complete it a little more quickly.

The contract remained with Wm. Denny, and she finally appeared towards the end of 1947.

Although she was a more utilitarian ship than would have been the case had she been constructed before the war, she was superior in all ways to her predecessors and became the largest ship to serve Stornoway until then. She was 229 feet (70m) in length and had a tonnage of 1089. Her name, written as two words, broke with 'house style' of 'Loch' names being written as a single word, which had been started many years earlier. The design of the new ship was a development of the *Lochness* in many ways, with large high bows (no doubt to slice through the waves of a Minch storm), but all her cargo holds were located forward, leaving the rest of the ship for passenger accommodation. This was considered to be much superior, particularly for third class passengers, the third class lounge being thought to be better than the first class saloons of older steamers. Cabins were provided for both first and third class, and an innovation was the provision of cubicles, with basic bed, rug and pillow, also for both classes. The first class lounge on the observation deck was quite luxurious, apparently modelled on that of the *Queen Mary*, with large armchairs on which to relax and watch the ever-changing scenery through large windows. Accommodation for the officers and crew was also vastly improved. She was also the first MacBrayne ship to be fitted with radar.

A contemporary description of the ship gives a good impression of her:

> The first thing to catch the eye on the plans is a large observation lounge, the full width of the ship, on the boat deck. The smoke room and bar is away down on the lower deck between the engine room and the stern. There is a large lounge for third-class passengers on the promenade deck aft, corresponding roughly to the area occupied by the first-class deck cabins on the *Lochness*. Nearby is a little hospital. The ticket office is on the same deck, and there is plenty promenade space for both first and third class passengers. One aspect in which the *Loch Seaforth* is infinitely superior to the *Lochness* is the amount of sleeping accommodation both for first and third-class passengers. Some apartments are described as "Third-class sleepers", others as "Railway sleepers" and others again as "Rest Cubicles".
>
> There is no cattle deck aft as on the *Lochness* – for once passengers come first. The only cargo space is forward of the bridge. There seems to be ample space for cars and

> there is a three-ton electric hoist and slewing winch and two one-ton electric cranes which should make little noise. The comfort of passengers has certainly been given more consideration than on any vessel MacBrayne's have yet put on the Minch.

The writer did add, however, that 'the proof of the pudding is in the eating, and the proof of the *Loch Seaforth* will be somewhere round the Shiants with a stiff breeze blowing'.

The *Loch Seaforth* was launched on 19 May 1947, the ceremony being performed by Mrs H T Leith, wife of the general manager. Local colour was added by the Glasgow Transport Department Pipe Band playing 'The Road to the Isles' as the ship slid into the water. The *Stornoway Gazette* added, 'Let us hope that the road travelled by the *Loch Seaforth* will not have too many ups and downs'. As the ship was being fitted out, plans were also being drawn up for handling her in Stornoway. MacBrayne's were planning to speed up her turn-around with the provision of a new mobile crane. The Harbour Authority wanted to rope off part of the pier for the safety of passengers, while they were to recommend that the *Loch Seaforth* be turned round each night before coming alongside, and that the gangway should always be placed aft.

She arrived in Stornoway on the morning of 5 December 1947. A number of local public gentlemen were invited to inspect the ship, and then the Chairman and Directors of David

The assembled dignitaries at the launch of the *Loch Seaforth* on 19 May 1947

The *Loch Seaforth* after launching at William Denny's yard in Dumbarton

MacBrayne entertained them to a luncheon on board. When the guests arrived they were received in the third class lounge and they 'did not realise they were not travelling cabin', a tribute to the standard of the ship's accommodation! One councillor declared 'By Jove, there's not much third class about that', referring to the third-class lounge. Mr H T Leith, general manager of David MacBraynes, proudly stated, 'The *Loch Seaforth* is a luxurious small liner equal to anything on the British coast'. The response from the Stornoway councillors was equally fulsome in its praise, with comments such as John MacIver's when he said he had 'seen many ships but he had seen nothing better than the *Loch Seaforth*'. But the praise was also slightly tainted, reflecting the ding-dong battle which had taken place between Stornoway, London and Glasgow, with comments such as 'the people of Lewis would never be satisfied … Now that they had the *Loch Seaforth* they would soon be wanting the *Queen Mary*', and the request from Provost Mackenzie that, since they had wanted a vessel which could make the crossing in four hours and had been given one which was scheduled to take half-an-hour longer, MacBrayne's should increase speed during summer to reduce the journey to four hours using her 'ample reserve of power'.

One week later the *Stornoway Gazette* reported that the ship had a stowaway. 'The black cat which paced up and down the main deck opposite the gangway when she berthed at Stornoway on her maiden voyage appears to be a stowaway. No-one claimed her. It appears that she had joined the ship during her trials on the Clyde, and was now accepted as one of the ship's company. We take this as a good omen.'

It must have been a good omen, for her time on the Stornoway service lasted twenty-five years, during which she hardly missed a sailing. She quickly became popular with the Lewis folk and is fondly remembered by many today. Six days a week she would leave Stornoway at half past eleven at night (a quarter past midnight on Sunday nights), arriving at Kyle of Lochalsh around four in the morning before reaching Mallaig just after seven. At twelve, the passengers would stream down the pier from the station at Mallaig, and she would set off again for Kyle, where more passengers would join and the major part of the cargo was loaded. This regularly included bales of wool, sheep and, of course, a number of cars which were swung on to the deck by crane. This no doubt looked precarious to the car owners, but the crews would have been experts, any apparent casualness belying their expertise. She would then leave Kyle, scheduled at three, but often later due to the late arrival of a train or cargo loading, and head up the Inner Sound past the Crowlin Islands before crossing the Minch to reach Stornoway after a journey of four and a quarter hours.

There do not appear to be many descriptions of crossing the Minch on the *Loch Seaforth*. One voyage, which took place in the early years of the steamer, was described by Duncan Macpherson in his book *Lure of the West*:

> It was early afternoon in Spring when we set out to visit Stornoway … The T.S.V. *Loch Seaforth* lay alongside the pier. We climbed the narrow gangway, and hoped for the best. According to the published timetable, we were due to sail at 2.30, weather and circumstances permitting. As it happens, the weather makes no difference, but other circumstances seldom permit.
>
> This afternoon, the M.V. *Lochnevis*, which plies between Portree and Mallaig, had not arrived in time. No doubt, if we cared to enquire, we should have learned that the *Lochnevis* was not to blame, but that the connecting train had been late in reaching Mallaig.
>
> The train from Inverness was also overdue. Again, this would be owing to the lateness of the arrival of the south train at Inverness. We, who live there, realise that this unpunctuality is entirely caused by someone else – in the south. Anyway, what's all the hurry?
>
> There were a few passengers on board. One man was walking backwards and forwards along the deck, glancing frequently at his watch, and muttering to himself. Really, it is saddening to see anyone so impatient. At length, about three o'clock, boat and train arrived almost simultaneously.
>
> Passengers laden with cases, rugs, and packages, came along the pier in two sprawling rows. They met at the end of the narrow gangway, the only perceptible approach to the ship. It was difficult to decide the order of priority.
>
> Two elderly gentlemen, leaders of the converging streams, caused further delay by their excessive politeness, each insisting that the other should take precedence. At length one of them, a portly parson holding fast to his umbrella, took a few steps forward.
>
> Alas, this was the psychological moment that a stout, vivacious young woman, who had been on board for over an hour bidding a friend a voluble good-bye, chose to make a dash from the ship. She had suddenly realised that train and boat had arrived, and that the *Loch Seaforth* would be sailing. She did not stop to consider that the boat would not leave until all the passengers were on board.
>
> Now, that gangway – or one very like it – had been constructed fifty years ago. It was intended for use when a cargo boat, carrying a maximum of twelve passengers, came alongside. But the *Loch Seaforth* carries 500 passengers. It might be supposed that the harbourmaster might have provided a wider and more up-to-date one

to meet present day needs. Oh, no, we don't do that sort of thing.

Yet, if someone had suggested the need of a special platform for a piper to march up and down while he played a lament, we might have managed that. But a wider gangway! Away with these utilitarian notions! We have always used that gangway, and we do not intend to change. Hence Dorothy's regrettable collision with the parson. Fortunately the umbrella was undamaged.

At length all the passengers were safely aboard; all the good-byes had been said. The last hamper, the last bag of mails had been safely stowed away. A very important part of the perishable cargo consisted of a daily consignment of milk, stored in large sealed drums. For, Stornoway, the largest town in Ross-shire, is not too proud to buy from Inverness the nourishment which her own county is unable or unwilling to produce.

We sailed out through the narrow channel between Kyleakin and the lighthouse; then, Skye several miles distant on our left, we continued northward to the mainland of Applecross. Passing close to the deserted island of Crowlin, we skirted the mainland coast for several miles before entering Applecross Bay … The ferry boat drew alongside. The ferryman brought one passenger, he took off two; he also took with him several bags of mail and sundry packages. Ashore, at the small jetty, a number of people had assembled. For, the arrival of the mail-boat was the event of the day. We resumed our Northern voyage, through the Inner Sound, past Raasay and South Rona, and out into the Minch.

The *Loch Seaforth* is a finely built motor vessel, fitted with many luxury devices for the passengers' comfort. Unfortunately, these did not render us wholly impervious to the effects of high winds and tumultuous seas. In the circumstances our admiration for the scenery became dulled; and for a time we retired to the dining-room to test the virtues of a cup of tea. There we found several other passengers, besides the Captain and one or two of his staff.

Although Captain Mackinnon had only recently been appointed to the command of the *Loch Seaforth*, in succession to Captain MacArthur, he was well acquainted with the West Coast in all its moods. He has had varied experiences, and has come in contact with many interesting people. I had heard of his helpfulness while he was on the Outer Isles run, and I found his praises well deserved. He can guide you with practical advice, or cheer you with a good story.

Mr G N Adams, the wireless operator, was another helpful friend. Mr Adams who belongs to Aberdeenshire, has a strange aversion to certain types of ministers. I feel sure this must be due to his early associations, for our Highland ministers are most likeable.

After a time we made our way upstairs again, for, no matter how stormy, there is a limit to the amount of tea which one can consume. The lounge was exceedingly comfortable, and the view from its many windows unequalled. At one moment we saw a glorious wave towering above us, the next we gazed into a watery abyss. Everywhere there was water, in various shapes, glistening in the sun, tossed by the wind, limpid, vibrant.

At that moment a bell rang sharply on the bridge overhead. Almost simultaneously, mysterious noises came from the engines, and the vessel slowed down. There was bustle and the tread of hurrying footsteps, and the sound of excited voices. There followed a bang, and shouts appeared to come from the sea … A seaman appeared. He explained the lights of the lounge had been temporarily switched off as there had been no time to draw the curtains. There had been no break-down on our ship. On the contrary, we were helping another in distress.

It seemed that the engine of a fishing boat had failed, and that the rudder was also out of action. The boat had been tossing helplessly on the waters when our ship came to the rescue.

The *Loch Seaforth* had been stopped, and a rope thrown on board the crippled craft and made fast between the two vessels. This may sound a simple proceeding, but it must be remembered that we were not afloat on a mill-pond. For some reason, which I do not attempt to venture to explain, when our ship was on the top of a wave, the fishing boat was usually wallowing in the trough of another.

Even when safely fastened together, there had to be explanations. These were made in both English and Gaelic, in the course of which a number of words generally referred to as expletives, came into use. At last we resumed our interrupted voyage, and proceeded slowly with the fishing boat in tow.

Passing safely between Holm Point and Arnish lighthouse, we cruised safely into the waters of Stornoway Harbour. We passed Goat Island, obstructing the entrance to the inner harbour, and tied up alongside the wharf.

We had crossed the Minch.

The *Loch Seaforth* arrives at Stornoway in August 1965

The arrival of the *Loch Seaforth* meant that the *Lochness* was no longer required at Stornoway, although she did return to relieve the *Loch Seaforth* when that ship went for her annual overhaul. As had been planned, she was transferred to Oban to improve the service to the Outer Isles. In 1951 she became the company's spare steamer, before being sold in July 1955 to an Italian Company, Lloyd Mediterraneo S P A, who named her *Valmarino*. Three years later she was sold to S Billinis & Co., of Piraeus, to serve the Aegean Islands, being given a third and final name of *Myrtidiotissa*. Scottish passengers travelling to the Greek islands were intrigued by mural paintings of Loch Ness in her dining saloon, for the superstructure of the vessel had by now been so altered as to make her unrecognisable as a former MacBrayne's steamer. She was finally broken up in 1974.

The *Loch Seaforth* was involved in a variety of incidents throughout her life; most were relatively minor but some of a more serious nature. On one night in 1950, the ship's accommodation was vandalised: five cushions and three chairs were cut with a knife while a glass shelf and water bottle were wrenched from the wall of the ladies first class toilet. Passengers were warned it could lead to the withdrawal of comforts and facilities. Apparently there were three suspect groups on board that night – workmen returning to Skye, university students and Harris schoolchildren. All were asked to admit responsibility, but there is no information as to any culprit or ensuing punishment.

In June of that year, there was a five-day strike of dockers at Stornoway, and naturally this affected the *Loch Seaforth*. On her arrival on a Saturday night, an attempt was made to unload her cargo, but this was stopped by the MacBrayne's Manager, as he considered the situation threatening and that someone might be pushed over the pier into the water. The local kipper-sellers

Menu and wine list from the *Loch Seaforth* in 1967. Those using the dining room would have appreciated the linen table cloths and silver service. There was a choice of ten wines, available in half bottles varying in price from a 1955 Médoc for 8/3d (41p) to a vintage Moet et Chandon Champagne for 22/6d (£1.12)

wished their cargo to be loaded, but the *Loch Seaforth*'s crew refused to man the winches. This also meant that two cars could not be unloaded. However, the dockers decided to unload milk and mails; this was duly carried out at five o'clock on the Sunday morning when the tide was suitable. When the ship arrived back on the Monday evening, an area was roped off on the pier for safety, and again the essential milk and mails were unloaded, along with bacon which had been on board for two days. Ten tons of perishable goods were going back and forth across the Minch for several days before the dispute ended.

Later the same year in July, the *Loch Seaforth* suffered damage to her rudder and propellers coming alongside at Mallaig. Two tugs towed her to Ardrossan for repairs. The only vessel available to take her place was the *Loch Nevis*, the Portree mail steamer. She had accommodation for only 100 and needed to make two trips from Kyle to carry all the waiting passengers. She had a busy schedule, arriving at Stornoway at quarter past nine in the evening, reaching back to Kyle at three in the morning. She was back at Stornoway again at half past eight, and four hours later had returned to Kyle. After another trip to Stornoway later on that second evening, she was replaced by the *Lochness* which remained on the run until the *Loch Seaforth* returned.

In December the Stornoway Harbour Commission complained to MacBrayne's that the King Edward Wharf, where the *Loch Seaforth* berthed, was being damaged by the method of bringing the mail boat alongside. Timbers of a newly constructed extension to the pier were being subjected to repeated strain. The vessel was swung round at the south-west corner of the pier and stopped three hundred yards from her berth. From there the ship proceeded 'at high speed' along the face of the quay grazing the timbers. Apparently the Captain had already been asked to turn nearer his own berth, but nothing had been done about it.

A further complaint that year concerned the price of carrying a coffin to Lewis. From Inverness to Stornoway, the freight charge for a coffin was £13/1/9 (£13.08), and it was stated that a living person could make a return journey four times for less than that, while the charge of £59/6/3 (£59.32) from London was considerably more than the £42 which could then buy a fourteen-day cruise. But all was not either complaints or mishaps. For once, a councillor, Baillie MacLean, had something good to say when he commented at the start of a meeting that the '*Loch Seaforth* had passed in before the meeting started at 7.15. It goes to show that she can do it, if she gets away in time'.

Had anyone still been concerned about the seaworthiness of the *Loch Seaforth*, they would have been reassured during the 'great gale of '52'. This occurred in January, and afterwards Captain Ewen MacKinnon said the vessel behaved 'like a lady' after sailing her out of Stornoway into the teeth of the gale. Heavy seas meant she was slowed to seven knots. The skipper added, 'When we reached island of Tredda off the Skye coast we were alright, but it was still blowing hard and we "hugged" the Skye coast'. The *Loch Seaforth* docked at Kyle at 7 am, about three hours after the scheduled arrival time, and continuing high seas prevented her running to Mallaig.

The next few years were fairly uneventful. The *Stornoway Gazette* did report in January 1954 about 'one of the rare disruptions to the mail steamer'. The *Loch Seaforth* suffered engine trouble going into Kyle, blowing an air box, but it was decided to make the crossing to Stornoway on one engine. This took six hours and the prevailing good weather unfortunately did not last. The strong wind which arose made entry into Stornoway extremely tricky and carried the ship broadside on to the harbour. The following day's passengers were carried from Mallaig and Kyle of Lochalsh by the *Lochmor*, while a chartered BEA plane flew in the next day, a Sunday, with replacement parts for the engine. A 65 mph gale kept both ships in harbour, until the *Loch Seaforth* recommenced her duties on the Monday morning at 0900, being followed across the Minch by the *Lochmor*.

In 1956 the call at Applecross was terminated. This service had operated since early in the twentieth century, and was the main source of access for both passengers and goods for the remote communities on the mainland peninsula. Long after most of the towns and villages on the west coast had adapted from access by sea to the twin benefits of roads and railways, Applecross still depended on the Stornoway mailboat to Kyle and Mallaig. The vessel lay off the pier at Milltown, and was attended by a large rowing boat. The whole operation was somewhat precarious in bad conditions.

An advantage of the service was that in summer a passenger could catch the boat coming from Stornoway at three o'clock in the morning, and arrive in Glasgow via Mallaig and the West Highland railway line at two in the afternoon. A less attractive feature was that, at any time of year, indifferent conditions could prevent the ferryboat from making contact; so the unfortunate passengers for Applecross got a 'free' trip across the Minch to Stornoway and back again. Also, in 1929, it was agreed that the steamer would not call at Applecross on the winter run from Stornoway to Kyle, unless illness necessitated removal of a patient to hospital. This meant that those wishing to go to Kyle boarded the steamer at Applecross in the afternoon for a double trip across the Minch. They would leave Applecross at 1515 and get into the small open ferry boat to join the steamer—that is, if the steamer called at all. Frequently, because of the westerly gales, it was known to pass without calling on three consecutive days. Provided, then, that passengers reached the steamer, they would have had to cross the Minch to Stornoway, where, as has been described by a native of Applecross, 'the delights of that otherwise fine Lewis town soon palled when there was time to kill between nine in the evening and midnight, while nursing a sorely tried digestive system and waiting to repeat the trip!' They would then have to re-cross the Minch, to arrive at Kyle of Lochalsh at 0430 the following morning—that is, having left at three o'clock the previous afternoon. This was a distance of only twelve miles, but a trip of 112 miles had to be undertaken, lasting more than thirteen hours.

In 1952 it had been suggested that MacBrayne's should instigate a ferry running from Kyle to a pier built at Toscaig, but the company showed no interest in doing so. However, the situation changed and four years later on 1 June 1956 the *Loch Seaforth* made her last call at Applecross. A small motor fishing-vessel named the *Irene Julia* had been purchased in 1955, her fish hold converted for carrying cargo, and accommodation at the stern adapted for passengers. She was given the apt name *Loch Toscaig*, and provided a direct service linking Applecross with Kyle. The *Loch Seaforth* thereafter sailed directly to Stornoway. Captain John Smith on the mail boat reckoned that the only difference to the sailing schedule would be a saving of only ten or twelve minutes as the stop took no more than two minutes, and eight or ten were spent in slowing down and getting under way again. Perhaps summer visitors would miss the Applecross call, for it always added a little bit of romance and excitement to the crossing, but for the people of Applecross it was 'a release from bondage they had suffered too long'.

The ferry for Applecross alongside the *Loch Seaforth*. The call here ceased in 1956, when it was replaced by a direct service from Kyle of Lochalsh to Toscaig

The year 1956 saw another dockers' strike in Stornoway; this time the dispute involved the red containers which were now being used to carry cargo. Arguments continued over who should unload them, the dockers initially offering to unload them on the ship, and then put the cargo ashore on slings. Over fifty wagon loads of cargo piled up on the railway sidings at Kyle, while the cargo already on board travelled to and fro across the Minch. This included all the luggage and furniture of a Miss Campbell, the new matron at the Lewis Hospital, who was left with nothing but her uniform. Eventually the cargo was carried to Stornoway in the cargo steamer *Lochbroom*.

Another strike four years later, this time by seamen, saw the *Loch Seaforth* tied up in Stornoway for about a week. The main effect of the strike was a shortage of milk and provisions. Bread supplies were also threatened – there was plenty of flour but very little yeast. On the first sailing after the strike had ended, there were 450 passengers on board and twenty-one cars filled the hold. The first officer stood at the head of the gangway with 'a small counting machine', as over 500 were expected, but it is thought that a significant number of people waited to avoid any rush. A crowd of 300 watched on the pier, with police circulating among them to prevent trouble. One chaotic incident occurred in the middle of the strike when it was announced that the steamer would sail with a scratch crew, and hundreds of people bought tickets and went aboard only to be told the sailing was cancelled. The town Sanitary Inspector and a gentleman with a yachting master's certificate were to be among the crew, but a Customs Officer reminded Captain Smith that he must have twelve men with lifeboat certificates if passengers were to be carried, and this could not be complied with. The passengers were reluctant to come ashore; a stewardess attempted to address the crowd, but could not be clearly heard. It was 0100 before the bulk of the passengers returned ashore.

The boom defence vessel *Barbican* brought much-needed supplies to the island, but its arrival also led to some light-hearted moments. One outward cargo of mails from Stornoway consisted mainly of kippers which had been lying in the Post Office for four days, and it was suggested that in the heat of summer they might have been capable of delivering themselves, while a wholesale firm was not particularly pleased with its delivery of emergency food, which consisted mainly of a large amount of a well-known brand of table jelly. The hooting of a car horn in the village of Back on the morning the *Loch Seaforth* finally sailed was an important sign for a particular housewife: it was a pre-arranged signal that the steamer had sailed, and it was safe for her to make 'maragan dubha', or black puddings, for posting to London the next day!

A slight change to the *Loch Seaforth*'s schedule came about in 1959, when the proposal from a year before to introduce a morning return sailing between Mallaig and Armadale was initiated. A large notice was displayed on board the steamer stating 'Express service to Portree via Armadale and coach'. There was little evidence of any delay in arrival at Stornoway which this extra sailing might have caused; the fears of the critics, who included members of Stornoway Town Council, were unfounded, when she arrived before 2000 on the first night, and even earlier on the ensuing two evenings. The Council also took this occasion to complain about problems getting fish loaded at Stornoway, and that fewer cars were being carried than previously. This was perhaps the start of the push towards a replacement for a steamer which was only twelve years old, but whose design was now starting to look anachronistic. There may have been no connection with her extra duties, but towards the end of the year the *Loch Seaforth* suffered three breakdowns. On the third occasion she remained at her berth for a whole day, and the Portree steamer *Lochearn* took over the service, bringing passengers and mails from Kyle.

The only other change to the mail boat schedule occurred in 1964, when a proposal to operate a daylight service was put into operation. The plan was to start the new schedule when the *Loch*

The Stornoway Gazette entitled this picture, taken in the 1950s, 'The largest van in the Western Isles.' It illustrates both how cargoes of any size were handled by the steamers, and also the growing need for a car ferry

Seaforth was off the run for about seven weeks at the beginning of the year, being replaced by the then new car ferry *Clansman*. The departure time from Stornoway was to be at 0600, with arrivals at Kyle at 1030 and Mallaig at 1230. A thirty-minute turn-around there would mean an arrival back in Stornoway at 2000, only slightly later than before. It was further proposed that this service would continue with the return of the *Loch Seaforth*, and that she would be converted to one-class for that purpose. Some councillors considered the plan unreasonable, being concerned about the early hour people living in outlying districts of Lewis would have to leave home to catch the steamer, but the majority voted to agree to the daylight crossing. It also prompted the composition by a Lewisman clearly not in favour of the change of a poem entitled 'You never know with MacBrayne':

> A daylight boat
> In the middle of the night,
> Sailing for Kyle
> Before first light.
>
> Day boat? Night boat?
> Whichever do they mean –
> A ship, an ark,
> A submarine.
>
> Only MacBrayne,
> And it ain't no joke,
> Could call night, day,
> Or animals, folk.

The last line apparently referred to the notice, previously mentioned, carried on some steamers inferring that a certain space on board could accommodate passengers, if not occupied by cattle or other encumbrances.

The *Clansman* inaugurated the daylight service on 25 January 1965, when the *Loch Seaforth* was away for annual overhaul. Ross & Cromarty County Council, which represented the rural areas of Lewis, was not in favour; so it was agreed that the new service was to be on the basis that the timetable would continue until the end of that summer, and then be reviewed. The new timings found little favour with anyone, however, and as early as April David MacBrayne intimated that the service would be withdrawn at the end of that month. C B Leith, the General Manager, announced, 'I bring you this message of goodwill, right away, if the feelings of the island remain as unanimously as they were, and the Company will be very happy indeed to restore the night service'. By this time the *Loch Seaforth*'s accommodation had been converted to one class, and she returned to the run without the deep armchairs which had formerly graced her observation saloon.

Five years earlier, a very significant event of a totally different nature had taken place. A ceremony was held in honour of Mr George N Adams, who had completed forty years' service with the Marconi Company; for most of that time he had been the radio officer on the ships sailing on the Stornoway mail service. He was the first radio officer on board the *Sheila*, and was sailing on board her when she ran aground in 1927. He remained on board, and maintained wireless contact with the company for three days before being one of the last to leave by means of a rope over the bow, just before the ship was towed off by the steam drifter *Furze*. After the loss of the *Sheila*, he took over on the *Clydesdale* before transferring to the *Lochness* when she appeared on the run. He was the radio officer during the whole of her life on the run, including the years of the Second World War when Mr Adams sailed continuously for six years without taking any leave. He had one alarming moment during the War, when an object resembling a mine appeared alongside the *Lochness* as she entered Stornoway harbour. Fortunately it was nothing more sinister than a fishing buoy. Of a more serious nature was the night when a torpedo had been fired at the ship; the Navy was informed, and the submarine later cornered and accounted for. Mr Adams naturally transferred to the *Loch Seaforth*, and on her he completed his forty years' service. It was calculated that he had completed 24,000 crossings of the Minch, a record unlikely to be bettered.

Longevity of service was not a rarity. Only three men had captained the Stornoway mail boat between the arrival of the *Lochness* and the departure of the *Iona*. Norman MacArthur was in charge of the former vessel, never failing to cross the Minch on account of storms, and only on a couple of occasions due to fog or drift nets in Stornoway harbour; Captain Ewen MacKinnon took over on the *Loch Seaforth* until 1954, when John Smith assumed the helm on that vessel before opening the car ferry service to Ullapool. There was no 'two weeks on, two weeks off' in those days!

Two complaints concerning the mail steamer appeared on the front page of the *Stornoway Gazette* in January 1966. The first complaint was about the re-introduction of calls at Armadale. The mail boat was scheduled to make three calls there, one on the way down to Mallaig, one out from Mallaig and back, and the third on the run north to Kyle and Stornoway. From the way the calls had been fitted in to the timetable, it was thought that it was not possible for the steamer to arrive in Stornoway less than half-an-hour late; this was considered unacceptable by the Town Council. The second complaint was voiced later during the same Council meeting and involved the *Clansman*, which was relieving the *Loch Seaforth* at the time. Councillor Abraham Langley said he thought MacBrayne's would lose a great deal of traffic if the *Clansman* continued on the Stornoway run. He told the Council that, when his sister and her husband came to Stornoway on holiday on the *Clansman*, 'every single passenger on the boat was sick'.

Both these complaints were indicative of the groundswell that was building up against the deficiencies of both the route from Mallaig and Kyle and the vessels operating on it. Responses to both were forthcoming. The Stornoway Town

The *Loch Seaforth* aground at Kyle of Lochalsh in 1965

Clerk, Mr Alasdair MacLeod, countered the first complaint, and defended MacBrayne's, saying he understood that the times had been very well maintained by the *Clansman* since she came on the run to relieve the *Loch Seaforth*. The complaint about the supposed 'poor sea-going' qualities of the *Clansman* provoked an immediate response from seven of her officers, two mates, three engineers, the radio officer and the purser. In a letter to the *Stornoway Gazette* the following week, they refuted Councillor Langley's claims, stating:

> On no occasion have more than a handful of passengers been seasick and we fail to understand how anyone so sick managed to make a census of the other passengers' condition. It is unfortunate that critics are more vociferous than satisfied travellers. Over half the officers on this vessel (the *Clansman*) have served on the *Loch Seaforth*, and consider the *Clansman* a more comfortable ship in every way, especially in bad weather.'

They went on to conclude that the 'vessel is providing a very good service, with excellent time-keeping, and carries its passengers in greater comfort than quite a few of them deserve'.

Up until now, the *Loch Seaforth* had experienced few major few incidents, but as the years passed by she became more accident-prone. In December 1965 she grounded in Mallaig harbour and three months later she was slightly damaged when she hit a pile on the pier at Mallaig. This was the day before her steering gear failed, and she went aground just off the Lochalsh Hotel at Kyle of Lochalsh. This was a more serious incident, and for two days she defied the rescue efforts, before eventually being pulled off and taken to the Clyde for repairs. Passengers were re-routed by bus through Skye and on the car ferry *Hebrides* to Tarbert, while cargo ships carried the freight from Kyle.

According to the *Press and Journal*, the rescue attempts seem to have been rather along 'Whisky Galore' lines.

> They huffed and they puffed – but all they did at Kyle of Lochalsh … was to break two steel hawsers. The attempts to free the … *Loch Seaforth* from the rocks … assumed the proportions of a massive entertainment for the locals. People lined the shore as small boats fussed around the grounded steamer – and they raised a cheer when, in the late afternoon, a tug from Greenock appeared in the narrows. As the sun shone brilliantly from the Skye direction, over the half mile stretch of water a hawser was passed from the tug to the stern of the steamer. The water churned as the tug engines strained to the load – then the tug leapt forward as

Engineers inspect the damage to the bows of the *Loch Seaforth*. It can be seen that four feet of the hull is missing

> the hawser parted with a twang that could be heard on shore. Then someone had a bright idea to roll the steamer. The tug took the strain with another hawser. But instead of pulling the steamer straight back, she steamed round at an angle to try to pull the *Loch Seaforth* sideways. Again the hawser broke. Another rolling attempt was made. This time the hawser did not break, but the tug was brought short with her bows rearing in the air. The rocks of Kyle were not keen to give up their captive. Dusk was falling, and the crowds were starting to move homewards. The tug crew suddenly developed a hunger, and steamed away to Kyle pier to tie up for the night and make a meal. In the early spring night the riding lights of the *Loch Seaforth* were the only thing visible on the water. For her skeleton crew, it was another night aboard. For the tug crew it was a night of rest before another Herculean battle the next day.

The 'Herculean battle' was eventually won, for she was towed off and repaired.

Only months later, in May, the second national seamen's strike since 1911 brought much of Britain's coastal shipping to a standstill, with the *Loch Seaforth* one of the ships involved. There appeared to have been two views regarding the impact of the strike. The *Stornoway Gazette* announced, 'Islanders can only hold out for one week', and went on to describe an air of quietness around the main quays of Stornoway, with the *Loch Seaforth* seemingly abandoned at her usual berth. It further commented that most shops would have enough food for about a week, and that the Harris Tweed mills would run short of wool after a similar length of time. The converse view was that any impact 'bounced off most people', because with the crofting system being still very much alive, people still had a 'milking cow, chickens, sheep untethered by legislation, potatoes in the hopper and a boat down on the sea loch'. This was described as 'resilience by way of local food security'. It was also pointed out that with the steamer being tied up, a house was being communally built by striking seamen!

This latter point of view may have been a slightly rose-tinted one, for within a week of the strike commencing a Stornoway fishing boat had been chartered to bring fruit, vegetables and animal foodstuffs to the island. The following day a rumour suggested that a boat was coming to Stornoway carrying milk for the island's children; unfortunately MacBrayne's *Loch Arkaig*, for this was the intended ship, was not on her way. Aid was provided, however, in the form of a boom defence vessel, HMS *Barrage*, which arrived that evening carrying seventeen tons of foodstuffs, 457 bags of mail and oxygen cylinders for the hospital. Four days later a tank landing craft, the *Aachen*, brought another seventy tons of foodstuffs, with a similar vessel, the *Abbeville*, carrying a further 130 tons the following day. Several days later the local pubs closed as beer supplies had run out. Rumours abounded when the submarine, HMS *Otos*, tied up alongside the *Loch Seaforth*, but she was merely on a 'peaceful operation'. The strike was eventually settled, and the mail service resumed its regular pattern.

By the late 1960s, the complaints about the shortcomings of the *Loch Seaforth* were becoming stronger and more frequent. So some light verse in praise of the mail service, penned by a visitor to Lewis, came as a pleasant change.

> We like our comforts nowadays;
> We choose the shortest path,
> And even on Safari,
> We expect a daily bath.
>
> But we remember other days –
> The *Sheila*, *Clydesdale*, *Gael* –
> When sheep took precedence of folk;
> They smelt of vomit (stale).

It's good to hear MacBrayne's being praised
For clean and tidy ships,
And see folk swarm across the Minch
On real pleasure trips.

The *Loch Seaforth* went aground again in 1972. On the morning of 24 October en route from Stornoway to Kyle, she became stranded on the shore of the island of Longay, off Skye. She had left Stornoway at twenty-five past one in the morning, about two hours behind schedule. In a south-westerly Force 9 gale, she struck a sand and gravel shore north-west of Longay, leaving her bows high and dry and her stern in seven fathoms of water at high tide. The Mallaig lifeboat and the small passenger vessel, the *Western Isles*, which had been sheltering at Kyle, came to her assistance. The latter vessel managed to take off the twenty-eight passengers and a pet dog. Conditions by this time had calmed down and the passengers were in good spirits, being 'very co-operative and uncomplaining', with some of them 'joking about getting breakfast on board with the compliments of MacBrayne's'. The tug *Flying Falcon* arrived from Tobermory in the afternoon, and stood by the *Loch Seaforth*, but the sea was now calm and there was no apparent danger. By eight o'clock the following morning the vessel was refloated, and under her own power made her way to Kyle of Lochalsh and then to Greenock for repairs. Traffic was diverted through Skye until the *Clansman* took over the run. Comments about the incident, such as 'suspicious that only one engine was functioning', and 'the *Loch Seaforth* had done about 50,000 miles in bad conditions – as bad as any part of the world. What was wrong was the way her machinery was being "driven to death"', added to the dissatisfaction and ill-feeling that was now felt towards the steamer.

Shortly after this incident, the *Loch Seaforth* departed the Stornoway mail service, the run on which she had served since new in 1947. On 28 January 1972 the *Loch Seaforth* made her official farewell voyage out of Stornoway, handing over to the *Clansman* at Mallaig. She was transferred to Oban to relieve the *Claymore*, operating the Outer Isles service to Coll, Tiree, Barra and South Uist. Ten days later the *Loch Seaforth* returned once more to the Stornoway service, when she had to relieve the *Clansman*, which had been taken to the Clyde for repairs after a bad collision. On 30 March she left Stornoway for the final time, and never again did she see Lewis. She was then laid up in Greenock, but on 27 May left there for Oban to replace the *Claymore*. Although the *Loch Seaforth* was an older vessel, the *Claymore* having been launched in 1955, she could carry more cars, and having a higher speed was thus better able to cope with the increasing number of vehicles being shipped to the islands. Incidentally, the *Claymore* had been a visitor to Stornoway, functioning as the normal relief vessel on the mail service until the coming of the car ferries in 1964. The performance of the *Loch Seaforth* on the Inner Isles run was, however, not a complete success. In October she suffered a minor grounding at Coll, while the *Claymore* had to keep coming back to cover numerous breakdowns. However, after a major engine overhaul in December 1972, she behaved faultlessly. In January 1973 she began a thrice-weekly service to Colonsay, and in February paid her first visit to Islay, when she made a cattle run to that island. It seemed that she would be assured of at least two more years' service, but as will be seen, this was not to be.

Less than a year later she went aground again. On 22 March 1973, while on passage from Castlebay on Barra to Oban, she struck a rock in the Gunna Sound between the islands of Coll and Tiree. The passengers and crew were safely landed by lifeboat, and the steamer was then towed into Gott Bay and tied alongside Scarinish Pier. Initial inspection revealed a flooded engine room, with a hole 'the size of a man's fist' below the waterline. Later the crew returned to salvage what they could of the passengers' luggage. The following morning the members of the crew, including Captain Donald Gunn, who had stayed on board overnight, had to make a dash for safety when the vessel suddenly lurched over on her port side until her superstructure hit the pier. She then slowly sank in six metres of water, with waves covering her boat deck at high tide. It was thought that a bulkhead had given way, causing the remaining compartments to be flooded. There was concern that she might keel over on her starboard side, but she settled down on the seabed, to remain there for just under two months. During that period all passengers and cargo had to be ferried out to the *Claymore* which had taken over the Inner Isles service.

The following information regarding the subsequent recovery work on the *Loch Seaforth* is taken from the notes of Alan Thomas, one of the divers sent out to the stranded ship. They travelled out on the replacement ship, the *Claymore*, on 25 March. Their first task was to remove spirits from the bar at the aft end of the ship. This was carried out as a safety issue, as this part of the vessel was accessible at certain states of the tide. Perhaps someone in authority had visions of a second 'Whisky Galore' taking place on Tiree. Nothing more could be done then until a crane could be obtained to lift the ship from the seabed.

On 11 May, the divers returned and the following day a giant floating crane, the *Magnus lll* arrived from Germany. Over the next two days the divers fed cables beneath the *Loch Seaforth*, enabling her to be hoisted off the sea bed and dropped on the nearby beach. The three foot gash in the hull was patched and wooden wedges, which would swell and hold the patch tight, were fitted. While the work was being carried out the divers stayed on board the *Loch Seaforth*, in rather surreal conditions.

The end of an era. The *Loch Seaforth* under tow from Tiree to be broken up at Troon on the evening of 23 May 1973. She docked at Troon the following afternoon and breaking up commenced the following day

Alan Thomas described how 'being on board a dead ship at night was an eerie experience. We only had torches and had to make hourly inspections of every space below the water line, (in order to decide) whether to run a pump or not. All floors were covered in oil and mud from its time on the bottom. Thank goodness it wasn't rough.'

Finally on 23 May, after 300 empty fifty gallon oil barrels had been stacked in the engine room, presumably for buoyancy, the Board of Trade cleared the ship fit to sail and at 1800, in flat, calm conditions, she commenced her last voyage. A single tug towed her at about 7.5 knots from Tiree to Troon, where she finally arrived at 1400 to be broken up. It was an ignominious end to a fine ship which had served the people of Lewis well for a quarter of a century. It was an ironic coincidence that the demise of the *Loch Seaforth* occurred on almost the same date that the last regular sailing between Mallaig, Kyle of Lochalsh and Stornoway took place, the service being transferred to Ullapool on 26 March.

Chapter 20

The Decline of the Cargo Services

In 1949 the cargo service from Glasgow was now operated on a weekly basis. The *Lochgorm* returned to replace the *Hebrides*, but she in turn was replaced in 1951 by a much more modern cargo ship. This was the second *Lochdunvegan*. She was new to Macbrayne's, but had in fact been built in Sweden as the *Ornen* in 1946, and, presumably for working in the Baltic, she was designed with a strengthened hull for ice-bound conditions. It must be assumed that this provision was never called upon in the relatively warm waters of the Minch. Although MacBrayne's had owned motor vessels since 1907, she was the first ship powered by diesel engines to visit Stornoway regularly. She was originally intended to be named *Lochalsh*, but this did not happen. She took up the Glasgow-Stornoway run, and could be seen in Stornoway unloading cargo every Thursday evening, having left Glasgow the previous Monday. She too outlived her usefulness as a MacBrayne ship, and after assisting in the carriage of cars between Oban and Tiree in 1973, was sold for further service in Greek waters under the ownership of George

After the Second World War the cargo service from Glasgow was operated by the *Lochgorm* until she was withdrawn in 1951. This picture shows her at Stornoway

Stavrou and others and with a succession of new names, *Fanis*, *Vassilis* and *Maggy*. Her place was taken by the *Loch Carron*, built under the conditions of the 1949 mail contract. She was a typical cargo vessel of her time, with diesel engines aft and good accommodation for both officers and crew. In addition, she had accommodation for four passengers. All the cargo space was forward, including space for livestock, and cargo could be handled by two derricks.

As well as these two regular callers, the other post-war cargo ships of MacBrayne's were also to be seen in Stornoway from time to time. It was originally intended that the *Lochbroom* would become the regular Stornoway cargo boat after the war, but this did not come about, and she was to be only an occasional visitor. She had been built as the *Empire Maysong* by Messrs Scott & Sons of Bowling, on the Clyde, for service during the Second World War, but was not required for that purpose, and was thus available for purchase and conversion to a cargo ship. Another wartime-built and later-converted cargo vessel purchased by MacBraynes was the *Loch Frisa*, and she, too, called infrequently at Stornoway, either as a relief to the regular ship or with a specific cargo. Incidentally, she was the last steamship to join the MacBrayne fleet. The *Loch Ard*, launched in 1955 and the final cargo ship to be built for MacBrayne's, similarly called at Stornoway on only a limited number of occasions. Her first visit to the island was in January 1956, when she relieved the *Lochdunvegan*. Later, reflecting the importance of the cargo boats in carrying not only everyday goods but also specialised items, she featured in the local paper, having transported to the island a van which would be used to deliver 'Calor gas supplies and cooking apparatus' to all parts of the island. The *Loch Ard* was also the ship used to carry cargo between Kyle and Stornoway when the *Loch Seaforth* was aground in 1966.

The *Loch Dunvegan* (right) at Stornoway. For over twenty years she was to be seen on Thursdays and Fridays at her berth at No. 1 Quay. In this unusual view the car ferry *Iona* lies astern of the cargo boat

By the mid-1970s the *Loch Carron* had become the last regular coastal cargo ship operating from Glasgow. With the development of car ferries to Skye and Harris, more and more cargo began to be carried by road. In November 1972 Lewis District Council was informed that road haulage of goods from Glasgow had commenced, thereby denying traffic to the *Lochdunvegan*. Councillor James Maclennan said 'it did not require much imagination to appreciate what was behind the move … It is a deliberate attempt to phase out the *Lochdunvegan* at the earliest possible date.' In 1975 sailings from Glasgow were withdrawn, bringing to an end the direct steamer service between Stornoway and Glasgow, which had operated continuously for well over a century. The *Loch Carron* was now surplus to requirements, and followed the *Lochdunvegan* to the Mediterranean, being sold in 1977 to a Cypriot concern, Kopsi Shipping Co. Ltd, and trading under the name *Georgis K* until she sank during the 1980s.

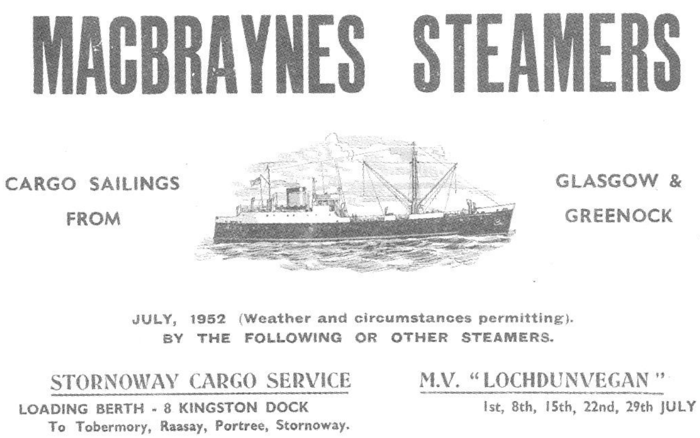

An extract from a 1952 MacBrayne's cargo poster. These were issued each month. It shows a drawing of the *Loch Carron*, the last cargo ship to operate regularly from Glasgow to Stornoway, sailings finally ceasing in 1975. It also gives the dates of the sailings for that month of the *Lochdunvegan*, the cargo steamer between 1951 and 1973

Fourteen years before the end of the Glasgow service, the other regular cargo service to Stornoway, operated by Coast Lines and running between Newcastle, Leith, Aberdeen, Stornoway and Belfast, had been withdrawn. The last run was carried out by the *Pacific Coast*. For almost forty years since the first Coast Lines vessel, the *Durham Coast*, had arrived in 1925, the company had been supplying the lifeblood of the community in Lewis. Groceries, provisions, wool for the Tweed industry, heavy machinery for factories, fertiliser and fencing materials for crofters' reseeding in springtime, had all filled the ships' holds, while up until their decline in the 1950s kippers contributed to outgoing traffic. The service had originally been once a fortnight, but on taking over the Antrim Line's sailing, it became weekly. While trade to Stornoway had stayed fairly constant; that between Newcastle, Leith, Aberdeen and Belfast had declined to such an extent that it was not worth the company's time to send ships round the Pentland Firth solely for the Stornoway cargoes. The mill owners were concerned about the loss of service, fearing that if all the wool had to be carried by the *Lochdunvegan*, it would lead to a bottleneck at Kyle. Never missing a chance to complain about the island's shipping services, one Stornoway councillor commented, 'This puts Lewis on a par with places like Fair Isle, Yell and Foula, where services are being cut off'. The withdrawal of the service was also thought to have strengthened the case for a vehicle ferry to Ullapool.

In 1964, three years after the Coast Lines' service had been withdrawn, a survey was conducted in Lewis to consider the effects of the closure. The results indicated that Stornoway had been adversely affected, with eleven out of eighteen firms interviewed stating that their business had suffered and fourteen claiming transport costs had risen. There had been delays, with Stornoway Builders and General Services Ltd having bulk orders held up for over three weeks at Glasgow, while the tweed industry was concerned about what would happen if there were severe weather conditions during winter, and roads to the mainland ports would become blocked as they had been in 1961–2. Stornoway Seafoods Ltd had to obtain special containers to export scampi, and even the small shopkeepers were unhappy with the service they were now getting. There was no mention in the survey of any improvements.

The history of the services leading up to that operated by Coast Lines started well before the 1920s, going back as early as 1861, when the North of Scotland, Orkney & Shetland Steam Navigation Co. extended their service from Leith and Aberdeen to Wick along the coast to Stornoway. This service continued on an irregular basis for almost forty years. In 1895 a sailing was advertised from Leith and Aberdeen leaving every Monday during May and June, returning from Stornoway every Thursday evening. Messrs M Langlands & Sons took over the operation in the late 1890s.

In 1863 this company had commenced a bi-weekly service between Liverpool, Aberdeen, Dundee and Leith, with a call en route at Stornoway, using the steamer *Princess Royal*. With their black funnels with two white hoops the 'Langlands steamers' were a regular sight in Stornoway harbour for over half a century. In the 1880s the two ships on the run were the *Princess Beatrice* of 1874 and the *Princess Alice*, built in 1866. The former was wrecked in Nova Scotia in 1890. In 1894 the company had the *Princess Victoria* built in Dundee. As well as continuing the regular cargo service she also provided West Highland cruises from Liverpool. In 1899 the *Princess Ena* had the distinction of carrying the first car to Lewis. It was unloaded on 26 August, and driven round the principal streets of the town carrying a few prominent citizens and causing no little attention. The vehicle was brought to Lewis by a Mr W K Miller, who had taken a lease of the Soval Shootings that year. The *Princess Victoria* was joined in the provision of cruises in 1912 by a new *Princess Royal*, a steamer capable of carrying two hundred first class passengers. Unfortunately both these vessels were sunk during World War l, the *Princess Victoria* being torpedoed off the Mersey estuary in 1915. Langlands lost all their ships during the War, resulting in the cessation of their service. Coast Lines took over Messrs Langlands in 1918, and re-introduced the Stornoway service in 1925.

Coast Lines also took over the Antrim Iron Ore Co. Ltd in 1929. Under their management, the two ships of the Antrim Co. were re-named using Coast Lines' standard nomenclature with the suffix 'Coast'. The *Glentaise* became the *Antrim Coast*, and the *Glendun* was similarly renamed the *Aberdeen Coast*. These ships had operated between Belfast and Stockton, including a call at Stornoway. Up to 12 passengers were carried, and it is said that, when returning westward through the Pentland Firth, the passenger food bill was often significantly reduced! Both were withdrawn in the early 1930s, to be replaced by two modern twin-screw motor vessels with engines aft and accommodation for twelve passengers. These were the *British Coast* and the *Atlantic Coast*, both of which first appeared at Stornoway in 1935, when they were placed on a fortnightly service from Liverpool to Middlesbrough, with calls at Belfast, Aberdeen, Dundee, Leith and Newcastle as well as Stornoway. Coast Lines operated a large fleet of ships around the coasts of the British Isles, and it is not surprising to find a number of their ships visiting Stornoway throughout the years. The *Pembroke Coast* called regularly between 1936 and 1940, while the *Dorset Coast* and a new *Antrim Coast* also brought cargoes to Lewis before the Second World War. While all these were modern aft-engined motor coasters, typical of their time, the *Adriatic Coast*, built in 1949 was of a rather unusual design, being described in the *Stornoway Gazette* on her first visit as having 'three holds, three cranes and two bridges, a main one and a berthing one in front of the holds'.

A number of other shipping concerns operated cargo ships to Stornoway. The Stornoway Shipping Co. Ltd, based in that town, ran a cargo service to Glasgow from 1914. The company had been formed in direct response to a decision made by David

The *Antrim Coast*, one of Coast Lines' regular cargo boats serving Stornoway, lies beyond the *Loch Seaforth* at Stornoway in 1960. The storage sheds, since demolished, behind the cargo boat were known locally as the 'Coast Lines sheds'

MacBrayne to debar traders from having any claim against them for loss of, or damage to, goods in transit. This decision by MacBrayne may have been taken as a result of the impending First World War. Whatever the reason, the Stornoway traders found themselves at a potential disadvantage with regard to exporting goods from Lewis to the mainland. There may have been other reasons as well which prompted the Stornoway traders to investigate the possibility of setting up a shipping company, and at a meeting of the Merchants Association of Stornoway on 4 December 1913, it was proposed and accepted that a company be formed. It was initially entitled the Lewis Steam Navigation Company Ltd, but this name was later changed to the Stornoway Shipping Company. Each subscriber was required to guarantee to use the shipping service within one month of its commencement. To begin with, this service was to have been solely to Glasgow, but it was hoped to extend the sailings to other west coast ports on the promise of additional trade. Much of the trade was expected to consist of the harvest of the winter herring fleet; during the first three months of 1914, close on 17,000 barrels of cured herring had been shipped to the Clyde, many for trans-shipment to America, and most of the local curers and other traders had promised to support the company with their trade. No time was wasted in obtaining a suitable ship; this was the *Lady Tennant*, with a tonnage of 180 and built in 1904 for Nobel's Explosives Ltd. She was under the command of a Captain Robertson. Her arrival in Stornoway in May 1914 aroused great interest, and crowds visited the pier, initially on a Sunday, to view the steamer, and then the following day to watch the discharge of her cargo. During her service she had one narrow escape. While she was loading in the Kingston Dock in Glasgow, a warehouse went on fire, and it was feared that this would spread to the ship. Forttunately the steamer managed to get clear of the dock 'with only a slight scorching', and as most of her cargo had been put on board, only a few packages were destroyed. Two years later she was sold in part exchange to Messrs Langlands & Sons, being replaced by the steamer

Between 1913 and 1915 the Stornoway Shipping Co operated the *Lady Tennant*, seen here at Stornoway, on a cargo service between Lewis and mainland ports

Earnholm. She was built as early as 1874 to sail from Glasgow to Limerick and had then passed to the Aberdeen, Leith & Moray Firth Steam Shipping Co. in 1882. When this firm came under the ownership of Messrs Langlands in 1914, she passed into the latter's fleet. On being sold to the Stornoway Shipping Company, she was given a Board of Trade Cattle Carrying Certificate, and in addition another Board of Trade Certificate for 'an increased number of Deck Passengers, not exceeding 185'. It had been intended that as soon as possible the company's ship would carry passengers; this would explain the change of ship, for she had accommodation for thirty-one first-class and fourteen second-class passengers, presumably in addition to those carried on deck. The *Earnholm* commenced her duties on 10 March 1916, under a Captain Wilson, and carrying a crew of twenty. Her last sailing was on 18 March 1917, after which the company seems to have faded away, finally ceasing operations in 1921.

In the mid 1930s, the Point Steamship Co. Ltd extended their service to include Stornoway, using steamers named *Rubaan*, *Rumore* and *Rustoer* (*Ru* is a reduced form of the Gaelic *rudha*, meaning point or headland). The *Rumore* was lost in February 1938, at which time the company ceased their service.

Since the demise of regular cargo services, there continued to be a number of shipping companies whose vessels served Stornoway from time to time. It is mainly bulk cargoes, such as coal, oil and salt, which are carried by sea today, loads which cannot easily be transported by road, and are cheaper carried in bulk. R Cunningham (Scalpay) Ltd was one such company, using Dutch-built coasters such as the *Isle of Harris*, the *Isle of Lewis*, and the *Eilean Glas*. The Glenlight Shipping Co, using their diesel-engined 'super puffers' such as the *Glenshira* and the *Glenetive*, brought cargoes from Glasgow and other mainland ports. In 1987 they carried 4578 tons of cargo, including

The *Red Duchess* is typical of the cargo vessels which bring bulk cargoes such as coal to Lewis at the present day. In this picture she is being towed into Stornoway by the Coastguard tug, *Anglian Prince*, in December 2010, after breaking down in gales off the island of Rum

Oil is regularly delivered to Stornoway by the coastal tanker *Sarnia Liberty*, pictured here alongside No 2 pier at Stornoway

583 tons of coal and 700 tons of salt. This company ended their services in 1993, and since then coal and salt have been brought to the island by a variety of shipping companies, including J & G Gardner and Aasen Shipping of Norway. Their coaster *Aasheim* was a welcome visitor to Stornoway in January 2011, when she delivered a cargo of salt to keep the island's roads free during a severe winter. Coal has also been carried by the *Red Duchess*, owned by the Coast Lines Shipping Co. On one of her voyages, in November 2010, carrying 1500 tonnes of coal from Londonderry, she experienced the worst winter weather conditions that the Minch can produce, and in a Force 7 gale suffered an engine breakdown. She was drifting helplessly towards the island of Rum, but the Mallaig lifeboat managed to secure a line aboard her, and hold her in position until the tug *Anglian Prince*, stationed in the Minch for just such an event, was able to tow her to Stornoway, a journey taking twenty hours.

The other main bulk cargo required in Lewis is fuel oil. This is delivered approximately twice each month by coastal tankers such as the *Sarnia Liberty*, owned by Jamesco 750, of Guernsey, and chartered by James Fisher Everard.

Chapter 21

Cruising with Coast Lines

Mention has already been made of the service provided by the ships of Messrs M Langlands & Sons. In 1870 they introduced cruises from Liverpool and Ardrossan to the West Coast of Scotland, with calls at Stornoway using the steamer *Princess Royal*. The popularity of this service led to the introduction of the *Princess Victoria* in 1894, so successful that in her first season, 'the profit on the bar more than covered the expense of the ship.' She was followed by the *Princess Maud* in 1902, the *Princess Alberta* three years later, and the *Princess Royal* in 1912. The last mentioned ship could carry 200 passengers, although much of her first-class accommodation could be removed to provide extra cargo space in winter. Unfortunately, Langlands' cruises ceased with the onset of the First World War, and all the steamers became war losses. The success of the cruises operated by Messrs Langlands and the increasing number of tourists carried on their own ships must have prompted David MacBrayne to compete in the cruising market, as has been seen with the introduction of the *Chieftain* in 1907. However, events already described cut short her career. In 1931 David MacBrayne replaced the *Claymore* with the *Lochbroom* to operate their West Coast cruises. To increase the latter ship's passenger numbers some of the cargo space was converted to cabins, enabling the *Lochbroom* to carry up to eighty passengers on the round trips she made every ten days from Glasgow to West Coast ports, with occasional services extended to Stornoway. She, in turn, was replaced in 1937 by the *Lochgarry*, which was lost during the Second World War. MacBraynes' cruises stopped at the onset of the War, and were not reintroduced after 1945.

Before the First World War, Messrs Langlands' steamers provided cruises round the northern coast of Great Britain, including calls at Stornoway

Messrs Langlands were unable to resume cruising after the end of the First World War, but the tradition was continued by Coast Lines, which re-introduced ships specifically designated for cruising to the West Coast in 1922. However, the first post-war cruise to call at Stornoway was made by the *St Ninian*, belonging to the North of Scotland, Orkney and Shetland Shipping Co, which called on 17 June 1925 having sailed from Scrabster before continuing to Lerwick. This revived, if only on one occasion, the service which had been operated by that company as far back as the 1860s.

MacBraynes operated the *Lochbroom* on cruises in the early 1930s. She mainly visited West Coast ports but did make occasional calls at Stornoway

It was almost two years after 1925 before one of Coast Lines' cruise ships, the *Killarney*, called at Stornoway.The *Killarney* was possibly the best known of the inter-war cruise ships. When she first arrived on the West Coast in June 1927, the *Highland News* was prompted to write,

> the arrival of the s.y. *Killarney* ... recalled pleasant memories of pre-war days when Messrs Langlands' splendidly equipped steamers, with their courteous and efficient officers and men called regularly each week and helped materially in the social activities of the town. We were delighted to welcome old friends in Capt. Rendall, in charge of the *Killarney*, Mr Mara, superintendent steward of the Coast Line; Mr Bell, chief steward, and Mr Duncan Fletcher, quartermaster, all of the former Langlands, with its traditions for courtesy and the care and comfort of the passengers. These have now been carried into the yachting business of Coast Lines.

The *Killarney* was not a new vessel, having been built for service on the Irish Sea. She was launched in 1893 as the *Magic* for the Belfast Steamship Co, before being re-named *Classic* in 1919, after which she sailed intermittently for the City of Cork Steam Packet Co Ltd. In 1924 she was transferred to this company and given a third name, *Killarney*. For her cruising duties to many West Highland ports and anchorages, including Stornoway, she was painted with a grey hull and yellow funnels. The original fees charged for a seven day cruise varied from eight guineas (£8.40) for a berth in an inside cabin on the main deck to twelve guineas (£12.60) for an outside cabin on the promenade deck. By 1939 a two-berth cabin on the main deck cost seventeen guineas (£17.85), with a reduction of ten shillings for passengers joining at Ardrossan. The onset of the Second World War saw the end of these cruises, with the *Killarney* making her final visit to Stornoway in August 1939.

A postcard produced for passengers on Langlands' cruises shows a view of the quays at Stornoway, with a large crowd on the pier awaiting the arrival of a steamer. It is dated 1903

Coast Lines' cruise ship *Killarney* regularly sailed from Liverpool and Ardrossan up the West Coast to Stornoway during the 1930s. She is seen here arriving at Kyle of Lochalsh

After the Second World War, it was left to Coast Lines to maintain the tradition of west coast cruising, as the ships operated by David MacBrayne from Glasgow to Stornoway could now carry only a handful of passengers. The *Killarney* had survived the war, but it was not considered worthwhile to spend a large sum of money renovating her, so she was sold in 1947. Coast Lines introduced the *Lady Killarney* as a replacement in April of the same year, and she became as popular as her predecessor operating cruises from Liverpool and Ardrossan. She was not a new ship, having been built as long ago as 1912 as the *Patriotic* for the Belfast Steamship Co., thereafter being renamed *Lady Leinster*, and subsequently *Lady Connaught* by the British & Irish Steam Packet Co., under which names she ran between Liverpool and Dublin. She was refitted for cruising, and appeared for the first three seasons with a buff hull and yellow funnel, giving her the appearance characteristic of a 'cruise liner'. The hull was then altered to green, and then finally to black, most probably on practical grounds, and her funnel was painted in the Coast Lines colours of black with white chevron. In her early days, before the installation of hot water in the passenger cabins, and when wash basins had only cold water on tap, hot water would be brought by stewards carrying cans. She gained a clientele who returned year after year; so it was with these regular passengers' regrets that she was withdrawn in 1956.

A typical cruise in the early 1950s is delightfully described by Ellen Pickworth in her book *By Sea to the Isles*. From a start at Liverpool, more passengers were picked up at Ardrossan, from where the *Lady Killarney* continued with calls at Brodick and Tobermory, where the steamer was known as the 'Rainy Killarney', because it always seemed to rain when the steamer called, and the locals took in their washing when she appeared round the headland. From Tobermory, the cruise headed west to Lochboisdale, returning across the Minch to anchor off Stein, on the west coast of Skye, from where a visit to Dunvegan Castle was made. Re-crossing the Minch took the cruise into Stornoway, after which the steamer returned south making further calls at Gairloch, Poolewe, Lochinver, Sheildaig, Portree, and Kyle of Lochalsh. The steamer was due at the last-mentioned port by tea-time for a cricket match at Kyleakin, the *Lady Killarney* versus the local team. Continuing south, the final visit was to Oban before passengers returned to Ardrossan and Liverpool.

The *Lady Killarney* was small compared to cruising ships of the twenty-first century, and in spite of post-war austerity conditions, including rationing, standards on board were redolent of an earlier age. Ellen Pickworth describes the 'old world' atmosphere of the ship as she investigates the facilities on board:

> Conducted by a pleasant steward, we go below to our cabins. Our Cabin Steward appears and he takes our cases below for us. We view our cabin – and our baggage (seven cases) – and we wonder how we can possibly accommodate everything in the two drawers and the one hanging wardrobe. We go along to the lounge where we find another pleasant young steward in charge of a pile of gay travelling rugs. "May we borrow one please? We are one short." "Certainly madam," and he searches the passenger list for our name and registers the withdrawal in the allotted space.
>
> Then on a voyage of exploration of our floating hotel (we discover) a comfortable lounge with innumerable easy chairs, writing desks well stocked with notepapers and envelopes, and yes, very nice coloured postcards of the ship. We glance down into the dining-saloon, tables gay with flowers, stewards hurrying around laying for the first sitting of dinner at 6.30 pm. Then (we) pass on to the "Ship Inn." A colourful corner, gay with red leather chairs, chintzy curtains, a piano and a Bar.
>
> And so to dinner. Here comes the Steward with the gong (known colloquially on board as the Hash-Hammer). We cover our ears as he goes past, beating it loudly so that it is

> heard in every nook and corner of the ship. (In) the library there are several books we should like to read (and we borrow some from) the Lounge Steward. At 10.0 pm there is a welcome rattle of tea-cups as the two lounge stewards pass around leaving six or seven cups and saucers on each small table and a heaped plate of sandwiches as well. (It is morning) and again a pleasant rattle of tea cups. A tap at the door heralds a smiling stewardess who gives us a pleasant "Good morning" and a welcome cup of tea and a biscuit. Then for a wonderful sea-water bath.
>
> At 10.30 there is boat drill, so we don our life-jackets and proceed to our "stations". We line up and the Chief Officer inspects us, tightens up a few loose cords, and then proceeds to address us through a microphone. The next duty is to contact the Chief Steward and book our permanent seats in the dining saloon. So we surrender our ration books and go up on deck to enjoy the fresh air and sunshine.
>
> During the morning a volunteer from each table has become a member of the "Sports Committee" and, after a meeting in the card room has taken place, the programme has been drawn up, the lists are ready and pinned up on the notice board in the Main Hall. Shall we enter for Deck Quoits or Shuffle Board or both? And what about Deck Tennis?

On the seventh day:

> the afternoon is spent at sea – deck games in full swing. In mid-ocean we pass the strange looking Shiants, with their steep cliffs and rocky caves.
>
> And so to Stornoway, another lovely picture as we sail into the sheltered harbour, with the castle in its beautifully wooded precincts dominating the scene. We had not expected to see so many trees and are charmed with this first glimpse of the busy little port. The harbour is very busy: trawlers coming into the creek, where they berth alongside the jetty and proceed to unload their catch. The *Loch Dunvegan* (sic) is moored near to us and is unloading enormous bales of raw wool for the tweed factory.
>
> We shall see it all again tomorrow morning, but tonight there is a "Highland Ball" and we must go below and dress for dinner. It is still twilight when we go ashore and along the Waterfront where the Harris Pipe Band has already arrived. Then follows a wonderful evening of colour and movement and the stirring music of the Pipes. There is a Grand March to open the ball and some little girls in highland dress then give a dancing display: the Reel of Tulloch, the Sword dance, etc, etc. Some of our officers come ashore and soon they have the girls merrily whirling with the rest of the dancers. "Strip the Willow" and "Petronella" – nothing is too intricate for them, as their partners steer them safely through these strange dances. Strange to the Sassenach that is, but as natural as breathing to these merry Highlanders. There is a delicious Buffet supper, more dances, and then at 1 am "Auld Lang Syne" and "The Queen", and shortly we are wending our way through the quiet streets, on to the docks, up the gangway and stealthily along the corridor to our cabins, tired but happy. These people of Stornoway certainly know how to enjoy themselves.

As mentioned above, the *Lady Killarney* included Kyle of Lochalsh as one of her mainland ports of call on the return journey. The steamer would be due to arrive there by tea-time to allow a cricket match to take place, the *Lady Killarney* versus the local cricket team. The competition had been started in 1922, and was played for the Edward Cup, which had been donated that year by A Edward, of Kintail, in Ross-shire. A very rare card from 1952 provides a fascinating insight into this unusual event. In addition to details of the fixtures it gives a brief historical description, under the caption, 'These Notes will interest you.' It then describes how 'the Competiton commenced in 1922, first with the "The Tiger," (sic) then "Lady Louth," and finally "Killarney," until September 1939, when the Kyle pitch was built over for war purposes. Games recommenced at Kyleakin, Isle of Skye, in 1947, and a total of 98 matches have now been played, Kyle scoring 7205 runs, Passengers 5672.' Examples of high scores are then mentioned before the feat of one of the locals is described, 'J. Humphrey, Captain of the local team from 1920 to 1951, played in 84 matches, batted 74 times, 31 occasions not out, total 1546 runs, with an average of 40. He has now left for Inverness. The Directors kindly presented him with a framed coloured picture of the S.S. *Lady Killarney*.'

Finally it was written that 'Both teams will be out to give of their best on the occasion of the 100th game due to be played on 28th June.' The reverse of the card gives further information, stating that 'Players will cross to Skye by Ferry from Small Pier. Return fare is 10d (5p),' and asking players to 'Please avoid lofting Ball towards windows. Rather hit the ball into the water.' It is also interesting to note that the ship's purser would confirm the fixtures, of which there were seven over the season, while the captain of the local team was M Livingstone, Steamer Office, Kyle.

The final chapter in the Western Isles cruising story was the short-lived cruising programme commenced by British Railways in 1958, using the Heysham-Belfast steamer the *Duke of Lancaster*, which made a trial sailing to Stornoway in September 1959. As holiday tastes changed passenger numbers dwindled, and although cruises were operated which called at Stornoway at the beginning of each summer between 1960 and 1965 she did not return after that date. It would be a number of years before cruise liners would again grace Stornoway harbour.

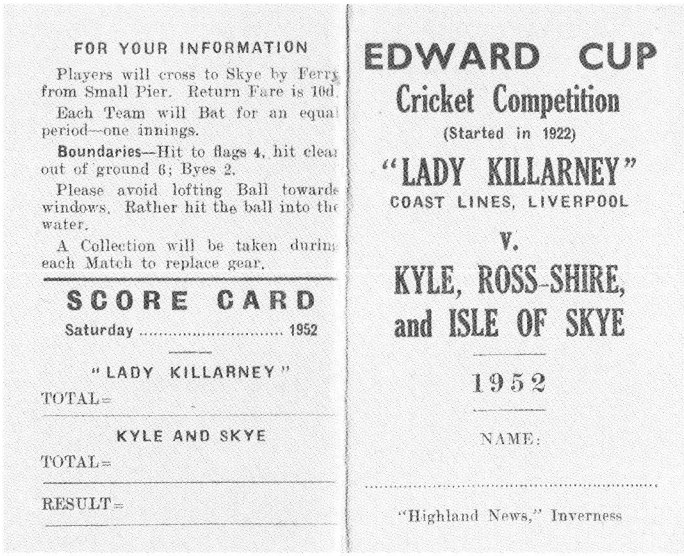

FOR YOUR INFORMATION

Players will cross to Skye by Ferry from Small Pier. Return Fare is 10d.

Each Team will Bat for an equal period—one innings.

Boundaries—Hit to flags 4, hit clear out of ground 6; Byes 2.

Please avoid lofting Ball towards windows. Rather hit the ball into the water.

A Collection will be taken during each Match to replace gear.

SCORE CARD

Saturday 1952

"LADY KILLARNEY"

TOTAL=

KYLE AND SKYE

TOTAL=

RESULT=

EDWARD CUP

Cricket Competition

(Started in 1922)

"LADY KILLARNEY"

COAST LINES, LIVERPOOL

V.

KYLE, ROSS-SHIRE, and ISLE OF SKYE

1952

NAME:

....

"Highland News," Inverness

After the Second World War, Coast Lines resumed their cruises using the *Lady Killarney*. She resumed the tradition, dating back to 1922, of her crew and passengers taking part in a cricket match against a team from Skye and Lochalsh when she called at Kyle of Lochalsh. This photograph shows a very rare example of a scorecard from one of these matches

In the 1960s the *Duke of Lancaster*, owned by British Railways, continued the tradition of cruising to Stornoway. She is seen here tied up at No. 1 Quay, dwarfing the *Lochdunvegan*

Chapter 22

The Car Ferry – 'It's Comin' Yet for a' That'

The first car ferries in the United Kingdom had been developed in the 1930s for service on the English Channel, and then, like ripples on a pond, spread northwards to the North Channel in 1939, to be followed by the introduction of three ferries, described as 'general purpose vessels', on the Clyde in 1954. Thanks to their success, the increase of car ownership in the 1950s, and the improvements made to roads in the Highlands and Islands resulting in ever-increasing amounts of goods being transported by road, it came as no surprise when, in 1960, C B Leith, managing director of MacBrayne's, announced plans for three new car ferries to serve the Western Isles. Two of these were to open up new short crossings, described as 'Marine Motorways', one linking Mallaig and Skye at Armadale, and the other creating a triangular service between Skye, North Uist and the Isle of Harris, thus opening up a new route to Lewis. The three ferries duly entered service in 1964.

Although the *Loch Seaforth* continued to operate the Stornoway mail service, the new ferries showed the way forward for Lewis. Sooner or later the *Loch Seaforth* would need to be replaced by a car ferry. As things turned out the change was a long and protracted one.

In 1960 there were encouraging signs for the advocates of a car ferry, when the Secretary of State for Scotland intimated that a subsidy or grant would be available for both pier facilities and a service. At the same time, it was acknowledged that the *Loch Seaforth* was 'completely inadequate' with regard to vehicle accommodation, with long waiting lists, and bookings having to be made 'weeks and even months in advance'. In December of that year, there was such strength of feeling against the mail steamer that a petition was sent to the Secretary of State for Scotland asking for a ferry to be established from Stornoway to Ullapool.

Stornoway Councillor Angus J MacLeod suggested that the Council should run the ferry. He had been in contact with MacBrayne's who stated that their preference was for the shorter crossing between Skye and Harris; Councillor MacLeod thought that this would not be the 'best thing for Stornoway'. The supporters of a ferry envisaged two possible types of vessel. One would have been 'a large transport ferry of the type used in the English Channel', of which several were thought to be laid up at the time. The other option was to use a tank landing craft. Both had disadvantages: the former would have proved extremely costly, while the latter would have been 'deficient in speed'. Whichever was to be adopted, it was considered that it would have to carry forty or fifty vehicles which could be driven aboard on an adjustable ramp, allowing loading and unloading at any state of the tide. It would carry cars, and lorries laden with fish products and tweed, which could proceed straight on to delivery points beyond Ullapool, the lorries returning with wool for the mills in Stornoway. It was thought that the ship would run full to capacity in summer, while there would be a steady trade in winter.

Provost Donald Stewart of Stornoway was clearly in favour, saying, 'It's a grand idea all right. I was in Ullapool in the summer and there were plenty of tourists with cars. If there had been a vessel offering them transportation to the Western Isles in an hour or two … they would have taken the chance'. He ended prophetically, 'There will be plenty of difficulties to overcome, but I feel that "it's comin' yet for a' that."' The Council, however, did not pursue this scheme any further when they heard that a 'certain business man' had plans for a ferry.

This mystery man turned out to be a Stornoway businessman, Charles Alexander, who was convinced that the future of island communications lay in a fast ferry service. He proposed to build a 1,400 ton ship, 240 feet (73m) in length, with a speed of seventeen knots, and capable of carrying forty to fifty cars or lorries and three hundred passengers. It would be a ship as large as, if not larger than, MacBrayne's vessels, similar to cross-Channel ferries, with passenger accommodation on the upper deck, and all the underdeck used for motor cars and 'motor vehicles with merchandise'. Sailings would be in daylight, but sleeping accommodation would be provided for long-distance lorry drivers. The crossing would take three hours and the ship would load and unload by means of a floating ramp, supported by containers of compressed air. Armed with this information, a delegation of Ross-shire County Councillors travelled to meet with the Secretary of State. It would appear that nothing came as a result of this meeting, and, in fact, over two years elapsed before anything more was heard.

In January 1963, Charles Alexander and a group of businessmen from Stornoway and elsewhere formed a company named Stornoway-Ullapool Ferries Ltd. The company had obtained an option to purchase a Danish car-ferry to operate between Stornoway and Ullapool. This was the *Isefjord*, a ship which could carry sixty vehicles, 360 passengers, and had thirty-two cabins. She was capable of making two round trips daily between the two ports. If the necessary harbour facilities were provided, then it was possible that the vessel could take up service on the run by the summer of that year. There were a number of reasons why there was no guarantee that these facilities would be in place. As yet, no official approach had been made to the Stornoway Pier and Harbour Commission for their provision. Even if it had been, it was doubtful if they would have been able to finance the development, unless Government assistance was made available. It was then pointed out that the Government had a financial interest in both the *Loch Seaforth* and the planned Skye and Harris ferries, with which the new ferry would be competing. The Pier and Harbour Commission were aware of the planning, and asked Stornoway-Ullapool Ferries Ltd to provide details of the ferry and the facilities it required, stating they could not procede without details, including the ship's size and draught. It was agreed to give the matter 'sympathetic consideration', as the Commission had already approved in principle a car ferry from Lewis to Ullapool. The scheme finally came to nothing when the Board of Trade did not pass the vessel as suitable for the service.

Undeterred, Mr Alexander then proceeded with plans to build a new ship, to be ready within a year, and using the existing quays at Stornoway at suitable states of the tide if roll-on/roll-off facilities were not ready. On a visit to Denmark he had been impressed by the vessel *Kattegat*, which operated on the Sound of the same name. He stated that the Kattegat Sound experienced similar conditions to the Minch, and its width was a similar distance to that between Stornoway and Ullapool. Six firms were invited to tender for the construction of this new vessel, which was to be on the same lines as the *Isefjord* but with less superstructure. 'It is the right kind of ferry for here,' said Mr Alexander. 'The cars will drive on to the boat through an opening in the bow and drive straight through ready to disembark at the stern. It will be able to take vehicles weighing up to forty tons and will hold ninety-three cars and 500 passengers.'

The new vessel, if it was to be built, would not be ready until the following summer, and Mr Alexander planned to charter a ship to open the service earlier. 'This ought to have been done fifty years ago,' he said,

> It has been the lack of quick transport that has been the ruin of Stornoway. If this ferry comes off, it should put the fishing trade back where it should be, on its feet. With its speed of sixteen to seventeen knots our boat will cross the Minch in two-and-a-half hours and lorries could be in Inverness with fish in a remarkably short time. For the loading and unloading of the ferry sixty-five foot ramps would have to be built at Stornoway and Ullapool.

It was clear that the proposed ferry meant more to Mr Alexander than a very profitable business venture. 'It's my life's ambition now to see her afloat,' he said.

Further weight was put behind the cause of the ferry by Provost Donald Stewart, when he suggested that its introduction would bring further benefits to crofters on the island. There would be cheaper winter fodder and the cost of transporting cattle to the mainland would also be less. The news in June 1963 that Coast Lines were to terminate their Stornoway service also strengthened the case for a ferry.

The next stage in the saga was the news that Stornoway-Ullapool Ferries Ltd had been offered another Danish ferry. It would be available to enter service in April 1964 at the 'very latest'. The vessel, of similar size to those already considered, could carry fifty-six cars and 300 passengers. She seemed to be 'the most promising so far', and, having been built as recently as 1961, the company considered that there would not be any problem in having her passed by the Board of Trade. Nothing further was heard of this venture, but in January 1964 an article in the *Stornoway Gazette* carrying the headline, 'Boat Bought for Ferry', reported that the service was to start as early as May. This time it was to be a German ship, only one year old, and currently operating in the Baltic Sea for a Swedish company. It could carry seventy cars and had accommodation for 600 passengers. With a crossing time of two-and-three-quarter hours, it was planned to make two or three return sailings per day as required. The vessel would be available in February, with the start of the service in May allowing for ramps to be constructed at both Ullapool and Stornoway. Things did not go according to plan, and when May arrived, no ferry was there to commence the new service. Instead, the press reported that the proposed ship had 'struck a few snags', and a vessel could not now be delivered before autumn at the earliest. Mr Alexander explained that, as this was not the best time to start a new service, it would probably begin in spring of the next year. It will never be known what might have happened if Ullapool-Stornoway Ferries Ltd had obtained their vessel, and ramps had been provided at Ullapool and Stornoway, for in 1965 Charles Alexander died suddenly, and the company was dissolved. He was never to see his cherished dream of a ferry vessel from Ullapool entering Stornoway harbour.

With all these delays, it came as no surprise that there was more dissatisfaction on the island, and rumours about a new service abounded. The Leith-based ship-owning firm of Salveson had to deny that they had a vessel earmarked for the ferry service, although they admitted that Stornoway-Ullapool Ferries Ltd had been in contact with them regarding provision of a ship, adding, 'We are nowhere near reaching a decision, for we have only really started looking at the project. We have given the project some consideration but we are still very much in the early days yet'. A totally different idea was proposed by the Sea Express Shipping Company of London, which aimed to provide a weekly cargo service from Stornoway, with a fortnightly sailing to Belfast. There was no mention of what type of vessel they proposed to used, and the scheme never came to fruition. Ross and Cromarty County Council was stung into action, stating that a ferry service was required for the Island of Lewis, particularly for commercial traffic. One councillor stated, 'The prime need is to have the fastest, most suitable ferry service available to the mainland'. Another added, 'Lewis needs a ferry service direct to the mainland, suitable for transporting all the commercial traffic of the island and tourists as well if need be.

It needs it now'. It is interesting how the emphasis was on the needs of industry, with the development of the tourist trade in Lewis still in its infancy. There was concern that the Uig-Tarbert service would be confirmed as serving the whole of the Long Island (Lewis and Harris), with the result that the 'true needs of the Isle of Lewis may never be met'. The question of which would be the most suitable mainland port to serve Lewis also arose at this time, with a number of places being considered. Gairloch and Poolewe were dismissed, leaving the choice between Ullapool and Kyle. The distance by road was considered to be virtually the same; the crossing to Ullapool would be about an hour quicker, while Kyle had the advantage of having a railway connection. The Lewis councillors were adamant that whichever port was chosen, it should be solely for the benefit of their island, stating, 'We must not use the people of Lewis to advantage Kyle or Ullapool or Gairloch or Railways, or any consideration whatsoever except the prime needs of the Island of Lewis to have the fastest, most suitable ferry service available to the mainland'.

1966 opened with a call for a faster ferry, leading to a resolution being passed by a combination of Stornoway Town Council and Lewis District Council that the *Loch Seaforth* be replaced by a fast drive-on/drive-off stern loading ferry to operate on the shortest route to the mainland, which was to be Ullapool. This was passed to the Secretary of State. Little more was heard until September, when yet another meeting was held to discuss the provision of a fast ferry, this time between the local authorities in Lewis and the Highland Transport Board. The debate dragged on into 1967, when a completely new idea was added to the discussion. When Peter Walker, the then Shadow Minister of Transport, visited Stornoway, he suggested that a hovercraft might be the answer to the island's transport problems. He claimed it would be 'fast and efficient', and could easily cover the distance across the Minch, citing as a comparable example a 'Swedish Company (which) had recently applied for a landing stage at Folkestone to run a hovercraft service to Sweden'. The local MacBrayne's manager, James MacLeod, replied that this was 'a possibility which might be achieved within the next ten years'. It was another scheme which quietly faded away.

Only a week later, a brake was put on the impetus for a new ferry when the Highland Transport Board suggested that it would be premature to remove the mail service from Kyle and Mallaig in favour of a 'major vehicle ferry plying direct from Stornoway to Ullapool or some other point on the mainland'. In their report on Highland Transport Services, it was stated that the *Loch Seaforth* still had ten years of service in her, and that the overland route through Skye and Harris might prove to be the most economic and efficient route to and from the Outer Hebrides. While accepting that the days of conventional passenger/cargo ships were numbered and that the future of sea transport to the islands lay with vehicle ferries, the report said that a number of considerations had to be taken into account. It acknowledged that there had been strong representations for the *Loch Seaforth* to be replaced immediately by a ferry, but considered such action would be hasty. It went on to state, 'It must be recognised that owing to the exposed nature of the waters which lie between Stornoway and the mainland, any such vessel would require to be of substantial size and therefore high capital cost, while the frequency of the service could not be great owing both to the distance and the likely volume of transport'.

Events progressed the following year. In February the Town Council again pressed for a fast ferry. Six months later came the first definite sign that a change might actually take place. Provost Donald Stewart announced to a meeting of councillors representing Stornoway, rural Lewis and the Loch Broom district, and members of the Ullapool Pier Trustees, that, following discussion with the General Manager of David MacBrayne, Mr C B Leith, the Company proposed initiating a service from Ullapool to Stornoway in 1969, using the *Loch Seaforth* to operate a twice-daily service. Considerable discussion ensued. There was general agreement that Ullapool should be the mainland terminal, although concern was expressed about the amount of available space on the pier. There was less agreement about using the ageing mail steamer. It was pointed out that the *Loch Seaforth* was twenty years old, and ex-Provost A J Mackenzie felt that 'if they agreed to using the *Loch Seaforth* it would be there permanently'. The Chairman of the Lewis District Council, Mr John Patterson, countered this by saying, 'I am quite confident that MacBrayne's are going to get rid of the *Loch Seaforth* as soon as possible', adding that a ferry would be cheaper to operate as it would have a smaller crew and would not require dockers. Other suggestions included asking to have one of the three planned car ferries operating on the route, and keeping the Kyle and Mallaig mail service, while the Ullapool route was introduced to ascertain which was the more popular and successful. There was concern as well that the *Loch Seaforth* might not generate enough traffic on the new route, which could jeopardise the chances of obtaining a new ferry. Councillor Sandy Matheson expressed the feelings of the majority that, 'Half a loaf is better than no loaf at all', and that if the opportunity was overlooked, then it would leave the islanders in a very bad position. It was decided finally to support the idea, with Ullapool being the favoured mainland port and the *Loch Seaforth* to operate the service until a new ferry became available.

Later in the year, Ross and Cromarty County Council also agreed on using Ullapool, but was not in favour of the *Loch Seaforth* being transferred to the service. Finally, during the last week of 1968, a proposal was announced by David MacBrayne stating that a new twice daily service would start to Ullapool. They stated that they might use the *Loch Seaforth*, stressing that the ship 'has the power and the ability, and that she could manage the crossing in three hours, allowing a daylight service to be operated. The Town Council in Stornoway immediately rejected this 'entirely', only to be encouraged a month later by the Highlands and Islands Development Board to back the transfer of the *Loch Seaforth* to Ullapool, declaring 'Get the right route and then go for the right ship'. The arguments continued: the Conservative candidate for the Western Isles and the Western Isles Crofters Union both came out against using Ullapool, while Lewis District Council agreed to push for any mainland terminal, including Aultbea, Kyle and Ullapool. Meantime David MacBrayne revealed that they might not transfer the *Loch Seaforth* to Ullapool. Towards the end of 1969 the Scottish Transport Group produced a report on proposals for developing ferry transport, and Ross and Cromarty County Councillors were annoyed that no mention was made of a ferry from Ullapool, and that traffic for Lewis would be encouraged to use the route through Harris.

Finally, the Scottish Transport Group gave an assurance that an early decision would be made regarding the ferry service to Lewis, and on 12 December 1969 Willie Ross, the Scottish Secretary, announced that he expected to receive detailed proposals about the Stornoway-mainland ferry from the STG within the next few weeks. The STG and the relevant local authorities met early in 1970, and a decision was taken that the mainland terminal would be Ullapool, but this was far from the end of the arguments. Colonel P M Thomas, the STG chairman, announced at the meeting that, if the Stornoway-Ullapool service came into being it would almost certainly mean that the *Lochdunvegan* would be phased out. Stornoway Town Council responded that she should remain as long as she was needed. Eventually, in April, David MacBrayne announced that that they intended to inaugurate a Stornoway-Ullapool service with the *Iona*, which was then under construction, and that Ullapool pier would be rebuilt to accommodate a vessel 250 feet in length and of 50 feet beam.

It might be thought that this would be the end of the matter, but there was to be a further plea to make Aultbea the mainland terminal, citing a route 11.6 nautical miles less than that to Ullapool and no congestion from fishing boats, while a group of island businessmen set up an Action Group to resist the phasing out of the *Lochdunvegan* and to retain Kyle as the mainland port. Finally, in December 1970 Stornoway Town Council agreed not to re-open the Ullapool question. Earlier in June the Scottish Transport Group had submitted its proposals for the Stornoway-Ullapool service, but it was not until after six months of consultation that in January 1971 they were at last formally approved by the Secretary of State. It was announced that there would be two daily crossings with a sailing time of three hours, and that the *Loch Seaforth* would be replaced by a ferry with a speed of no less than sixteen knots.

If it was to be thought now that all would be plain sailing, then events quickly proved this to be far from the case. Stornoway Town Council was not willing to approve the new timetables, unless they obtained certain written guarantees from the STG and David MacBrayne. Most of their concerns related to the suitability of the *Iona* for service on the Minch. It was considered that David MacBrayne was 'economising by replacing a worn out vessel with a new vessel not designed for our waters', this referring to the fact that, although the *Iona* had been designed for the Islay service, a lack of appropriate piers caused her to make her debut on the more sheltered waters of the Clyde. Councillor William Lucas went so far as to say, 'I have come to the conclusion that the *Iona* is nothing but a glorified version of a Clyde paddle steamer'. Another councillor, Baillie Albert Nicoll, announced that he 'had never been on the *Iona*, but all the reports he had heard about her had been adverse. We should have a newly built vessel for the job'. While his motion to reject the *Iona* was unsuccessful, the Council did agree to send a delegation to inspect the ship. The visit to the Clyde to study the new vessel was a partial success. The Town Council accepted the *Iona*, being satisfied with her loading and unloading capabilities, but they were still unhappy about the passenger accommodation. Baillie Nicoll summed up the position by saying the 'vessel needs alterations. *Iona* was a marvellously slick handler of vehicles and there was a degree of luxury in the bar and smoke-room', but there was a 'total lack of settees, no cubicles or cabins'.

Chapter 23

Roll-On Roll-Off

The *Iona* arrived to take up the Stornoway-Kyle-Mallaig service on 1 May 1972. She was the first drive-through roll-on roll-off ferry both to be built for David MacBrayne Ltd, and to serve the island of Lewis. She was not the first drive-on drive-off ferry to have been seen in Stornoway, for on 23 July 1969 the *Sound of Jura*, owned by Western Ferries, laid claim to that distinction when she called on her maiden voyage en route from her builders in Norway to her home port of Kennacraig. The *Iona* had been built by the Ailsa Shipbuilding Co. Ltd at Troon, and was launched on 22 January 1970 by Mrs P M Thomas, the wife of the Scottish Transport Group chairman. With a length of 230 feet (70m) and a breadth of 44 feet (13m), her dimensions were only slightly greater than those of the *Loch Seaforth*.

In appearance the two ships had little in common, apart from a red and black funnel, although in the case of the new ship this was a dummy, there being twin exhausts aft, painted white to appear part of the superstructure. The *Iona* had a high bow, incorporating a lifting visor and vehicle ramp, astern of which was a car-deck capable of carrying forty-seven cars and the height of two decks to allow commercial vehicles to be carried. This ran the length of the vessel, opening out at the stern on to a low open deck with a stern ramp. There was also a hoist with two side ramps, enabling her to operate at piers which did not have a linkspan. She was driven by two Paxman diesel engines with fixed pitch propellers, giving her a maximum speed of seventeen and a half knots, although her normal running speed was about a knot less. The propellers were driven by geared transmission rather than direct drive; unfortunately these gearboxes were to prove troublesome on a number of occasions. Compared to the *Loch Seaforth*, her passenger accommodation was somewhat limited. There was a full-width lounge, seating 101, on the boat deck, but small windows and the high bows made it difficult to justify the term observation lounge. Also on the boat deck, further aft, was a cafeteria which could seat ninety-seven. The bar and smoke-room were below the car deck, and no sleeping

A sign of things to come. Western Ferries' *Sound of Jura* became the first roll-on roll-off ferry at Stornoway when she called en route on her delivery voyage from Norway to the Clyde in July 1969

accommodation was provided. A criticism of the vessel was that open deck space was limited.

Because she had no sleeping accommodation, a new timetable involving only daylight sailings was introduced. This meant a departure from Stornoway at 0600, with Kyle being reached at 1000 and Mallaig at 1215. There was only a fifteen minute turn-around making it possible for the ferry to arrive in Stornoway at 1900. After only seven days on the service, the Stornoway Town Council changed its mind and rejected the new ferry. A number of reasons were put forward. These included a general dissatisfaction with the morning departure from Stornoway, which meant that some islanders had to make an extremely early start, and it was no longer possible to connect with the early trains to Glasgow. There were also complaints that the ship could carry only nine commercial vehicles, and that seven of the spaces were permanently booked by MacBrayne or other nationalised hauliers, leaving insufficient space for local companies. The standard of the passenger accommodation

The *Iona* leaving Stornoway (drawing by the author)

came in for more criticism, and it was proposed that there should be 'a comfortable lounge with armchairs and settees, similar to the *Loch Seaforth*', and that 'cubicles and suitable toilet facilities should be provided'. A rapid response was made within a week when two representatives of the Highlands and Islands Development Board gave an assurance that there would be a new vessel available within two years.

Only a month later, questions were being asked about the seaworthiness of the *Iona*, with comments being made that the ship 'will not be able to travel in a gale' and she 'would spend half the winter in port'. The situation was not helped when the *Iona* broke down, for the second time in three months, with gearbox failure, and traffic had to be diverted via Tarbert. The Town Council became so incensed that they wrote a letter about the problem to the Prime Minister, Edward Heath. In August it was hinted that a rebuilt *Clansman* might become available to be used on the service, and this was confirmed in December when details of the alterations were announced. The *Clansman* was one of the three original car ferries built by Hall Russell at Aberdeen for David MacBrayne in 1964. She had operated mainly on the Skye ferry route between Mallaig and Armadale, and also to Lochboisdale and Castlebay. She had visited Stornoway on a number of occasions, as she was the vessel used to relieve the *Loch Seaforth*. The vessel had also been used as a winter relief ship on the Pentland Firth crossing between Scrabster and Stromness, and in addition her travels had taken her as far as London as an exhibition ship. She was originally 220 feet (67m) in length, and this was increased by an additional thirty-eight. Her passenger accommodation was raised five and a half feet to create more headroom on the vehicle deck. Stern and bow ramps were fitted, while the hoist and side ramps were removed. The alterations gave her a rather unbalanced appearance, although the extra length did create a new open deck for passengers. Twin rudders were fitted, and the engines were adapted for control from the bridge. No new engines were fitted, and this resulted

In 1973 the *Clansman* was lengthened and converted to become a drive-through ship. She is seen here in dry-dock on the Clyde undergoing the final stages of her conversion

in the *Clansman* becoming slightly underpowered and therefore lacking in the required speed.

In 1971 Government grants and loans allowed the relevant authorities to proceed with the provision of a suitable pier extension at Ullapool and linkspans both there and at Stornoway, to be operational early in 1973. The linkspan at Ullapool was ready for operation towards the end of March, but completion of the one at Stornoway was delayed, partly due to bad weather and also as the result a trawler colliding with the construction work. It had been intended that the *Clansman* would open the service from Ullapool, but an almost farcical series of events resulted in the honour of operating the first service to Stornoway from Ullapool since 1885 falling to the *Iona*. Had the *Clansman* been ready in April as scheduled she would not have been able to operate the service, as she now had no hoist and thus could not load in Stornoway. As it turned out, the alterations fell behind schedule and she missed this deadline. The *Iona* therefore made the first crossing from Ullapool on 26 March, using her hoist and side ramps at Stornoway. Mr W M Little, deputy chairman and managing director of the Scottish Transport Group, informed the press that, 'Unfortunately, because of the delay with the terminal, we are unable to provide, from the start, the true roll-on roll-off service which was our aim,' adding that, 'The matter will be even better when the *Clansman* … becomes available to take over from the *Iona*.' Two sailings each day were operated, leaving Stornoway at 0530 and 1300 and returning from Ullapool at 0915 and 1700, with a crossing time of three hours.

Finally, work on the linkspan at Stornoway was completed, and a true drive-on drive-off service could be offered. The *Clansman* was still in dry dock, and therefore the *Iona* continued to provide the service, inaugurating the Stornoway linkspan on 23 May, almost two months after the facility was available at the mainland terminal. The Provost of Stornoway was on the quay to welcome the first car to drive off the *Iona*, in recognition of the importance of the new facilities to the people and the economy of the island. Somewhat surprisingly, the *Stornoway Gazette* was very low-key about the new service, devoting only a small space on its front page to the event. It simply stated that the new service was 'inaugurated by the *Iona* which made her last crossing to Kyle the previous Saturday,' that 'the vessel carried 31 commercial vehicles and 30 private cars on the first day,' and that bookings were being received at a 'pretty fast rate.' Describing the initial crossing, Mr J Macleod, the local manager, said, 'There were little teething troubles which were overcome and the vessel is expected to be in good time today.' After only three and a half weeks, the Stornoway linkspan broke down, and for three days the *Iona* reverted to using her hoist. It was providential that the arrival of the *Clansman* had been delayed.

With the drive-on facilities repaired by 17 June, it might have been thought that normal service would have been resumed and indeed so it was, but only for the next five days. The *Iona* was by now in poor health, and broke down on the twenty-second. For the next few days she operated the service on one engine, managing a speed of ten knots, and with her runs bearing no relation to the timetable. Finally her crankshaft broke, and she was tied up alongside the pier at Stornoway. The *Columba*, a sister ship to the *Clansman*, but in her original condition, was drafted in from Mallaig to relieve the build-up of traffic. This she did, although progress was slow, as she had to use her hoist to load and unload. After two days she was needed elsewhere, and so for a couple of days there was no ferry. Eventually, on the thirtieth, the *Clansman* arrived around lunchtime, and it was assumed she would be able to operate the afternoon sailing. As she approached Stornoway, however, she collided with the *Iona* as the latter lay alongside the pier for repairs. This caused a further delay, and it was not until late in the afternoon that the *Clansman* eventually sailed on her first crossing to Ullapool. Even this crossing was not without its problems, for she developed an electrical fault, further delaying traffic. On her return to Stornoway late on the Saturday evening, she had difficulty in berthing at Stornoway and then experienced a serious problem with her bow visor. The outcome was that the vehicles on board were not able to drive ashore until quarter to eight on the Sunday morning. The third sister side-loading ferry, the *Hebrides*, was brought from Tarbert that day, and both ships operated Sunday runs to clear the backlog of traffic.

After this inauspicious start, the *Clansman* settled down to operating the daily double crossing between Ullapool and Stornoway. One advantage over the *Iona*, with her lack of sleeping accommodation, was the cabins which had been retained on the *Clansman* during her conversion. This meant that passengers from the rural districts of Lewis did not have to start their journeys at an extremely early hour in the morning, but could board the ferry in Stornoway the evening before, sleep overnight, and wake up to breakfast as the ship made her way into Loch Broom.

The *Iona*, no longer required at Stornoway, moved to Oban where she operated the service to Castlebay and Lochboisdale, before finally taking up the run for which she had originally been intended, from Kennacraig to Port Ellen and Port Askaig on Islay. Her final duty for Caledonian MacBrayne, as the company had now become, brought her back in 1997 to Mallaig to operate the Skye ferry to Armadale. She was then sold to Pentland Ferries to provide a service across the Pentland Firth to Orkney, being renamed *Pentalina B*. She spent the next four years laid up, before this route was initiated. She made three very brief returns to the west coast. The first was in April 1998 when Caledonian MacBrayne chartered her to operate the Oban-Craignure service, when the *Isle of Lewis* broke down, and the *Isle of Mull* was sent to cover the Stornoway-Ullapool sailings. Her second visit will be mentioned later, while on the final occasion she returned in April 2009 to cover for the *Isle of Arran* between Kennacraig, Port Askaig and Oban.

The *Clansman* was not going to be a long-term solution for the Stornoway service. Her lack of speed, described on one occasion as 'pathetic', was a constant problem, and she was beset by a number of mechanical problems. In spite of this, at a reception held on board, Col. P M Thomas of the Scottish Transport Group described the ship as 'The Best in the West', with a 'carrying potential of 400 tons per day compared with 50/60 tons daily with the *Seaforth* and 600 tons weekly with the *Dunvegan*'. He also described the passenger capacity as 'ample on any voyage summer or winter'. Despite this glowing praise and a plea to 'give the ferry a fair chance', complaints about the service continued. The situation was not helped when the *Clansman* broke down on 28 July with generator trouble. What ensued was described as 'a week of chaos and frustration'. Passengers were stranded at both terminals; no replacement vessel was

The *Clansman* framed by the linkspan on No. 1 pier as she approaches Stornoway

provided initially, but a few days later the *Lochdunvegan* took cars to Ullapool, while foot passengers were taken by coach to Tarbert, and then by ferry to Skye. Not surprisingly, this resulted in strong protests coming from various people. Ian Horne, the Western Isles Tourist Officer, hit out, saying, 'Many tourists have expressed annoyance at the "couldn't-care-less" attitude of those in authority … it is for the Secretary of State for Scotland to … use all his powers to expedite emergency actions to relieve this situation.' After a special meeting, Stornoway Provost Sandy Matheson signed a telegram from the Council to protest to the Secretary of State, insisting that 'the present situation is no longer (an) operational matter for the company,' and demanding 'that you … supply (an) immediate vessel to take over the Stornoway-Ullapool run … even to the extent of using the Royal Navy.'

By September the situation was described as 'beyond a joke', and the STG was asked to make an application to the Secretary of State to make £2 million available for a suitable vessel. It was also considered in Lewis that Western Ferries should be approached to provide a twice-weekly service to Kyle. The situation reached a head in January 1974, when the *Clansman* was mentioned in a debate in the House of Commons about shipping services to the islands. It was at this time that it was announced that the decision had been made to place an order for a new custom-built ferry. Caledonian MacBrayne therefore started to look around for a replacement vessel. A Norwegian ferry, the *Basto V*, less than one year old, was for sale. The reason for this was that the local authority who owned the pier from where she would operate was slow in enlarging the facility, a problem not unknown to Caledonian MacBrayne. It appeared that the vessel would be suitable for service on the Minch, but on close inspection it was discovered that her design, for service on the more sheltered waters of the Oslofjord, would not meet the standards required for British shipping. There was, however, an identical ferry under construction at the shipyard of Moss Rosenberg Vaerft A/S in Norway. The vessel was purchased on the stocks, and the design was suitably altered to meet the standards required.

The new ship arrived at Gourock in August 1974, having been given the name *Suilven*. This was a new name for the fleet, but it was an appropriate one, Suilven being the name of an iconic mountain near Lochinver, part of the distinctive profile of the hills north of Ullapool, which can be seen when crossing the Minch. With a length of 284 feet (86.5m) and a breadth of 51 feet (15.5m), she was not significantly larger than her predecessor, but her carrying capacity was almost double. She could carry 120 cars and 500 passengers at a working speed of just less than sixteen knots. Power was supplied by two Wichman 7AX diesel engines, and she was fitted with two bow propellers. She was described as having two complete decks; the lower car deck was fitted with 'hoistable car platforms', or mezzanine decks, while the deck above contained cafeteria, saloon, hall and toilets. Six four-berth cabins were provided on the bridge deck.

The *Suilven* made a 'show the flag' tour of west coast ports before arriving at Stornoway on 29 August. It had been planned that her first duty would be to sail to Ullapool the following morning with only invited guests on board, but she was immediately pressed into service to carry stranded passengers and vehicles to Ullapool, the result of the *Clansman* breaking down with piston trouble and failing to make the mid-day crossing. The 'invitation trip' took place the next day as planned, with Caledonian MacBrayne 'taking the bull by the horns' by showing off their new ship to previously critical members of the local Councils, the Stornoway Chamber of Commerce and local businessmen. They appear to have been suitably impressed, for there were few negative comments about the *Suilven*, although some people considered that, for all her qualities, she lacked the character of the older ships. John M Macleod, in an article 'Remembering the *Seaforth*', wrote:

> Today we can wander out of the *Suilven's* fuggy plastic cafeteria, and take a polystyrene cup of grey coffee for a walk round her oily metal decks. She is far more modern than any of the mailboats, of course; her crew enjoy better facilities than their forbears ever did, and she is fitted with all of the state of the art technology now deemed essential to West Highland operation – bowthrust units, sonar, autopilot, variable pitch propellers, bridge-controlled engines. The islands and its drivers have never had a better service from this efficient, reliable, hi-tech and utterly boring ship.

The *Suilven* quickly settled down on the run for the next twenty years, although some of these years were not without their problems and troubles.

After the arrival of the new vessel, the *Clansman* was used on a variety of other services, principally running between Ardossan and Brodick, before being sold in 1984 to Torbay Seaways for a service to the Channel Islands. This deployment did not take place, and she was sold in the same year to Mira Shipping Line Ltd of Malta, where she was renamed *Tamira*, and operated as a ferry between Malta and Gozo. A further change of ownership, still in Malta, led to another name, *Al Hussein*. She was last mentioned in Lloyd's Register in 1995, now named *Al Rasheed*, and was later abandoned off the coast of Sudan.

At the end of 1974, the pier at Ullapool needed updating and there were fears that this would interrupt the *Suilven*'s schedules. There was even speculation that Oban might be used as the mainland terminal while major repairs were carried out. Oban was the nearest mainland port with a linkspan, which would have meant a journey time of between twelve and fourteen

The *Suilven* operated the ferry service between 1974 and 1995 when she was replaced by the *Isle of Lewis*. The two ferries are seen here at No. 1 Pier, the latter dressed overall to announce her new arrival

The *Suilven* arriving at Stornoway on her last crossing from Ullapool in 1995, before being sold for service in New Zealand

hours. Fortunately, it was decided that it would be possible to continue using Ullapool, while the repairs were completed and the necessary extension to the pier was made.

In April 1975 the *Suilven*'s seaworthiness was put to the test when she took five hours to cross the Minch, having to cope with a northerly wind gusting to gale force, and with blinding snow and hail showers. 'All we could do,' said one passenger, 'was clutch the person next to us as the ship rolled and plunged. It was terrifying. Crockery smashing, clanging from down below, probably from the car deck, furniture shifting around. We were told over the loudspeaker to stay where we were, but we couldn't have moved even if we had wanted to.' There were some injuries, fortunately none serious, to some of the passengers, while the officers and crew were commended on accomplishing the crossing. A comment at the time suggested that the *Suilven* was an 'ideal ship for a cruise up a Norwegian fjord, but not up the Minch'. The following year it was the *Clansman*, relieving the *Suilven*, which experienced stormy conditions. In one week in January, she sailed on the Monday to Ullapool, but could not berth and had to return to Stornoway. Weather conditions forced her to remain tied up all Tuesday, while on Wednesday she sailed, waited in Loch Broom in vain for conditions to improve, and then returned across the Minch sixteen hours after leaving Stornoway. Other incidents included the *Suilven* breaking down in July 1984; the *Hebrides* was drafted in from Tarbert on a Saturday night to carry out a Sunday sailing to clear the traffic. Five years later, it was the linkspan at Stornoway which broke and on this occasion, again a Saturday, the *Suilven* had to divert to Tarbert eventually to unload sixty-one cars and three lorries in the early hours of the Sunday morning.

The success of the *Suilven* on the crossing led to an ever-increasing amount of traffic. As early as 1982, she had to leave 140 passengers and a number of cars at Ullapool at Easter weekend. She became fully booked on an increasing number of occasions, and when she was relieved by the smaller *Isle of Arran* in 1986, there were more complaints about lack of space. In 1989 it was announced that plans were being made to introduce two extra night sailings each week in the following year's summer timetable, leaving Stornoway at 2130 and returning from Ullapool at 0130 to cope with the traffic, as it was thought that these runs would be used principally by commercial vehicles. When the National Mod was held in Stornoway in October of the same year, the *Suilven* and the *Isle of Mull* changed places, with the former vessel operating between Oban and Craignure. This reflected the fact that the *Isle of Mull* could carry almost twice the number of passengers. The accommodation on this vessel was looked on favourably by passengers, and when a replacement for the *Suilven* started to be considered, similar facilities were wanted for the new vessel.

That was one of the few times when the ferry diverted from her normal run. One other occasion took place earlier, in 1977, bringing back memories of the excursions of many years ago. The ship was chartered by the Stornoway Round Table for a cruise to mark the fiftieth anniversary of that organisation. Described as a 'novel Hebridean adventure, the like of which has not been seen in Stornoway for many a long year,' it was planned that the *Suilven* would make a short voyage on the east coast of the island, anchoring in Broad Bay, at which point a dance would be held on the car deck. As events turned out, the vessel left Stornoway around 1930, and after sailing to Tiumpan Head, made for Loch Shell, eventually arriving back around 0030.

The first call for a replacement ship came in 1988, when the Stornoway Pier and Harbour Commission asked for a new fast ferry for the crossing, arguing that 'the *Suilven* had not been built for the Stornoway run but had been built for service in the Norwegian fjords'. The response from Caledonian MacBrayne was that there would be no new ferry before 1993 at the earliest, and that it would be unlikely that a two-hour crossing would be possible, as fuel costs would 'go through the roof'. Colin Paterson, the Managing Director, stated, 'There is nothing wrong with the operation of the *Suilven* to justify changing it early'. Within a year, however, Caledonian MacBrayne was backing a replacement, as the *Suilven* was now working to capacity, and there were fears that she would not cope the following year. At the end of 1989, the Scottish Development Department confirmed that there would be no new ferry before 1994, but, perhaps spurred on by the *Suilven* suffering further engine trouble in the summer of 1992, the Scottish Secretary announced that funding was to be made available for a new ferry, with an initial capital grant of £10.5 million which would possibly increase to £16 million. Caledonian MacBrayne finally placed an order for a new ferry with Ferguson Bros of Port Glasgow in 1993.

Chapter 24

The *Isle of Lewis*

While the new ship was under construction, she was known simply as number 608. When she was launched on 18 April 1995 by HRH Princess Alexandra, she was given the name *Isle of Lewis*. Nearly 1,000 people came to watch her slide into the Clyde, five weeks ahead of schedule. Colin Paterson, Managing Director of Caledonian MacBrayne, announced, 'The *Isle of Lewis* will be a great boost to tourism in the Western Isles, and more importantly provide a faster, luxury service for those who live in the islands'. Over the next three months, fitting out took place, and she ran her sea trials, her two Mirlees Blackstone K6 Major engines producing a speed of nineteen knots. She then sailed north, testing the berthing facilities at Uig, Lochmaddy and Tarbert en route, before arriving at Stornoway on 27 July. A crowd of over 2,000 gathered on the quayside to watch the new ferry enter the harbour, accompanied by a flotilla of small vessels. It had been intended to have a new linkspan and berth for her, but this was not ready and she had to use the existing facilities. There was some embarrassment when her bow door could not meet the linkspan, but this was shrugged off as 'teething troubles'.

The *Isle of Lewis* under construction at Ferguson's shipyard on the Clyde

It had originally been the intention that the inaugural crossing of the *Isle of Lewis* over the Minch would be for 350 invited guests, and this she undertook on Friday 28 July 1995. As she made her way up Loch Broom, she passed the *Suilven* making her penultimate trip to Stornoway, and the coming changeover was heralded by loud blasts on the ships' horns. On the return trip from Ullapool, the guests were joined by about fifty passengers and their vehicles; they had expected to cross on the *Suilven* but had been left as she was fully loaded. All were treated during the crossing to music by members of the Lewis and Harris Accordion and Fiddle Club, who gave a repeat performance exactly a decade later to celebrate the tenth anniversary of the *Isle of Lewis* on the service.

The basic statistics of the *Isle of Lewis* read as follows: a length of 331 feet (101m), a beam of 61 feet (18.5m) and a draught of fourteen feet (4.2m), with a gross tonnage of 6753. She could carry 123 cars, with two mezzanine decks, and 680 passengers, making her the largest vessel yet to serve Stornoway. Her service speed of eighteen knots enabled her to make the crossing to Ullapool in two and a half hours, and it was pointed out that she could 'go almost as fast backwards as the *Suilven* could forwards'. The increase in her breadth compared to her predecessor meant that her stern ramp had to be offset to port to allow her to use the linkspan at Ullapool. These bare facts do little to give an impression of both her size and the facilities provided for passengers. In flowing hyperbolic terms, the journalist Fred Silver painted a picture of the luxury hinted at earlier. He 'wandered in a daze from lounge to lounge, lingered in the long, wide corridors, paced out the restaurant to see how many football pitches could fit in, and, whenever possible, gasped with amazement'. He went on to describe how 'guests waded through plush carpets, passed the TV lounge, the children's play area and the special dog corner – complete with tiled floor and drain. (They) suffered exhaustion and agoraphobia crossing the entrance lobby'.

There were some who doubted the ship's capabilities, with comments being made; such as 'She's ugly compared to the *Suilven*' and 'She's too high out of the water', while 'some ungrateful soul could be heard warning against high winds on the higher-sided ship'. Colin Paterson insisted such criticism was 'completely misplaced as the ship has been extensively and scientifically tested'.

With the arrival of the new ferry, the *Suilven* was put up for sale. It was considered unlikely that she would see further service in the United Kingdom as her safety standards were

The launch of the *Isle of Lewis* on 18 April 1995

Crowds throng No. 1 pier at Stornoway to gain a first glimpse of the *Isle of Lewis* in July 1995. A fleet of small vessels had surrounded her as she entered the harbour

The *Isle of Lewis* shows her sea-going qualities in heavy seas when on trials of Tiumpan Head

now out of date. This proved to be the case, for after she made her last crossing of the Minch, just days before her twenty-first birthday, she was sold to the Straits Shipping Co. of New Zealand, to operate as a cattle carrier between Wellington and Nelson. After leaving Scotland from Troon, she passed through the Panama Canal and en route to Auckland protested at Mururoa where the French were carrying out nuclear tests. The Stornoway Gazette reported that 'French helicopters were hovering above wondering where on earth this vessel came from.' From Auckland she made her way to Wellington. On the day after she arrived Strait Shipping had a promotional day; more than 500 visited the ship, including a significant number of expatriot Lewis people. The following day she commenced her new role, a four hour journey across the notorious waters of the Cook Strait. On this route she became a minor celebrity, when she was photographed in sea conditions far worse than anything she would have experienced in Scottish waters. In 2004 she was again sold, to Bligh Water Shipping of Fiji, where she operated an inter-island passenger service under the name Suilven Shipping, this name being painted in large lettering on

In New Zealand the Calmac lion on the funnel of *Suilven* was replaced by a happy smile

her hull sides. Finally in 2012 she was advertised to be sold for scrap, the broker in charge of the sail explaining she had 'simply reached the end of her useful life'.

The *Isle of Lewis* made her first scheduled crossing on 31 July 1995, and settled into a routine of two crossings per day in winter and either two or three during the summer season. For the first few weeks, there were a number of teething troubles. The main problem was the incompatibility between the ship's bow ramp and the Stornoway linkspan, which resulted in delays of up to two and a half hours. With the opening of the new terminal in May 1997, this issue was resolved. A second concern was a series of loud bangs when the ship was hit by strong waves; this aroused considerable alarm amongst passengers, causing rumour to spread about the safety and seaworthiness of the ship. The problem was solved by removing eight feet of fendering on either side of the vessel's bows.

With these minor problems resolved, the *Isle of Lewis* now provided a virtually incident-free service, and in fact it was relief vessels which made the news over the next few years. In 1996 there were complaints about empty shelves in the shops in Stornoway, as the *Isle of Mull* could not carry all the lorry traffic. In February 2002 the *Clansman*, the new ferry built in 1998 for the Outer Isles service from Oban, grounded on Seid Rocks when she was leaving Stornoway. It was stated that the vessel was 'swinging too slowly, south of the safe track', and she went aground close to an unlit beacon. She was immediately manoeuvred into safer water and checks were made to ascertain if she was taking in any water. This task was made more difficult as vehicles on the car deck blocked access to sounding pipes in the void spaces below. There was no serious hull damage, and the *Clansman* was able to proceed to Ullapool. The following day divers examined her hull and found 'scrape marks and indentations' on the starboard side. Less than a month later, it was reported that the *Isle of Arran* was involved in a 'near collision' with the Coastguard tug *Anglian Prince*. The weather had been poor and visibility limited, but there had been 'no real danger'. The *Isle of Lewis* was involved in an accident in March 2003, when she hit the pier at Ullapool while docking, resulting in a hole in her stern. Vehicles had to be unloaded through the bow door, after which the ship proceeded

The *Isle of Lewis* may be the largest vessel to serve Stornoway but here, in August 1997, she is dwarfed by two cruise liners visiting Stornoway, the *Aegean* and the *Sea Bourn Pride*

to Aberdeen for repairs, with the *Clansman* being brought in for the five days she was absent.

With the development of tourism, vehicle traffic steadily increased, and there was growing dissatisfaction over the amount of space occupied by commercial vehicles on the *Isle of Lewis* at the expense of visitors' cars. This problem might have been alleviated to some extent by the attempts of rival concerns to operate freight-only services, but as will be considered later, none of these became established on a permanent basis. By 2001 the situation was such that Caledonian MacBrayne decided to operate a freight service in addition to the existing timetable. The *Isle of Arran*, a smaller ferry built in 1983, was brought to Stornoway, immediately causing speculation that she was to replace the *Isle of Lewis*, but any fears were soon quelled by an announcement that she was there merely for berthing trials and as a relief vessel. In September of that year, the *Isle of Arran* returned to start up a freight service, with the *Lord of the Isles* replacing her for five days in November. Unfortunately, neither ship could convey all the lorry traffic. To solve this problem the *Isle of Lewis* was switched to the overnight freight service, with the other two ferries operating the *Isle of Lewis*'s schedule. The lack of speed of the smaller ships meant that the passage time between Stornoway and Ullapool was now three-and-a-half hours, resulting, not unexpectedly, in numerous complaints. A typical comment was that these older vessels 'set the island's service back years'. CalMac was sympathetic, stating 'it's not ideal, it's temporary'. In February 2002 it was announced that the *Isle of Lewis* would return to her daytime duties, and a new freight ship would replace the *Isle of Arran*.

The new vessel arrived in the form of the *Hascosay*. She was chartered from NorthLink Ferries, and appeared at Stornoway with the light blue hull of that line. She had been built in Norway in 1971, and could carry 65 trailers and twelve passengers. In September 2002, she in turn was replaced by the *Muirneag*. This vessel had been launched in 1973 for a Danish company under the name *Mercantile Carrier*. In 1985 she had been purchased

In 2002 the *Hascosay* was chartered from Northlink Ferries to operate the overnight freight service, replacing the *Isle of Arran* which had been operating the run

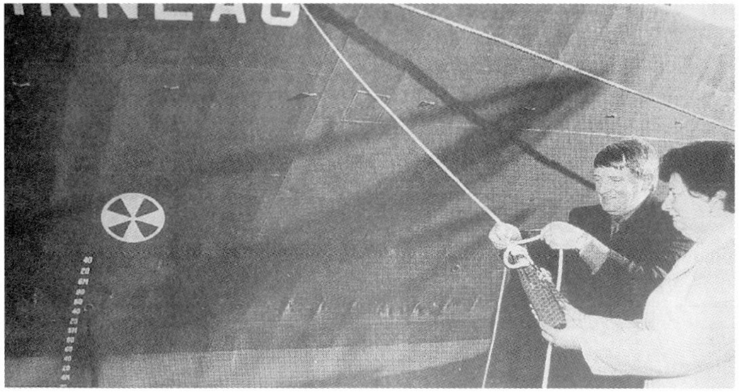

The freight ferry *Muirneag* is officially 'launched' by Mrs Morag Macdonald, wife of the Council Convenor

by P & O Ferries to operate their service between Belfast and Ardrossan. She was renamed *Belard*, reflecting the two ports she served. During the 1990s, she sailed to the Netherlands, and then on various routes including those to the Isle of Man and to Orkney and Shetland. In 2002 she had been purchased by Harrisons (Clyde) to operate for Caledonian MacBrayne. She was given the name *Muirneag*, after a hill in Lewis. Unlike the rest of the ships in the fleet, she has always had her hull painted blue. She was officially 'launched' on the service on 10 October, when Mrs Morag Macdonald, wife of the Council Convener, smashed the 'traditional bottle' against her hull at Stornoway. Before long, however, she was 'causing concern', and with a number of crossings being cancelled, was being referred to as the 'Olympic Flame', because 'she never goes out'.

This piece of 'CalMac bashing' was exaggerated, for she made crossings in conditions which were far from benign. These included the sailing from Ullapool on 11 November 2005, which took fifteen hours in winds of over 80 mph and waves of fifteen metres in height. The press described how there were 'scenes of chaos on board the vessel as it veered miles off course', and that 'cars slammed about the deck, crashing into other vehicles', while 'freight was catapulted off trailers and oil and cargoes of fish farm food were spilled'. One passenger was quoted as saying, 'I really believed I was going to die', while another 'wrote a farewell letter to his wife and children believing he would never see them again'. As a result, local hauliers called for the ferry to be withdrawn, and the Vice-Convener of the Western Isles Council raised questions about the vessel's reliability, but CalMac insisted the vessel had exceeded reliability targets and had no plans to replace her, claiming in addition that there were no other suitable ships to charter.

In spite of all the adverse comments about the *Muirneag*, she would appear to have been involved in only a few other incidents. One of these was when she ran aground in Stornoway harbour in July 2008. The crew managed to refloat her, but it was necessary for her to go to Aberdeen to be repaired. While she was away, her duties were covered by the *Isle of Lewis*. On a second occasion, in November and December of the same year, Stornowegians could have been led to think they had been transported back

In July 2008 the *Muirneag* went aground in Stornoway harbour while attempting to berth. Here she lies on the shore of the Castle grounds, attended by the Stornoway lifeboat

The *Iona*, now renamed *Pentalina B* and owned by Pentland Ferries, returned to her old haunts in November and December 2008 when she was chartered to relieve the *Muirneag*

to the 1970s, when they saw what appeared to be the *Iona* tied up at the linkspan on No. 1 quay. It was indeed the same ship, in her new guise as *Pentalina B*, chartered for several days from Pentland Ferries to relieve the *Muirneag*. When she arrived at Stornoway, her first sailing was not, as would have been expected, to Ullapool, but instead she crossed to Uig on Skye, as the former port's linkspan was then under repair.

Thus, since the start of the twenty-first century, the shipping services to Stornoway have operated on a settled basis, with all regular services running to one mainland terminal at Ullapool and the same two vessels, the *Isle of Lewis* and the *Muirneag*, carrying out these duties. The only other CalMac ships to visit Stornoway are those which relieve the two regular ferries, such as the *Lord of the Isles* for the latter, and the *Clansman* which covers the passenger services when the *Isle of Lewis* is away. There have been visits by two former Caledonian MacBrayne ships, both under new ownership. The *Hebridean Princess* was formerly the *Columba*, the third of the original car ferries built in the 1960s. In 1989 she was sold to Hebridean Island Cruises, and refitted at Great Yarmouth. Now capable of carrying fifty passengers in luxury accommodation, she makes regular cruises around the Hebrides with Stornoway being one of her calls. In 2006 HM Queen Elizabeth chartered the ship as part of her eightieth birthday celebrations, with the voyage terminating at Stornoway. The other vessel was the *Waverley*, now owned by Waverley Excursions Ltd, and promoted as the last sea-going paddle steamer in the world. She dates back to 1947, when she was built to operate on the Clyde, for most of these years being owned by the Caledonian Steam packet Co. Ltd. In 1973 ownership passed to Caledonian MacBrayne Ltd before she was sold for a nominal sum to her present owners. As part of her annual cruising programme, she regularly includes some west coast ports. In May 1989, Stornoway was included as a port of call, and she made two cruises from there. A morning cruise was organised mainly for about 600 schoolchildren from all parts of the island, who boarded the ship for a four-and-a-half

The cruise ship *Hebridean Princess*, formerly MacBrayne's car ferry *Columba*, visits Stornoway from time to time during her cruising season on the West Coast. Normally she would berth at No. 1 pier, but on this occasion in 2010 she lies alongside No. 3 pier with the *Isle of Lewis*, showing how the ferries have increased in size since the 1960s

hour trip to the Shiant Islands. In the evening, a similar-sized crowd boarded the steamer for a trip along the coast of Lewis to Loch Erisort. Local musicians, singers, dancers and a piper on board added to the occasion. The following year she returned to take about 800 passengers to Tarbert and back, followed by an evening cruise to the Shiant Islands which attracted about 600. After a gap of five years a third visit was made, but this time only about 250 passengers boarded for a cruise to the Shiant Islands. It must be assumed that the venture north was no longer viable, and the *Waverley* has not since returned.

During recent years, a number of minor adjustments have been made to the timetable. With the arrival of the *Muirneag*, it was no longer necessary for the *Isle of Lewis* to make night-time sailings, but increased traffic led to three sailings rather than two on certain days. In 2009 the ferry switched to using Intermediate Fuel Oil to reduce her 'carbon footprint', with Caledonian MacBrayne announcing that the 'change of fuel had been in the pipeline for a considerable time'. The ship now fuelled

The paddle-steamer *Waverley* passes Arnish Lighthouse on one of her cruises from Stornoway in 1989

at Ullapool, and this required a slightly longer turnaround time. In 2010 the company responded to demands for a later evening sailing on Saturdays from Ullapool, allowing island people longer time in Inverness, and benefiting sports teams visiting the mainland. A year later, turn-around times were extended again to cope with ever-increasing traffic, resulting in sailings starting earlier and finishing later.

The biggest change to the sailings came in 2009, when Sunday crossings were introduced. It had long been a tradition that no shipping services in the Western Isles took place on a Sunday. In the days of the mail steamer, there was no sailing from Stornoway on a Saturday night, and no return trip from the mainland the following day. Before World War Two, the steamer did depart at 2300 on Sunday nights, this being deemed a 'work of necessity'. During the war, as has been mentioned earlier, the departure time was put back until after midnight. In 1945, after the cessation of hostilities, Stornoway Town Council voted to return to the pre-war Sunday timetable. This went against the wishes of some Sabbatarians, but the decision was finalised when David MacBrayne Ltd announced that it was 'not practicable for them to alter the sailing hour of the *Lochness* on Sunday nights when the pre-war timetable (was) resumed'. Several years later, the departure time was moved back until after midnight, as it was now possible to arrive in Kyle of Lochalsh to connect with the morning train. From time to time, the question of operating Sunday sailings reappeared, and by 2006 Lewis was the only major Hebridean island with a six-day service. In 2001, a report for the Western Isles Council by the Fisher Group included Sunday sailings amongst their proposals, while a campaign for a seven-day service was also set up on the island. In 2002 Sunday flights commenced operating to Stornoway, adding to the pressure for Sunday sailings. In 2008, after the *Isle of Lewis* had made a Sunday crossing to clear a backlog of traffic, CalMac stressed that they were not proposing to establish 'official' Sunday sailings. Little more was heard for almost a year, when in March 2009 CalMac stated they would make no decision for three years. However, less than a month later there was speculation that CalMac would give the go-ahead for a Sunday service within the near future, although the Company remained 'tight-lipped'. In early July a CalMac spokesman then announced that a decision had not been made, but he 'did not rule out a crossing on July 19'. This, in fact, did become the date of the first Sunday sailing from Lewis, in spite of protests from the anti-Sunday ferry lobby, and a single Sunday crossing has operated since. Its success can be measured by the numbers using the Sunday crossing between the first sailing and 18 October 2009: an average of 253 passengers and seventy-eight vehicles were carried on each crossing. Fifty years ago, it would have been unheard of to cross the Minch on a Sunday, but the sight of the *Isle of Lewis* departing and arriving at the ferry terminal on that day has now become an accepted part of island life.

This cartoon appeared in the Stornoway Gazette in 1945 when there was dispute concerning the sailing time of the *Lochness* on Sunday nights. It was equally relevant – other than the ship's name – in the first decade of the twenty-first century, when plans for Sunday sailings were proposed and inaugurated

Chapter 25

The Rivals

The names of David MacBrayne and Caledonian MacBrayne have been almost synonymous with shipping to Stornoway, but, as has been seen, various attempts have been made over the years to break the monopoly. Since the coming of car ferries, a number of companies have planned to attract freight traffic away from the established operator. Some of the schemes were on a more solid foundation than others. In 1974 Mr A A Cunningham of Scalpay announced that he was setting up a new company to be known as Outer Isles Containers. It was to be a three-way partnership between Cunningham, Western Ferries and Marine Development Ltd of Glasgow. It was planned to provide and run a suitable container ship, possibly between West Loch Tarbert and Lewis, and operating on a weekly basis. No more was heard of this scheme. A proposal the next year suggesting that Messrs Fred Olsen would be willing to run a ferry service also went no further.

The next scheme appeared in March 1982, when Seabridge Marine of Oban planned to start a service between Stornoway, Oban, Islay and Larne, with three sailings per week. They considered that it would be 'viable and advantageous'. A roll-on roll-off ferry would operate the service, capable of carrying 400 passengers, and with overnight accommodation, a restaurant, a bar lounge and a children's playroom. The crossing from Lewis to Oban would take nine hours, and with a departure time of 0830 from Stornoway the ship would arrive at Oban about 1730, allowing Glasgow to be reached by 2100. The service was to start in May, but again it did not materialise. The same year an item in the *Stornoway Gazette* aroused the interests of a large number of people. A company called Landlink, described as a wholly owned subsidiary of the National Maritime Transport Group, was to introduce a hovercraft service between Mallaig and Stornoway, cutting the travelling time across the Minch by almost two-thirds. It was to be a passenger service with three return trips on Mondays, Wednesdays and Fridays and would create a 'new vital link'. The article explained that it was hoped to provide a vehicle service, but the craft would not be able to carry the weight. When it was found that the name of the hovercraft was to be *Maid of Ayr* and that the date of the article was 1 April, all hopes of this development were speedily dashed.

A more serious competitor appeared towards the end of 1986 with the announcement that Barra Shipping, a company based in Aberdeen, planned to operate a car ferry between Stornoway and Ullapool in competition with the *Suilven*. The company was considering a new ferry, or else it would convert the *Barra Supporter*, one of its two oil supply vessels, into a ferry capable of taking twelve forty-foot container vehicles. After it was discovered that a berth could not be guaranteed at Ullapool, the company stated they would investigate using Kyle of Lochalsh as a mainland terminal. Once again the scheme never got off the ground, and CalMac had the crossing to themselves for another three years, when the announcement was made that a Greek company planned to start a Stornoway-Ullapool freight service. A P & A Shipping and Trading of London intended to use a 1,159 tonne roll-on roll-off ferry, capable of carrying eighteen to twenty lorries, and making six sailings a week. Again, there

The first of several short-lived competitors for commercial vehicle traffic in the 1990s was the *Highland Carrier*, owned by the Streamline Shipping Co.

were difficulties in obtaining suitable berthing facilities, but the company claimed they were going 'full steam ahead'. Nothing was heard for four months, after which prospects appeared to be fading. A P & A withdrew their interest, but were replaced by another Greek company, Pegasus Ocean Services. Only a month later, the *Stornoway Gazette* printed the headline 'Greek Ferry Unlikely', and that was the last that was heard of that scheme.

It was not until 1998 that the next opposition appeared, and this time a service actually started. Highland Haulage, an Inverness based road haulage company, acquired the *Highland Carrier* and introduced her on a service from Kyle and Ullapool to Stornoway. She had been built by Ube Dockyard in Japan in 1981 as the *Leichhardt*, becoming the *Trinity Bay* in 1998. As such she traded between Cairns and Thursday Island on the Australian Coast. She was 177 feet (54m) in length and fitted with a twenty-five tonne crane and a stern ramp. After being refitted at Hull she was painted in Scotline colours and arrived in Kyle on 7 November, sailing for Stornoway the following day. It was planned that she would carry a mixture of containers and pallets, including fish farm equipment and containers for the Co-operative supermarket in Stornoway. Trailers were also carried, being loaded and unloaded using the ship's crane. She was scheduled to leave Kyle at 0200 and take seven hours on the crossing to Stornoway.

Not quite roll-on roll-off! A trailer is unloaded at Stornoway from the *Highland Carrier* using her own crane

The service was discontinued one year later, but before then further opposition to CalMac appeared. Only months after the arrival of the *Highland Carrier* came news that another freight service was to start up. It was announced that Aberdeen based Streamline Shipping proposed to open a new service between Ullapool and Stornoway. Little information was forthcoming; the company would not comment on the service, nor confirm that they had contracts with island hauliers, nor that their vessel was to be a 1,500 tonne, 233 feet (71m) long, roll-on roll-off ferry, capable of carrying twenty articulated lorries. Then in March 2001, the Norwegian registered *White Sea* appeared. She was a 7,000 tonne vessel which had space for twenty-eight lorries on her main deck and a further fourteen on a lower deck, with a lounge, cafeteria and cabins for drivers. She was to be operated by Taygran Shipping Ltd, and had been chartered for four months, after which another vessel would take over. The *White Sea* had the appearance of a typical modern cargo vessel, with engines and accommodation aft, but had a large ramp at the stern indicating her function as a ferry. She was not ideally suited for the service and at times had difficulties docking at Stornoway.

It appeared that this time the rival company was operating on a firmer basis, agreements having been made with a number of local haulage companies to use their service, and claiming that the ferry was taking 60% of the freight traffic. CalMac reported that the number of commercial vehicles they had carried in June that year was 555, compared to just over 1,000 in the same month the previous year. They did not appear to be too concerned, stating the 'opposition do not appear to have any back-up in the event of mechanical breakdown or weather disruption', always a problem with a 'one ship' company.

In May the company announced that it had purchased a replacement ship, a faster passenger and car ferry. This was the *Taygran Trader*, a vessel built in 1975 for Townsend Car Ferries Ltd, and originally named *European Trader*. As well as operating on the English Channel, she saw service on the Irish Sea before arriving in Stornoway. She started on the service on 15 June, but only as a freight carrier. The service did not run as

The second rival, the *White Sea*, had problems berthing at Stornoway. Here she has been driven against No. 3 pier while attempting to tie up at No. 1

The third, and last, of the rivals, the *Taygran Trader*, operated between Stornoway and Ullapool for a few months before being withdrawn in 2001

smoothly as Taygran Trading would have liked; some sailings were cancelled due to mechanical problems, and the ship was not fast. It was pointed out that on one occasion the *Taygran Trader* left Ullapool ninety minutes before the *Isle of Lewis*, but traffic on the latter vessel had landed at Stornoway first, meaning much later deliveries to supermarkets. Worse was to come: early in August a writ was issued by the Stornoway Pier and Harbour Commission to the sum of £52,260 for non-payment of harbour dues. This meant that sailings were discontinued until payment was made, with the ship tied up in Stornoway. Meantime local haulage companies returned to using the *Isle of Lewis*, increasing Taygran's financial problems. The debt was duly paid, and the ship was able to sail again. When she left Stornoway, however, it was not to Ullapool but to Aberdeen, where it was thought that she was to be refitted for carrying passengers. Graham Thomson, owner of the vessel, announced, 'The *Taygran Trader* will be back! We never went away', but this did not happen. Taygran Shipping went into receivership, with the *Taygran Trader* detained at Leith. She was later sold to an Egyptian company, El Salam Maritime, and renamed *Lina Trader*, finally being scrapped in India in 2006. Since then there has been no more opposition, and Stornoway has been served from Ullapool solely by the *Isle of Lewis* and the *Muirneag*.

Epilogue

Looking Back, Looking Forward

It would be interesting to consider what the reactions of the first travellers to Stornoway by steamship would be, if they were to cross the Minch today. In just under two hundred years, both the journey and the ships making the passage have altered almost out of recognition. In the early nineteenth century, conditions would have meant a somewhat haphazard voyage based on a timetable measured in days rather than hours. Travel was an adventure, and there would have been relatively few 'comings and goings' from and to Lewis. The steamer would have been slow and not especially reliable, and would have provided the minimum of comforts. Black smoke from coal-fired boilers would have snaked out from a tall funnel while paddle wheels thrashed the water. Over the years, improvements were made to the means of propulsion, journey times and standards of accommodation. Today a ferry over 100 metres in length and towering above the quayside loads cars and lorries through bow or stern doors while passengers settle into a comfortable observation lounge or restaurant. Complaints are muttered if the departure is minutes late, as people expect the crossing, taking less than three hours, to operate to its schedule. There is still smoke from the funnels, but it is from environmentally-friendly oil-fired diesel engines.

The ships may have changed almost out of recognition, but a number of other aspects have remained almost constant, while certain 'themes' have occurred and recurred in a cyclical manner. The name 'MacBrayne' has become synonymous with West Highland shipping, services to Stornoway having been provided since the mid nineteenth century by a company either with a MacBrayne at the helm or in the name. In 1851 David MacBrayne became a partner in David Hutcheson & Co., changing the name to David MacBrayne in 1879. When his son became chairman in 1905, the title was altered to David MacBrayne Ltd. Twenty-three years later, the company withdrew from the mail contract, but a new company, David MacBrayne (1928) Ltd, was set up to maintain the service, with the name reverting to David MacBrayne Ltd in 1935. In 1969 the state-owned Scottish Transport Group took over operations, and in 1973 the MacBrayne fleet was merged with that of the Caledonian Steam Packet Co. Ltd to form Caledonian MacBrayne Ltd, with this last company often being known simply as CalMac.

The inhabitants of Lewis would have found life much harder had the company not managed to continue serving the island under its various guises. Whether from Glasgow or the north-west mainland, the service was a lifeline, carrying essential foodstuffs and general cargoes as well as passengers, including many emigrating, leaving the island for work on the mainland, or returning on holiday. Yet there would have been few occasions when the service was profitable, especially during winter months, and from the earliest days the services were promoted to encourage tourists, either for cruises or to visit Lewis. Evidence of the importance of tourists can be seen in the timetables provided over the years, which have included details of cruises offered, and of tourist attractions and accommodation on the island, as well as the basic departure and arrival times.

Steamers carrying tourists also brought trade to the inhabitants of Stornoway. For example, Donald Maciver, owner of a drapery shop on Bayhead Street in Stornoway, boosted his trade by sending 'small boys down to the quay when the ... *Clansman*, *Claymore*, and *Chieftain* of MacBrayne's, and the *Princess Maud*, *Princess Olga* and *Princess Beatrice* of M Langlands and Sons, called with tourists to sell them lengths of Harris Tweed'.

Even with the added income from tourists, the service was not profitable and ways had to be found to maintain the island's lifeline. In the last decade of the nineteenth century, David MacBrayne tried to solve the problem by purchasing older, second-hand steamers. Unreliability and unsuitability led to an unsatisfactory service, with complaints reaching as far as Westminster. The situation could not continue and eventually a new ship appeared, the *Sheila*. The First World War, its aftermath and the economic depression of the 1920s also took their toll on the Stornoway service and David MacBrayne Ltd as a whole. The resulting takeover in 1928 has already been mentioned, and since then the company has relied on government subsidies.

It is not surprising, therefore, that there has been little competition to provide a service to Stornoway. For many years, there was no opposition, but during the latter part of the twentieth century, when roll-on roll-off ferries were being introduced and developed, there were a number of attempts to provide an alternative and 'better' service. As has been seen, they either did not materialise or, if a new vessel did appear, it did not last long. This can be accounted for by a combination of a lack of subsidy and the difficulties of operating a 'one-ship' company.

Many of the ships serving Stornoway spent many years on the same run, becoming as familiar as the name MacBrayne. The first *Clansman* was a regular visitor to Stornoway for thirty-nine years, and the *Claymore* for forty. The *Sheila*, the *Lochness* and the *Loch Seaforth* all operated the mail service for over twenty years, and more recently the *Iona*, the *Suilven* and the *Isle of Lewis* have each spent more than a decade on the service. These ships became part of the landscape of Stornoway harbour, and were a part of the islanders' lives. The long-serving captains and the crews, to a great extent comprising Lewismen, were also a part of the role played by the steamers in the life of the island. In his tribute to the MacBrayne Centenary, Hector McNeil, then Secretary of State for Scotland, wrote, 'Much of (the) progress is due to the men who have manned the ships. We do well to remember the skill of the officers and crews of the MacBrayne fleets, many of them colourful characters, and as such remembered with affection'. Today the relationship between passengers and the masters and crews of the vessels is not as close as it was in the days of Captain Cameron of the *Sheila* or Captain John Smith of the *Loch Seaforth*. This may be because the ferries now have more than one master, or because the crews are less visible as a result of fully enclosed bridges, and crew accommodation is more private.

The islanders also considered, and still do, that with regard to communication with the mainland, they have a right to the best – the best ships and the best possible service available. On many occasions, local councillors and others have had no hesitation in expressing their dissatisfaction with existing services, when they have not reached the expected standards, or in putting forward their ideas of what the next improvements should be. Their cases have always been for bigger, better and more comfortable vessels, and a faster service.

The arrival of a new vessel has always been greeted with announcements, from both MacBrayne management and local dignitaries, extolling the virtues of the accommodation, speed and other attributes of the new ship. Usually this is accompanied by the remarks of a few detractors, who would accept nothing less than their ideal. The cycle from new to old would then work its way through, over the years, as demonstrated by the comment made in 1995, when the new ferry first arrived at Stornoway that 'of course, like anything new, the *Isle of Lewis* will become commonplace'. Then, with a ship becoming older, her facilities dated, and her engines slowing and becoming less reliable, the knives would come out, and what had once been praised as 'state of the art' would now be dismissed as unsuitable. In 1970, as the mail steamer neared the end of her days, a councillor stated that 'a vigorous, developing community must not be dependent on an old, superannuated tub like the *Loch Seaforth*'.

At the present time, the 'ship cycle' is coming to the end of another round. The *Isle of Lewis* is now seventeen years old, and although she is still providing a satisfactory service, it will not be too long before the growing crescendo of complaints will surely be heard. The *Muirneag*, which has always had her detractors, will require to be replaced by 2013 on account of her 'age and the costs of sustaining an ageing vessel'. In 2007 a report was prepared for the Western Isles Council by the Fisher Group, and one of its conclusions was that the *Isle of Lewis* and the *Muirneag* were 'no longer acceptable'. It proposed three possible options for the future. These were to replace the existing ships with two new vessels, or with one larger ferry, or to keep the *Isle of Lewis* and supplement her sailings with a fast ferry in summer which would cross in one-and-a-half hours. They suggested that a fast ferry could be available in two or three years, while it would take six or seven years to provide new traditional ferries. The Western Isles Council decided that they should then look at new and innovative ways of delivering the ferry service. In 2008 there were calls for a trial service using a catamaran. The use of such a craft had been proposed previously, but the reaction from CalMac had been lukewarm; 'they were not going to buy (one) in for the sake of buying (one) in'. It was at this time that Pentland Ferries had commenced operating a catamaran on their service across the Pentland Firth to Orkney, and Councillors met with Andrew Banks, the owner of Pentland Ferries, to consider a

The unusual sight of four Calmac ferries at Stornoway on 16 November 2004. From left to right, the *Muirneag*, the *Isle of Arran*, the *Clansman* and the *Isle of Lewis*. The ship at the linkspan is the Coastguard tug, the *Anglian Prince*

trial. He considered that a catamaran the size of the *Isle of Lewis* would be able to operate in waves of up to four metres in height, and would be 'faster, use half the fuel, and require half the staff' of the existing ferry.

The *Stornoway Gazette* reported in April 2010 that 'a new ferry to replace MV *Isle of Lewis* and MV *Muirneag* … could be on the horizon. The Scottish Government is fully aware of the importance of the Stornoway-Ullapool route to the Western Isles communities and is considering options for improving ferry links on the route. A decision will be taken in due course'. When pressed for a timescale, the spokesman added, 'Our position on timing is due course (sic)'. The Scottish Government did confirm that they were looking at options for 'improving transport links' between Ullapool and Stornoway. At the same time, a campaign to 'Replace the MV *Isle of Lewis*' was established, claiming that the ferry had been plagued with problems and frequently cancelled, and comparing her unfavourably with her predecessor, the *Suilven*. A petition to CalMac was also being considered.

Three months later, the *Stornoway Gazette* gave brief details of what was being proposed. The new ferry would replace the two existing ships; she would be 525 feet (160m) long, and be 'more powerful and more manoeuvrable' than the *Isle of Lewis*. She would be 'powered by diesel-electric engines to improve reliability', while 'the proposed new design would remove the need for a central core in the car deck', allowing her to carry 'twenty more articulated lorries or about sixty extra cars'. The commissioning of the new ferry would be the 'number one priority' of the Scottish Ferries Review. It was also mentioned that the pier at Ullapool would be extended to accommodate the new ferry.

Further details of the new ship were announced in March 2011 by Guy Platten, chief executive of Caledonian Maritime Assets Ltd. It was generally accepted that having two ferries plying their way across the Minch would provide a much better timetable for locals and tourists alike, as well as allowing travel at more convenient times. Under the 'extremely challenging financial climate', however, a single large vessel, 25% larger than the present one, and capable of doing four crossings a day was the best compromise. The option was there of adding a second vessel should this be dictated by demand. The recommendation which would then go to the Scottish Government was for a 380 feet (116m) ferry to meet predicted capacity levels until 2025. It would be a Euro Class B passenger/vehicle ferry powered by four diesel electric engines, allowing an optimum speed of nineteen knots which would reduce crossing times by fifteen minutes. The vessel, of 1530 tonnes, would be capable of carrying up to 153 cars, 20 lorries and 600 passengers. The ferry would be highly manoeuvrable and stable, being fitted with a pair of fin stabilisers, two bow thrusters and two azimuth thrusters that revolve through 360 degrees. It had been estimated that the ship would save £750,000 per annum on fuel compared to the combined consumption of the *Isle of Lewis* and the *Muirneag*, due to fuel-efficient engines and advanced hull form. Three daily crossings were planned, with freight normally accommodated on an overnight crossing, while a fourth sailing could be added during peak periods.

No further information appeared for over a year. The *Stornoway Gazette* of 7 June 2012 reported an 'urgent need for (a) new ferry' and that there were 'huge concerns about the lack of movement on plans for the new ferry'. A report to be considered at the Comhairle's Transportation and Infrastructure Committee the following week stated 'it is of considerable concern that there has been no apparent progress in announcing plans for a replacement of MV *Isle of Lewis* and MV *Muirneag*'.

Only a week later, the Scottish Government announced that a £41.8m ferry was to be commissioned. The announcement confirmed that the new ship would be similar to what had been previously mentioned, but with capacity for 700 passengers. She would be designed to be much more energy-efficient and more

The 'Stornoway fleet' in October 2012: the *Muirneag* lies alongside No 1 pier while the *Isle of Lewis* arrives from Ullapool

The shape of the future: an artist's impression of the new ferry to be delivered in 2014

reliable in bad weather than the *Isle of Lewis*, capable of berthing in a 40 knot wind, and able to operate at her full service speed on only one engine, using electric generators to maintain power. Her hull form was designed with a moderate bow flare and without the chine-type body of her predecessor, thus reducing the amount of 'slamming' in heavy seas.

A German shipyard, Flensburger Schiffbau-Gesellschaft MBH & Co. (FSG), was chosen to build the ferry. This company beat off forty-seven other yards for the tender, their bid being the most economically advantageous in terms of cost, quality, delivery, operating costs and emission reductions, having exceeded the technical specifications. The ship is due to be launched in March 2014, and delivered in June, before entering service in mid-July the same year. The *Isle of Lewis* would be kept as a stand-by vessel 'until the foreseeable future and until users are satisfied with the reliability and resilience of the new vessel and its operation'.

A number of problems required to be addressed before the arrival of the new ferry. While the facilities at Stornoway could cope with the new ferry in 2014, an extension of the pier at Ullapool would be required but this would be completed before her arrival. A second concern which required to be addressed was a gap of nine months between the removal of the *Muirneag* in 2013 and the arrival of the new ship. Towards the end of 2012 it was rumoured that this gap would be filled by the *Isle of Arran*. In December of the same year the *Arrow*, a ro-ro freight ferry, larger than the *Muirneag*, owned by Seatruck, called at Stornoway to try out her suitability to berth stern-to at the linkspans, having already tested the facilities at Uig.

A CalMac spokesman said:

> We are considering a number of options for the replacement of the MV *Muirneag* when she comes out of service in October next year, one of which is the MV *Arrow*.
>
> The opportunity to carry out trial berthings in Stornoway presented itself recently and we felt it prudent to take advantage of the this while she was in the area, however nothing has been ruled in or ruled out at this stage and we are continuing to investigate all options.

Thus the story does not end. The people of Stornoway and the Isle of Lewis will continue to be dependent on a ferry service to the mainland, and tourists will travel in increasing numbers to the island. For the foreseeable future, it would appear that this essential link will continue to be provided by Caledonian MacBrayne, with a new ferry which may well come to be another integral part of the landscapes and lives of Ullapool, the Minch and Stornoway.

Some Poetic and Personal Perspectives

Inspiration for Poets

It has been seen already that steamers to Stornoway have featured in a number of pieces of literature, and from time to time have caused correspondents in the press to compose verses either praising or criticising the ships. Such was the esteem in which the ships were held that they also inspired several Gaelic poets to compose songs. Some poems were composed about a particular vessel, while others made reference to a steamer in verses about the poet's homeland. There are also examples in which a minor reference is made to one of the steamers, although it is not a major part of the poem. An example of this is a brief reference to the *Clansman* in a humorous poem entitled 'Oran na Mulachaig', or 'Song of the Kebbuck', composed by John MacFadyen, from Mull. In this poem, people from various islands brag about the sizes of cheese from their particular areas. The man from Mull claimed that a kebbuck from his island was so large that

> Thug sinn do Chreag an Iubhair i,
> Los a cur sa *Chlansman*,
> Is thog iad leis a' chran às a bhàt i.

> We took it to Craignure
> To put it on the *Clansman*,
> And they had to raise it from the boat with a crane.

The first four examples which follow all refer to particular steamers which served Stornoway. The earliest was written in the late nineteenth century by Mary MacPherson, popularly known as 'Màiri Mhòr nan Oran' ('Big Mary of the Songs'), a native of Skye. In the poem she laments the departure of the *Clydesdale* to serve other islands from Oban. The poem about the *Clansman* follows a common theme in Gaelic poetry, that of an exile longing for his homeland of Lewis. In it, Lachlainn Donn, a poet from Harris, sings about an exile who has probably left home to seek work on the mainland. *Sheila*, composed by both Alasdair MacIllFhialain (Alasdair Uilleig from Grodhaigearraidh) and Dòmhnall Iain Dòmhnallach (South Uist), is about the first-named returning home on leave during the First World War. Both show by their reference to the steamers how these provided such an important link between the writers, their lands and people. 'Leaving Greenock' is also a war poem, this time composed in the Second World War, as it is the *Lochness* which is mentioned. It composed by Dòmhall Ailig MacLeòid, a native of Lewis, and describes how the poet's longing for home is heightened when he espies the *Lochness* as he is carried up the west coast, perhaps on a convoy bound for the Atlantic or Russia. The fourth and most recent poem, by another Lewisman, Tormod MacLeòid, was composed specially to mark the departure of the *Suilven* from Stornoway to sail in Antipodean waters. In doing this, he illustrates the affection with which the ships were held, and the way in which they became a part of island life. The final poem was written towards the end of the twentieth century by a celebrated 'modern' Gaelic poet, Derick Thomson, also from Lewis. It is of a more general nature, describing feelings on the crossing to Lewis, and the loss of precise identification with the island.

Oran do *Dhail na Cluaidh*

Beannachd leat, a *Dhail na Cluaidh*,
Gur iomadh bliadhn' a threabh thu 'n cuan,
Fàgail Ghlaschu mòr nan stuagh
Mu thuath gu tìr mo dhùthchais.

Gur iomadh oidhche fhliuch is fhuar
Ri frasan sneachda 's gaoth a tuath,
Chuir thu Mhaol le saothair chruaidh,
'S gun bhiadh ach gual is burn dhut.

Nuair a dh'èireadh i na glinn,
Gun snàmhadh tusa bhos an cinn,
'S do chuibhlichean a' bleith nan tonn
Mar mholltair ann an òpar.

Nuair rachadh an t-sian na luaisg,
Is cathadh mara mu do chluais,
Chan fhaict' thu ach mar eun sa chuan,
'S tu cumail suas do chùrsa.

Gur iomadh frachd thug thusa leat,
Rinn fuasgadh oirnn an àm a h-airc,
Nuair chaidh an tuath a chur fo smachd
Le achd nan daoine mòra.

Nuair lìbhrigeadh tu a' mhin 's an tea,
Gum faigheadh tusa càise 's im,
'S bhiodh toradh mara agus tir
A' falbh air pris don Ghalldachd.

Gur iomadh diùlnach agus òigh
Thug thusa leat à Tìr a' Cheò,
A' falbh a chothachadh an lòin,
'S gu leòr dhiubh nach do thill ann.

'S a' chuid a thilleadh dhiubh air ais,
An dèidh an duais a chur ma seach,
'S ann air do ghnùis a bhiodh an tlachd
Nuair thachradh iad bhith cruinn ort.

Nuair a ghabhadh cuid an smùid
Dhen stuth a bh' agad anns a' chùil,
Cha tigeadh fàilinn air do ghlùn,
Ged bheirte surd air danns' ort.

'S gum bi 'n *Ceann-cinnidh* còir fo sprochd
Mur coinnich thu rithe anns gach port;
Nach cluinn do cheòl 's nach faic do thoit,
'S gur goirt bhios iad gad ionndrainn.

Nuair choinnicheas sibh air druim a' chuain,
An dàrna tè a-mach à Cluaidh,
'S an tè eile ruith a-staigh gu luath,
Le cual à tìr nam beanntan;

Gun èigheadh an *Ceann-cinnidh* còir,
'A bheil sibh uile air ur dòigh?
Bheil naidheachd mhath agaibh air bòrd
Bheir sòlas dhomh ri chluinntinn?'

Gun freagradh *Dail na Cluaidh* gu fòill,
'Tha naidheachd mhath agam air bòrd –
Tha iasgach math an Tìr a' Cheò,
Is mòran na mo bhroinn dheth.'

Ma chuir thu nise rinn do chùl,
'S nach faicear tuilleadh leinn do smùid,
Ar mìle beannachd na do shiubhal,
A h-uile taobh gan triall thu.

Song on the *Clydesdale* (transl. Donald Meek)

Farewell to you, O *Dale of Clyde* –
Many a year you've ploughed the brine,
Leaving great Glasgow of gables high,
To head north to my home country.

Many a cold and rainy night,
With showers of snow and northern blast,
You rounded the Mull by striving hard,
With no food but coal and water.

When the sea would rise in glens,
You would swim above their heads,
As your fly-wheels ground the waves
Like grain inside a hopper.

When the storm would stir the seas,
And spume would rise about your ears
You were like a bird at sea,
As you steered your course with rigour.

Many a cargo you conveyed
Which saved us in the hour of need,
When the folk were kept under heel,
Through the deeds of the great nobles.

When you would deliver meal and tea,
You would get butter and some cheese,
And the produce of land and sea
Would seek a price in Lowlands.

Many a youthful lad and lass
You took away from the Isle of Mist,
As they went to earn their keep,
And many did not return there.

And those of them that would come back,
Once their pay was safely banked,
Your face would wear a joyful laugh,
When they chanced to be on board you.

When some would succumb to haze,
Because of the stuff you had tucked away,
Your knee would not tire in any way,
Though they would set you dancing.

The friendly *Chieftain* will be sad,
If you do not meet her in each port;
Without your music or your smoke,
They will miss you sorely.

When you both met on ocean's back,
One from the Clyde on an outward track,
And the other running in so fast,
With cargo from the Highlands.

The kindly *Chieftain* would then call,
'Are you all in the best of form?
Do you have any news on board,
That would cheer my soul to hear it?'

The *Dale of Clyde* would then assert,
'I do have news to lift your heart –
There's fine fishing in the Misty Land,
and much of it's inside me.'

If you have now turned your back,
and we'll no longer see your smoke,
our thousand blessings in your wake,
wherever you may travel.

An *Clansman*

Horò, tha mi muladach
Cho fad's a chuir iad bhuam thu;
Horò, tha mi muladach
'S mi cuimhneachadh na dh'fhuiling mi
'S na deòir a' ruith cho cumanta,
A' sruthadh air mo ghruadhean.

Ged thèid mi Là na Sàbaid
Don eaglais airson sàmhchair,
Cha tuig mi srann den cànan –
'S i Ghàidhlig a bha bhuamsa.

Ach tha na Goill ag ràdh
Nach d' fhiach a' chainnt a' Ghàidhlig –
'S an Tì a rinn gach cànan,
Cha do dh'fhàg e Ghàidhlig suarach.

Fir thèid dhachagh sàbhailt',
Innis dhaibh mar tha mi –
Thoir beannachd gu mo mhàthair
'S a dhà dh'ionnsaigh Ruairidh.

Ach tha mi an dùil 's an dòchas
Gun dean mi fhathast seòladh
'S gun toir an *Clansman* coir
Air a' bhòidse dhan Taobh Tuath mi.

Horò, tha mi muladach,
Cho fad 's a chuir iad bhuam thu;
Horò, tha mi muladach.

The *Clansman* (transl. Margaret Stewart)

Horo, I am downhearted
At the distance they have put between us;
Horo, I am downhearted
Recalling how much I've suffered
And the tears flowing so freely,
Streaming down my cheeks.

Though I should go each Sunday
To church for some peace,
I do not understand the hum of their speech –
It is Gaelic that I speak.

But the Lowlanders say
That Gaelic is of no value,
But He who created all languages
Did not leave Gaelic without worth.

You who will return home safely,
Tell them how I fare –
Bear greetings to my mother
And two-fold unto Ruairidh.

But my expectation and hope
Is that I shall yet sail,
And that the *Clansman* will take me
On a voyage to the Northern lands.

Horo, I am downhearted
At the distance they have put between us;
Horo, I am downhearted.

Sheila

Hi horaibh o hi horaibh o,
'S ann chuireas mi luinneag an òrdugh dhuibh,
Hi horaibh o hi horaibh o,
Air fòrladh Alasdair Bhàin.

Dh'fhalbh mi dh'ionnsaigh an stòdhair leat
'S gun tugadh iad aodach is brògan dhut,
'S gum biodh tu gu math air do chòmhdach
Dol air an fhòrladh cuide ri càch.

Fhuair thu gach nì a bha feumail dhut:
Thug iad fèileadh is seacaid is lèine dhut,
'S gu ruigeas na numerals fhèin,
Chaidh iad an èideadh Alasdair Bhàin.

Nuair ràinig thu Lunnainn, bu shunndach thu:
Bha trèana gad fheitheamh is smùid aiste,
'S cha b' fhada cur seachad na dùthcha i,
'S i giùlan Alasdair Bhàin.

Nuair ràinig thu 'n Caol bha an dìl' agad;
Chan fhaigheadh tu stiomair an oidhche sin;
Cha robh aig a' chidhe ach a' *Sheila* –
"Thèid mi innt'," thuirt Alasdair Bàn.

'S nuair fhuair a' *Sheila* air bòrd innt' thu,
'S ann ghabh i leat tarsainn gu Stèornabhagh,
Ach thàinig an t-Admiral còir
'S chuir e patrol le Alasdair Bàn.

'S dh'fhaighnich iad dheth an robh 'phìob aige
'S gu seinneadh e port aig an dìnnear dhaibh –
Thuirt Alasdair, "Seinnidh mi pìobaireachd
Agus pìosan math dhan *Chocade*."

Nuair ràinig iad Loch nam Madadh leat,
'S ann a leum tha air bòrd dhan a' *Hebrides*,
Ach dh'fhan ise 'n air an acair
O Dhisathairn' gu madainn Dimàirt.

'S ged a thachair dhomh teannadh ri bàrdachd dhut,
Cha bu mhath leam gun tachradh droch càradh dhut;
Mo dhùrachd thu ruighinn gu sàbhailte
Gu do mhàthair, Alasdair Bhàin.

Sheila (transl. Margaret Stewart)

Hi horo o, hi horo o
I shall put a little ditty in order for you,
Hi horo o, hi horo o
On Alasdair Bàn's furlough.

I sallied forth to the store with you
In order that they'd give you clothes and shoes,
That you might be well dressed
Going on furlough with the others.

You received all that you required:
They gave you a kilt, jacket and shirt,
Even down to the insignia,
Which were put on Alasdair Bàn's shirt.

Upon arrival in London you were in fine spirits:
A train awaited you, blowing steam,
And she didn't take long to pass over the country
Bearing Alasdair Bàn.

When you arrived in Kyle there was a deluge;
You couldn't get a steamer that night,
Only the *Sheila* was moored at the quay,
"I shall go aboard", said Alasdair Bàn.

When the *Sheila* had you aboard,
She carried you across to Stornoway,
But the kindly Admiral arrived and
He put a patrol on Alasdair Bàn.

They asked him if he had bagpipes,
So that he'd play a tune at dinner for them –
Alasdair said, "I shall play a pibroch
And a good piece of the *Cockade*.

When they arrived at Lochmaddy with you,
You jumped aboard the *Hebrides*,
But she remained there at anchor
From Saturday till Tuesday morning.

Though moved to compose a song for you,
I wouldn't wish misfortune to befall you
My wish is that you would arrive safely
At your mother's, Alasdair Bàn.

A' Fàgail Ghrianaig

Chuir sinn cùl ri Grianaig mu mheadhan-là Diluain,
'S nuair sheòl i tro na caoiltean bha cùrs againn ri tuath;
Nuair shoilleirich an là dhuinn bha fearann air gach taobh:
Bha Steòrnabhagh air fàire dhuinn is beanntan àrd mo ghaoil.

Ri dol seachad air na h-Eileanan bha 'n *Lochness* a' tighinn dlùth;
Air bòrd bha mòran sheòldairean air aiseig chun a' Chaoil:
Bu tùrsach iad san àm sin a' cur cùl ri àit' an gaoil –
Gun chrath sinn làmh gu brònach riu, is sheòl sinn air ar cùrs.

Gun mhiannaich sinn san àm ud a bhith 'n Steòrnabhagh fad oidhch',
Gum biodh sinn measg ar càirdean, le òrain gràidh gan seinn,
'S le seanchas anns a' Ghàidhlig – 's i chainnt as milse leinn,
An cànan thug ar màthair dhuinn nuair bha sinn na ar cloinn.

Cha robh ann dhuinn ach cianalas bhith tighinn dlùth don àit',
Bhith faicinn ceò nan dachaighean bha dhuinne riamh cho blàth,
Ach O! gu feum sinn gèilleadh leis, gu faigh sinn sìos an nàmh,
'S a-rithist nì sinn còmhnaidh ann an Lèodhas nam beann àrd.

A-nis bha àm na faire ann is dh'fheumadh sinn dhol suas;
Bha 'n oidhche gheamhraidh muladach, le frasan fliuch is fuar;
Bha cùrs don Chuan a Siar again, le smùid bho bhàrr nan stuagh,
'S mi fuar an siud ri smaoineachadh air Lèodhas beag nam buadh.

O mharaiche nan stuaghan 's nam buadhan uasal àrd,
Gu eilean rìomhach buadhmhor an t-sluaigh a thoill mo dhàn,
Gu eilean beag na luachair tha cruaidh is buan fo bhlàth,
An fhraoich is nam beann uasal – buaidh dhut is till gu slàn.

Leaving Greenock (transl. Margaret Stewart)

We left Greenock around mid-day on Monday,
And when we sailed through the narrows we continued on a course to the north;
When the day dawned for us, we could see land on either side:
Stornoway on the skyline and my beloved homeland hills.

When passing the islands, the *Lochness* was approaching;
And on board were many sailors on their way to Kyle:
Sad were they at the time, leaving behind their homeland –
With heavy hearts we waved to them, and sailed upon our course.

We wished, at that time, that we could be in Stornoway overnight,
We'd be amongst our own people, with love songs being sung,
And tales being related in Gaelic, the language most dear to us,
Which we received from our mothers as children.

For us it was but nostalgia to be so close to the island,
And seeing the chimney smoke from the homes which were so hospitable;
But oh, we must now resign ourselves to putting down the enemy,
And we will dwell once more in Lewis of the high hills.

It was now time for night-watch and we were required to go on deck,
The winter's night was dark, with wet and cold showers;
We were on a course to the Western Ocean, with sea-spray flying off the wave crests,
And I was shivering there, thinking of the noble little island of Lewis.

O proud and virtuous mariner of the waves, may you return uninjured and victorious;
To the beautiful blessed island of the folk who deserve my song,
To the little island of rushes, hardy and lasting in bloom,
To the island of heather-moorland and fine mountains.

Suilven

Tha *Suilven* a-nochd fo sheòl
À tìr nam beann 's nan glean 's nan òb,
An Cuan a Siar aice fo sròin
'S i togail cùrs' air Panama.
Tha seòldairean a' sileadh dheòir
A bh' innte fichead bliadhna 's còrr,
Ach b' fheudar fuasgladh dhith nan ròp –
Bha bith-beò 's a lòn air allaban.

Nuair a ghluais i mach bhon àit',
Thug i osann chruaidh neo dhà,
Leigeil soraidh leis a' bhàgh
Far an d' fhuair i blàths is carthannas;
Dh'fhag i Troon deas air Cluaidh,
Tha 'n Cuan a Siar ga bualadh cruaidh;
Chan fhaic i nis na h-eileanan uain' –
Tha beanntan cuain gam falach oirr'.

'S fhad' i nochd bho thìr a gaoil,
O uisgeachan is caoil Loch Bhraoin,
O Eilean Fada suairc' an Fhraoich
Far 'm bu tric i ri taobh nan calaidhean.
'S e Kiwis th' aic' a-nis air bòrd
An àite seòldairean à Leòdh's,
Ach m' dhùrachd dhaibhsan mach tron bhòids'
Gu laigh i stòld' a Wellington.

Nuair thèid a' mhaighdeann ud gu sàl,
Bidh cuirm is ceòl air feadh gach àit'
Aig fògarraich tha tàmh san àit'
A' gabhail slàint' na caileige –
Nach b' eòlach mi air a h-astar còir,
Air Port Boats 's Federal 's gach seòrs',
'N New Zealand thall, an t-àit' as bòidhch',
Nuair bha mi òg 's mi aineolach.

Suilven (transl. Margaret Stewart)

The *Suilven* is tonight under sail,
From the land of the hills, glens and bays.
She has the Western Ocean under her bow
And is setting a course for Panama.
Sailors who worked on her for twenty years and
More, are now shedding tears,
But were obliged to untie her mooring ropes,
Their livelihood and income now gone.

When she moved away from the quay
She gave a heavy sigh or two,
Farewell to the bay
Where she had received warmth and friendship.
She left Troon, south of the Clyde,
The Western Ocean is hitting her hard;
She cannot now see the green islands,
The mountainous seas conceal them from her.

Tonight she is far from her beloved land,
Far from the waters and straits of Loch Broom,
Far from the gentle Long Island of the heather
Where oft she lay in the harbours.
Now they have Kiwis on board,
In place of the Lewis sailors,
But my most sincere wish for them throughout the voyage
Is that she will berth safely in Wellington.

When that lady goes to sea,
There will be feasting and music all over,
By emigrants who live in that place
Drinking to the health of this lady –
Well acquainted am I with her journey,
On Port Boats, Federals and all sorts,
To far New Zealand, the most beautiful of places,
When I was young and innocent.

Air an Aiseag gu Leòdhas

A'leth-aithneachadh gach duine air a chuideachd,
aithne gun chuimhne,
is cuimhne gun aithne.
Tuigse a' tulgadh.
Tha am muir seo glas-
neulach, chan eil beatha
a' snàgadh tuilleadh bho na cladaichean,
tha am protoplasma
gun chumadh.

On the Ferry to Lewis (transl. Derick S. Thomson)

Half-recognising each by his kin,
a knowing-without-remembering,
and a remembering-without-knowing.
The understanding pitching.
The sea is grey-
filamented, no life
slithers any more from the shores,
the protoplasm
has no shape.

An Irreverent Look at the Mailboat

Over four decades of the twentieth century, George Morrison, a native of Lewis, writing in the *Stornoway Gazette* under the pseudonym of 'The Breve', took an irreverent look at many aspects of life on the island. His gentle satire, laced with Stornoway's own brand of humour, did not spare the blemishes and foibles of the mailboat. Some of his observations which follow relate to events which have previously been described in this book.

In the 1930s, dissatisfaction with the *Lochness* provided plenty of scope to disturb the consciences of those in authority. Morrison pointedly picked out a number of pertinent issues relating to the steamer:

> With infinite delight we notice that the Pier and Harbour Commission has noticed that the *Lochness* is not just what it might be, although being gentlemen, the Commissioners don't utter their real thoughts. They desire support from public bodies to voice a protest to the P. M. G. (Post Master General). As a public body ourselves we heartily welcome the support of the Commissioners. Our grievances against the *Lochness* began in August, 1929.
>
> We think the Commissioners' joke at the expense of MacBrayne's deck notice about the "sheep, cattle and other encumbrances" in bad taste. After all, the sheep, the cattle and the Skyemen have got feelings.
>
> The floor of the steerage and the deck round the crooning winch are to be marked out in neat oblongs for the scientific packing of fisher girls.
>
> We understand that among the titbits in the overhauled *Lochness* will be the painting of the steerage lavatory green, to go with the verdigris on the tap in the wash-hand basin.
>
> We do rejoice that the uppah ten (Town Councillors) are taking some interest in the travails of the poor, i.e. the steerage passengers. It has taken the rulers of Lewis nine years to realise that while cattle travel on the mailboat with all the comforts of a byre on land, and first-class passengers with all those of a home, the huddle of poor folk in the steerage must either freeze beneath the stars or rot beneath the deck. Even in this, their cry of woe to MacBrayne's and the Government, the Council shows a biased point of view. They cry for speed. It is not speed the third-class folk need but comfort, at least comfort is their first cry.
>
> We think it a good plan to interview the M.P. M.P.'s are experts on sitting on benches. Perhaps they could sleep even in the steerage of the *Lochness*.

The call at Applecross did not escape his pen, for he wrote,

> Dear me, dear me, so picturesque, don't you think? It would be a pity to lose sight of that moth-eaten coracle, bearing away its burden of three trunks, two boxes of margarine, a dear English lady, and the two strong silent Presbyterian(s) at the oars.

Neither did the *Loch Seaforth* miss out on well-meaning criticism:

> A wearied Glasgow Fair traveller suggest(ed) that the *Loch Seaforth* might be renamed the *Politician*, from her curious and unique ability to jump in umpteen different directions at the same time. Even the aim of the gull is said to suffer.

When it was announced that John Smith, a native of Ness in Lewis, was to become captain of the mailboat in succession to a long line of skippers from Skye, the 'Breve' wrote that

> we understand that Captain Smith of the *Loch Seaforth* is now hard at work cultivating a Skye accent to enable him to keep from disappointing trans-Minch travellers who could hardly be expected to accept such an anomaly as MacBrayne's having a Lewisman to skipper a Lewis mailboat.

It will come as no surprise that the *Iona*, with all the controversy that surrounded her arrival, came in for comment:

> St Columba came to Iona to save and succour and instruct. The *Iona* came to the Hebrides to deride, discomfort and inflame. A peripatetic cinema structure, ill-shaped without and worse within, with its hard bottomed seats like those in a Seceder church, enabling one to see the nothingness of the Minch at the cost of strangulation of the hip joint, the tramping on other folk's toes, and a general malaise which not even a visit to the subterranean bar can appease.
>
> The bar, for the benefit of T. Teasers, Weans and all Clergy, is situated in a cavity projecting – apparently – from the womb of the vessel, wherefore 'tis a hard task for a man four or eight pints heavier to regain the promenade deck. On that deck you cannot promenade, at least only as much as in a Japanese jail – four paces forward and five paces back, depending on whether there be a man from Achmore debating a point of Scripture in the way.
>
> We have one or two solutions for the situation created by this nautical absurdity and present them freely to the Anti-Trans-port board for the Western Reproaches.
>
> (1) Refloat the *Sheila*. She has been lying on the bottom, off Applecross, for only 45 years and should still be in good shape – for MacBrayne. Given a Lewis skipper and a Skye boatswain, and a Clyde engineer and a couple of good A.B.'s from Point (a district in Lewis) she would give a hiding in every way to the vessel which, with a name hallowed, is an unhallowed monstrosity. Maybe she is fast but so is a fast dame.
>
> (2) Why should we not seek amongst the Greek Islands of the blue Aegean and see if the *Lochness* be still around Delos, and Melos and Mytilene, while coming back to smell out the Piraeus? True she was no beauty. She had no forward protruding bridge out-thrust like the bosom of Mae West, but at least there were occasional spots where a weary head might lie down atop of an outstretched body. Not so the *Iona* – no cubicles, no cabins, no couches, no luggage racks, nutin' at all. And all over the place notices which say – "Ship's Personnel Only". By grace of MacBrayne the toilets are not so postered.
>
> (3) The timing of leaving SY should be altered to 3.30 a.m. which, give or take summertime, is Biblical cockcrow. By this resort 100 per cent of travellers would be inconvenienced, whereas the 6 a.m. start gathers in only 98 per cent. Surely the Transport folk and MacBrayne's cannot but accede to such a reasonable request. By doing so you could get to wherever you are going four hours later instead of two as at present.

The 'Breve' was also able to deal with the problem of intending passengers who wished to spend the night on board at Stornoway but 'who arrived too late to catch the pier office open for a ticket and could not get aboard the *Iona* overnight'.

> We put the problem to one of the Skye crewmen and he summed it up this way in good Snizort English: "Eff you

> was late for the offish you cannot get a tuicket. Eff you have not got no tuicket you cannot get abord. Eff you cannot get abord you cannot sleep abord all night till the next morning".

The Stornoway dockers who unloaded and loaded the *Loch Seaforth* each evening also gained a reputation under the pen of the 'Breve'. Their supposed lack of speed in working made him claim that 'chess is very popular', one docker saying, 'Yon's a great game, you don't have to make a move more than once in twenty minutes'. But he did have sympathy for the dockers:

> Let us think kindly of (them) as they traipse round the monstrous containers lovingly engirdled in slings in and out, in and out of the *Loch Seaforth*. Of the refrain of Victor Sylvestor Dance band rhythm "Slow! Slow! Quick!" they cannot accept the latter half, but who shall blame them since, if the fable be true, 'twas the tortoise that won the race.

It is to be wondered what the 'Breve' would have made of the *Isle of Lewis*, Sunday sailings and all the other changes of the present day.

Bibliography

Anderson G and P: *Guide to the Highlands and Islands of Scotland*, John Murray, 1834

Anderson I F: *Across Hebridean Seas*, Chatto & Windus, 1937

Atkinson G C (Quine D A ed): *Expeditions to the Hebrides*, MacLean Press, 2001

Atkinson R: *Island Going*, Birlinn, 2008

Baddeley M J B: *Scotland (Part 1), Thorough Guide Series*, Dulau, 1895

Black W: *A Princess of Thule*, McMillan, 1875

Black W: *A Glance at the Island of Lewis*, in Harper's Magazine, July 1875

Bowman J E: *The Highlands and Islands, A Nineteenth Century Tour*, Allan Sutton, 1986

Bray E: *Discovery of the Hebrides*, Collins, 1986

Cameron A D: *Go tell it to the Crofters*, Acair, 1976

Comet Centenary Celebrations, 1912

Cooper D: *Road to the Isles*, Routledge and Kegan Paul, 1979

Cowsill M, Hendry J, MacDuff L: *Caledonian MacBrayne – the Fleet*, Ferry Publications

Daniel W: *A Voyage round the Coast of Scotland and the adjacent Islands 1815–1822*, Birlinn, 2006

David MacBrayne Ltd: *One Hundred Years 1851–1951*

Deayton A: *MacBraynes Steamers*, Tempus, 2001

Dixon J H: *Gairloch in North-West Ross-Shire, its Records, Traditions and Natural History*, Co-operative Publishing, 1866, (reprint, 1980)

Duckworth C L D D & Langmuir G E: *Clyde River and Other Steamers*, Brown, Son & Ferguson Ltd, 1972

Duckworth C L D D & Langmuir G E: *Clyde and Other Coastal Steamers*, Stephenson, 1939, 1977

Duckworth C L D D & Langmuir G E: *Railway and Other Steamers*, Stephenson, 1966

Duckworth C L D D & Langmuir G E: *West Highland Steamers*, 1935, 1950, 1967, 1987

Dunlop J: *The British Fisheries Society 1786–1893*, John Donald, 1978

Good Cruising – *What you should know about ships and the sea*

Grant J S: *Stornoway and the Lews*, James Thin, 1985

Haldane A R B: *New Roads Through the Glens*, David & Charles, 1977

Holmes D T: *Literary Tours in The Highlands and Islands of Scotland*, Alexander Gardner, 1909

Hogg J: *A Tour in the Highlands in 1803*, Alexander Gardner, 1888

Knox J: A *Tour through the Highlands of Scotland and the Hebride Isles in 1876,* (reprint James Thin, 1970)

Lockie C: *Travels with my Tammie*, Tional, April 2009

MacBrayne D: *Summer Tours in Scotland*, 1883,1895, 1901

Macdonald D: *Tales and Traditions of the Lews*, Birlinn, 2004

MacGregor A A: *Behold the Hebrides*, Chambers, 1925

MacHaffie F G: *The Short Sea Route*, Stephenson, Prescott, 1975

Mackay C: *It Must Be Stornoway*, Argyll Publishing, 2008

Mackay L: *The St Kilda Steamers*, Tempus, 2006

Mackenzie J M: *Diary 1851*, Gairm, 1994

Mackenzie W C: *History of the Outer Hebrides*, 1903 (reprint James Thin 1974)

MacIver K: *The Night the Sheila Went Down*, Eilean an Fhraoich Annual, 1988

MacLean M and Carrell C: *As an Fhearann*, Mainstream, 1986

Macleod J C: *Seven Weeks' Holiday*, Journal of the Stornoway Historical Society, 2000
Macleod J M: *Remembering the Seaforth*, Eilean an Fhraoich Annual, 1998
Macpherson D: *Lure of the West*, Eneas Mackay, 1950
Mais S P B: *Isles of the Island*, Putnam 1934
Mather A S (ed): *Third Statistical Account of Scotland*, Scottish Academic Press, 1987
McArthur I C, McCrorie I, MacHaffie F G: *Steamers of the Clyde & Western Isles*, 1964, 1965
McCrorie I: *Royal Road to the Isles*,Caledonian Mac Brayne,
McCrorie I: *Sea Routes from Mallaig*, Caledonian MacBrayne, 2003
McCrorie I: *Steamers of the Highlands and Islands*, an Illustrated History, Orr, Pollock & Co, 1987
McCrorie I: *The Three Ships Hebrides*, Caledonian MacBrayne, 2001
McCutcheon C: *St Kilda – a Journey to the End of the World*, Tempus, 2002
McIntosh A: *Where Now 'Hell and High Water'?*, ECOS, vol 30, Dec 2009
McNeill D B: *Irish Passenger Steamship Services Vol 1*, David & Charles, 1969
McQueen A: *Clyde River Steamers of the Last Fifty Years*, Gowans & Gray, 1923
McQueen A: *Echoes of Old Clyde Paddle Wheels*, Gowans & Gray, 1924
Meek D E: *Caran an t-Saoghail*, Birlinn 2003
Meek D E: *Na Bàtaichean-Smùide*, handout of 10pp used for a lecture to stornoway Historical Society
Meek D E: *Steamships and Social Change in the Highlands and Hebrides*, published in Veitch K (ed), *Scottish Life and Society: Transport and Communications*, Volume 8 of *A Compendium of Scottish Ethnology*, John Donald, 2009, pp 227–273
Meek D E: *Steamships to St Kilda*, Islands Book Trust, 2010
Meek D E & Peter B: *From Comet to Calmac*, Ferry Publications, 2012
Memoirs and Portraits of One Hundred Glasgow Men, MacLehose, 1886
Millar W J: *The Clyde from its Source to the Sea*, Blackie, 1888
Moir P & Crawford I: *Argyll Shipwrecks*, Moir Crawford, 1994
Morrison G (The Breve): *One Man's Lewis*, Stornoway Gazette
Morton H V: *In Search of Scotland*, Methuen, 1929
Mursel W A: *Isles of Sunset*, Wyllie, 1931
Napier Commission Report, 1884
Newall Captain J T: *Scottish Moors and Indian Jungles*, Hurst & Blackett, 1889
Nic a'Ghobhainn M: *Sheòl mi 'n Uiridh*, Acair, 2009
Osborne B D: *The Ingenious Mr Bell*, Argyll, 1995
Paterson L: *The Light in the Glens*, House of Lochar, 1996
Patton B: *A MacBrayne Memoir*, Brian Patton, 2009
Patton B: *Irish Sea Shipping*, Silver Link Publishing, 2007
Pennell J & E R: *Our Journey to the Hebrides*, T Fisher Unwin, 1890
Pickworth E: *By Sea to the Isles*, Pickworth
Reid J T: *Art Rambles in the Highlands and Islands of Scotland*, Routledge, 1878
Report of the Rural Transport (Scotland) Committee, HMSO, 1919
Robins N: *Coastal Passenger Liners of the British Isles*, Seaforth Publishing, 2011
Robins N S & Meek D E: *The Kingdom of MacBrayne*, Birlinn, 2006, repr. 2008
Sea Sorrow, Stornoway Gazette, 1960
Sebak P K: *Titanic's Predecessor*, Seaward, 2004
Scottish Tourist's Steam-Boat Pocket Guide, McPhun, 1835
Sketches of Highland Character: Sheep-farmers and Drovers: 1873
Smith A: *A Summer in Skye*, Birlinn, 1995
Statistical Account of Scotland 1791–1799
Stephen I (ed): *Siud an t-Eilean*, Acair, 1993

Stornoway Port Authority: *Arrivals and Sailings 1865–1992*
Thomas J: *The Skye Railway*, David & Charles, 1977
Thompson F G: *Minefields in the Minch*, Journal of the Stornoway Historical Society, 2004
Thompson F G: *Old Stornoway Revisited*, Stornoway Historical Society, 2001
Thompson F G: *The Stornoway Shipping Company*, Journal of Stornoway Historical Society, 2001
Weir M: *Ferries in Scotland*, John Donald, 1988
Whittle J: *Speed Bonny Boat*, Saltire Communications, 1980
Williamson Capt J W: *Clyde passenger Steamers 1812–1901*, SPA Books, 1987

Newspapers, periodicals, etc.

Highland News
Inverness Advertiser
Inverness Courier
Inverness Journal
John O'Groat Journal
Scottish Highlander
Stornoway Gazette
The Glasgow Herald
The Herald

Web sites

Am Baile
Applecross Historical Society
Hansard
Hebrides News
Lochs Community
Pairc Historical Society
Royal Commission on the Ancient and Historical Monuments of Scotland
Scotland's Places
Ships of Calmac
Stornoway Historical Society
Uig Historical Society

Acknowledgements

In writing this book I am indebted to many people who contributed to its production. My thanks go to Donald Meek and Andrew Clark, who both encouraged me to write the book as well as so willingly giving help, advice and photographs; a second mention of Donald Meek, who patiently read and corrected my text, must also be made. I must give my wholehearted thanks to John Randall of the Islands Book Trust for agreeing to publish the book, and to also to Donnie Morrison and Alayne Barton of the Trust for their help and advice in its production. Thanks, too, to Nick Robins, John Newth and Graeme Dunlop for information on specific ships; to the staff of Stornoway Library who were always happy to answer questions, and to search the shelves and archives for sources; also the staff of Inverness and Wick Libraries. My appreciation goes to those who gave permission to reproduce published material: Peter Burns of Birlinn Ltd (for extracts from 'A Summer in Skye' and 'Island Going'), the late Professor Derick Thomson, Norman Macleod, Mary Morrison, Donald Mackenzie, Robert Maclellan, Malcolm Macdonald and the Stornoway Historical Society, the Stornoway Gazette and the Pairc Historical Society; to Michael Maclennan for supplying photographs (and chat about Stornoway steamers); to Alan Thomas who supplied information on the recovery of the *Loch Seaforth*; to Margaret Stewart who provided translations of the poems and to Mary Smith for valuable assistance; also to the Stornoway Port Authority for allowing access to their records. Last, and certainly not least, heartfelt thanks to my wife, Anna, for her encouragement, forbearance and tolerance, as well as her proof reading. If I have omitted anyone please accept my apologies and gratitude. To everyone who contributed, 'mòran taing'.

Illustrations

Thanks to the following for giving their permission to reproduce their photographs:

Dan Macdonald collection, courtesy Ballast Trust: sailing smacks, *Claymore*; Donald Meek: *Chieftain*, *Chieftain* advert, *Loch Seaforth* launch (2), cricket card; Clyde River Steamer Club: *Chevalier*; Hugh MacDonald (Viewfield House, Portree): *Claymore* at Portree; School of Scottish Studies Archives (J Lennie, photographer): ferry at Arisaig; Scottish Tramway and Transport Society: *Sheila*; Stornoway Gazette: cartoons, loading van, *Clansman*, *Sound of Jura*, *Suilven* funnel, *Isle of Lewis*(2), *Muirneag*, *Pentalina B*, *Waverley*, *Highland Carrier*; Inverness Courier: steamer advertisements (2); Fraser G MacHaffie: *Dolphin*, cargo handbill; Ian McCrorie: David MacBrayne, *Sheila* aground; Stornoway Historical Society: *Earnholm*; Michael Maclennan snr: *Duke of Lancaster*, *Suilven* (2), *Red Duchess*, *Isle of Lewis*, *Hascosay*, *Muirneag* aground; *Highland Carrier*, *White Sea*, *Taygran Trader*, 4 Calmac ships; Chris Murray: *Isle of Lewis*; Andrew Clark: *Lochiel*, *Lochness*, *Lochbroom* brochure, *Lochdunvegan*, *Clydesdale*, *Lochgorm*, *Antrim Coast/Loch Seaforth*, *Iona/Lochdunvegan*, Langlands brochure; Malcolm Macdonald: excursion crowd; Gairloch Heritage Museum: *Claymore* at Diabaig; Colin Burt: buskers; Alan Thomas: *Loch Seaforth* en route to breakers; William Foulger: *Clansman*; Birlinn: loading car; Gordon MacRae: *Isle of Lewis*; CMAL: new ferry; Langlands postcard courtesy of Western Isles Libraries; the photo of the *Clansman* at Stornoway is copyright of Highland Council, reproduced with permission of Highland Council Planning & Development Service.

THE ISLANDS BOOK TRUST – high quality books on island themes in English and Gaelic

Based in Lewis, the Islands Book Trust are a charity committed to furthering understanding and appreciation of the history of Scottish islands in their wider Celtic and Nordic context. We do this through publishing books, organising talks and conferences, visits, radio broadcasts, research and education on island themes. For details of membership of the Book Trust, which will keep you in touch with all our publications and other activities, see www.theislandsbooktrust.com, phone 01851 880737, or visit Ravenspoint at the address below where a good selection of our books is available.

LIVING HISTORY
THE ISLANDS BOOK TRUST
URRAS LEABHRAICHEAN NAN EILEAN

The Islands Book Trust, Ravenspoint, Kershader, South Lochs, Isle of Lewis, HS2 9QA (01851 880737)